THE EUROPE BOOK

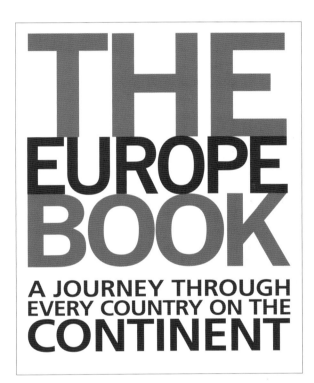

THE EUROPE BOOK
A JOURNEY THROUGH EVERY COUNTRY ON THE CONTINENT

CONTENTS

TEXT LAETITIA CLAPTON

INTRODUCING EUROPE

VISIONS OF EXTREME CONDITIONS, JAW-DROPPING SPECTACLES OR WILD WEST–STYLE ANTICS MAY NOT IMMEDIATELY FIGURE IN YOUR WARM AND FUZZY DAYDREAMS OF EUROPE, BUT PEEL BACK YOUR BLINKERS AND YOU'LL SEE THIS SUPERLATIVE CONTINENT IS SURPRISINGLY DIVERSE.

EUROPE WINS

Starting with the statistical stuff, there's the world's largest country (Russia), which boasts the deepest lake (Lake Baikal) and the longest river (Volga); there's the largest island (Greenland); and the smallest country (the Vatican). Andorrans have the world's highest life expectancy (83½ years), Moscow has more billionaires than any other city, and Scotland has the highest proportion of natural redheads. Slovenia has the oldest vine in the world, Armenia is home to the last Caucasian leopards and Malta's megalithic temples are the oldest freestanding structures. And if that doesn't impress you, there's the astounding contribution that Europe has made to global culture and science.

PRIZES FOR CULTURE & SCIENCE

Ancient Greece and Rome were breeding grounds for great thinkers such as Socrates, Aristotle and Plato (from the former) and Ovid, Virgil and Cicero (from the latter). After a fairly bleak Middle Ages, art fancied a slice of that ancient magic, and thus the Renaissance was born. Spurred on by the arrival of Byzantine scholars fleeing Turk-conquered Constantinople, this boom in European art and architecture was also inspired by the first printing press, invented in Germany by Gutenberg circa 1450, which began to spurt out classical texts. Italy epitomises the era with Brunelleschi's cathedral dome in Florence and Michelangelo's perfectly sculpted *David*.

Around the same time, Polish astronomer Nicolaus Copernicus made a breakthrough, rocking religion with proof that the earth revolved around the sun.

Hot on his heels, Galileo Galilei invented the telescope in Italy and started to map planets. In the following centuries, Englishman Sir Isaac Newton and German Albert Einstein crafted theories of gravity and relativity, which revolutionised mathematics and physics. In the 18th century, the British-born Industrial Revolution thrust the mechanisation of industry and improved transport networks upon Europe and beyond. As most Europeans came to grips with technology, others worked on the human body. Frenchman Louis Pasteur devised medical microbiology in the 19th century with German Robert Koch, studying germs and producing vaccines, including one for rabies. In the 20th century a Scottish research scientist, Sir Alexander Fleming, cultivated penicillin.

Culturally things had hardly slowed down. The roll call of European literary, musical and artistic protagonists is remarkable – 'Picasso, Monet, Renoir, Mozart, Beethoven, Verdi, Hardy, Dostoevsky, Tolstoy, Keats, Shakespeare… ' barely scratches the surface.

NOT JUST A CLASS NERD

For all the eye-popping gifts Europe has bestowed upon the world, there are smaller sources of pride: Venice gave the world spectacles; Switzerland spawned absinthe and the World Wide Web (not simultaneously); Hungary produced the ballpoint pen, the Rubik's cube and discovered vitamin C. But Europe's not just a grade-A student – it's also great fun.

Different national identities, languages, cuisines, traditions and histories sit snugly side by side. Where else might you attend a Big Nose Championship, a

Wife-Carrying Competition or the Air Guitar World Championship? Where else would you opt to jump in and out of freezing water before being beaten by birch twigs, celebrate the summer solstice in a prehistoric stone circle, or be able to choose between sweltering beaches, semidesert, permafrost, glaciers, volcanoes, hot springs and the Arctic? Europe is the place. It's also where, in some parts, drinking your body weight in beer is a national obsession, the range of cuisines is mouthwateringly delicious, natural beauty and wildlife are satisfyingly accessible, and people believe in fairies.

IN THE BEGINNING

But let's go back to the beginning. The birth of Europe can be traced to the human settlers who came to the peninsula between the ice ages or, more intriguingly, to the legend of Europa. The mother of Minos and Minoan civilisation, this virginal princess was seduced by Zeus in his disguise as a pure white bull (each to their own), and then swept off to the shores of Crete. Thus Europa left her native Phoenicia (now south Lebanon) to make her home in ancient Greece, and the continent that now bears her name was born.

It took a while for her moniker to catch on. For a long time the area was known as Christendom; since the Romans adopted it in AD 313, Christianity was, and continues to be, Europe's major religion. This label was only dropped during the 18th century when the Enlightenment's preference for logic over religious belief led many writers, including Rousseau and Voltaire, to adopt the more neutral term, Europe.

WHERE NOW?

At its eastern limits, Europe is generally accepted as meeting Asia at the Ural Mountains (for this book we've included the whole of Russia). To the south, some geographers cut Europe off at the Black Sea and the Bosphorus, but political and cultural common ground make a more interesting border below Turkey, Armenia and Azerbaijan. On the other flanks, the Atlantic and Mediterranean split Europe from the Americas and Africa.

Internally, Europe's borders have merged and diverged over the years. Throughout history, wars and ideologies have created empires and dynasties, unions and alliances. It is hard to believe that less than a lifetime ago the continent was a bloody battleground at war with itself and the world. Or that a physical and symbolic wedge such as the Iron Curtain really bisected Europe, separating East from West. Today the focus is on coalition, expressed by many countries' eagerness to join the European Union. And yet not all wish to accede, and so the borders within this peninsula continue to shift.

There's no doubt Europe is an awe-inspiringly rich place, with global achievements, a fascinating history and plenty to titillate. For any globetrotter, it's considered a must-see, a place to be 'done' at least once. But it's rather like an onion – its multiple layers make it simply impossible to digest in one bite. More temptingly (and with less tears), it's an endless pass-the-parcel just begging to be unwrapped time and time again, as magical and exciting as you'd expect from the home of Father Christmas.

TIMELINE

850,000–700,000 BC »
Humanoid settlers arrive in the European peninsula.

1450 BC »
Santorini suffers the largest volcanic eruption on record, prompting the demise of the Minoan civilisation.

776 BC »
Greece hosts the first Olympic Games.

753 BC »
Rome is founded by the legendary Romulus, son of Mars (god of war) and raised by a she-wolf.

508 BC »
Ancient Athens introduces democracy.

AD 301 »
Armenia is the first country to adopt Christianity.

476 »
The Roman Empire falls.

800 »
Charlemagne is crowned Holy Roman Emperor, taking charge of Western Europe.

1096 »
The Crusades are launched to wrestle the Holy Land from Islamic control.

1278 »
The beginning of Hapsburg reign, for six centuries one of the most powerful dynasties in Europe.

1348 »
The Black Death sweeps across Europe, killing over a third of the population.

1431 »
Joan of Arc is burnt at the stake for heresy.

1453 »
The Ottoman Turks take İstanbul and quash the Byzantine Empire.

1508–12 »
Renaissance artist Michelangelo paints the ceiling of the Sistine Chapel.

1517 »
Martin Luther publishes *The 95 Theses*, kick-starting the Reformation.

1531 »
Henry VIII dumps the Catholic Church after it refuses to nullify his marriage (the first of six), and creates the Protestant Church of England.

1543 »
Nicolaus Copernicus asserts that the earth revolves around the sun.

1605 »
Guy Fawkes' plot to blow up the English Houses of Parliament is foiled on 5 November.

1784 »
Immanuel Kant writes 'Answering the Question: What is Enlightenment?' for a Berlin newspaper.

1789 »
The storming of the Bastille on 14 July kicks off the French Revolution.

1815 »
The battle of Waterloo is the nail in the coffin for Napoleon's European domination.

1899 »
Sigmund Freud's *The Interpretation of Dreams* outlines his first map of the human psyche.

1916 »
Over a million lives are lost during World War I's bloodiest battle at the Somme.

1917 »
The Russian Revolution sounds a death knell for the tsars and lays the groundwork for the Soviet Union.

1939 »
Nazi Germany's invasion of Poland sparks World War II.

1944 »
The D-day landings herald the liberation of Europe from Nazi occupation.

1989 »
The Berlin Wall crashes down amid frenzied celebrations; the Soviet Union follows suit two years later.

1992 »
The Maastricht Treaty creates the European Union.

1997 »
Princess Diana's death in a car crash prompts an unprecedented global outpouring of grief.

2002 »
The euro is introduced in 12 European member states.

2004 »
Madrid's transport network is struck by terrorists – three days later a general election unseats the People's Party, who had taken Spain into the Iraq War.

2012
London hosts the Olympic Games.

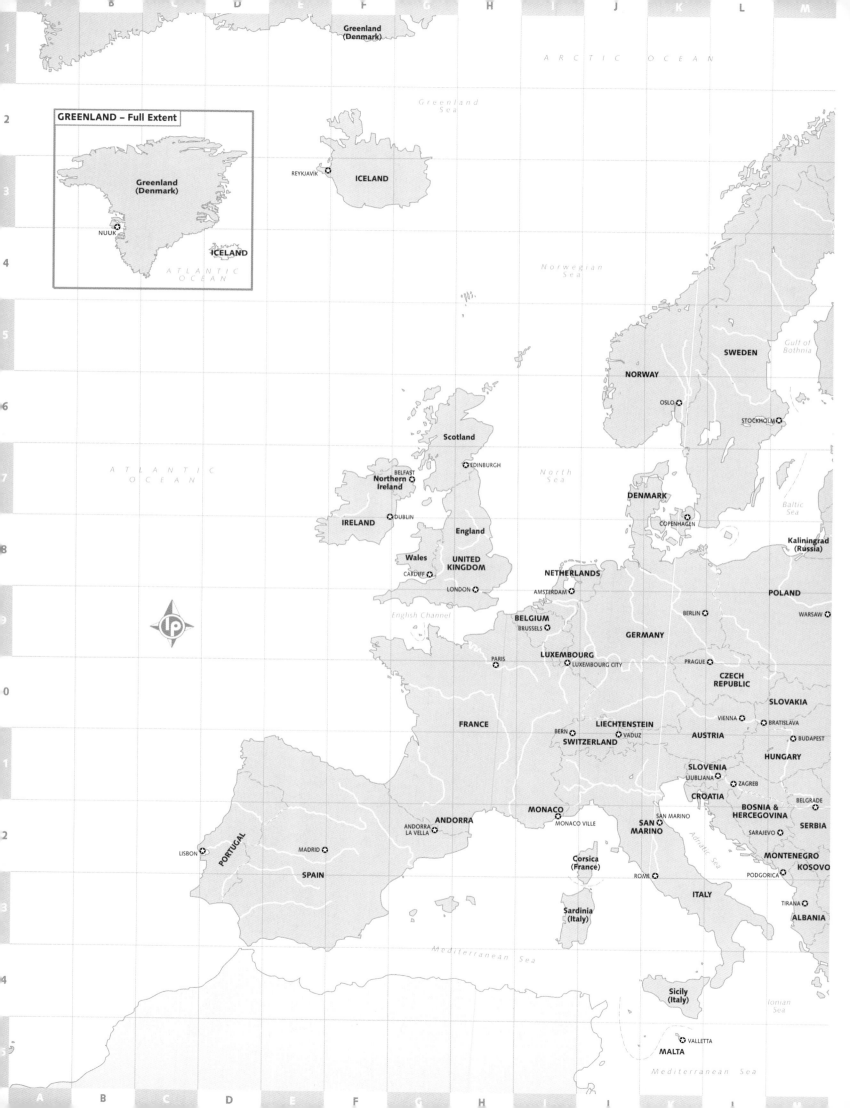

GREENLAND – Full Extent

Greenland
(Denmark)

NUUK

ICELAND

ATLANTIC
OCEAN

Greenland
(Denmark)

ARCTIC OCEAN

Greenland
Sea

REYKJAVÍK ICELAND

Norwegian
Sea

ATLANTIC
OCEAN

SWEDEN

Gulf of
Bothnia

NORWAY

OSLO

STOCKHOLM

Scotland

EDINBURGH

North
Sea

DENMARK

Baltic
Sea

BELFAST

Northern
Ireland

COPENHAGEN

Kaliningrad
(Russia)

IRELAND DUBLIN

England

Wales

UNITED
KINGDOM

CARDIFF

LONDON

NETHERLANDS

AMSTERDAM

BERLIN

POLAND

WARSAW

English Channel

BELGIUM

BRUSSELS

GERMANY

LUXEMBOURG

PARIS

LUXEMBOURG CITY

PRAGUE

CZECH
REPUBLIC

SLOVAKIA

FRANCE

BERN

LIECHTENSTEIN

VADUZ

SWITZERLAND

AUSTRIA

VIENNA

BRATISLAVA

BUDAPEST

HUNGARY

SLOVENIA

LJUBLJANA

ZAGREB

BELGRADE

CROATIA

MONACO

MONACO VILLE

SAN MARINO

BOSNIA &
HERCEGOVINA

SERBIA

ANDORRA

SAN
MARINO

SARAJEVO

ANDORRA
LA VELLA

MONTENEGRO

KOSOVO

PORTUGAL

LISBON

MADRID

Corsica
(France)

PODGORICA

SPAIN

ROME

ITALY

TIRANA

Sardinia
(Italy)

ALBANIA

Adriatic Sea

Mediterranean Sea

Sicily
(Italy)

Ionian
Sea

VALLETTA

MALTA

Mediterranean Sea

RUSSIA – Full Extent

RUSSIA

MOSCOW

Bering Sea

Barents Sea

FINLAND

RUSSIA

HELSINKI

TALLINN

ESTONIA

LATVIA

RĪGA

LITHUANIA

VILNIUS

MINSK

BELARUS

MOSCOW

KYIV

UKRAINE

MOLDOVA

CHIŞINĂU

ROMANIA

Caspian Sea

GEORGIA

TBILISI

BAKU

BUCHAREST

Black Sea

AZERBAIJAN

YEREVAN

BULGARIA

ARMENIA

SOFIA

SKOPJE

MACEDONIA

ANKARA

TURKEY

GREECE

Aegean Sea

ATHENS

NICOSIA (LEFKOSIA)

Crete (Greece)

CYPRUS

Mediterranean Sea

EUROPE AT A GLANCE

↟ ELIZABETHAN OPERATICS AT VIENNA'S STAATSOPER

↟ MONTE PELMO MAKES A PRETTY ITALIAN PICTURE IN THE DOLOMITES

↟ STAIRWAY TO HEAVEN AT THE VATICAN

POPULATION 817.2 MILLION | **AREA 23.1 MILLION SQ KM** | **COUNTRIES 52**
OFFICIAL LANGUAGES 40

SMALLEST COUNTRIES
Yes, grand things really do come in small packages – the Vatican is the smallest country in the world, followed by Monaco. Whether it's popes or playboys, no-one can question the influence that these countries have on the international stage.

LARGEST COUNTRY
From one extreme to another – at 17 million square kilometres Russia is the largest country in the world.

MUSICAL HIGH NOTE
Famous for its sensational sounds, Vienna's Staatsoper is the place to hear classical music and opera in Europe.

BEST BITE
If your smile needs a little tweak, thank Liechtenstein for being the world's largest exporter of dentures.

BALMIEST BEACH-HOPPING
With 1400 islands, of which only 170 are inhabited, sandy paradise is only a boat ride away in the Greek Islands.

SPOOKIEST SPOT
For serious shivers, Transylvania wins fangs down with blood-sucking vampires, werewolves and Count Dracula himself – make sure you don't forget your garlic!

PRETTIEST PICTURE
Thanks to mouthwatering art, beautiful buildings and a sexy populace, Italy is unquestionably the best-looking country in Europe.

HIGHEST MOUNTAIN
With towering twin peaks, one 5642 metres and the other 5621 metres, Russia's Mount Elbrus is the highest mountain in Europe.

BEST UNDERWATER ACTION
Caves, tunnels, reefs, genuine wrecks, a scuppered tugboat and marvellous marine life make Malta and Gozo's dive spots the best in Europe.

NOISIEST COUNTRY
After Japan, Spain is the noisiest country in the world. A quarter of all Spaniards are exposed to more than the 65 decibels deemed acceptable by the World Health Organization. Ssssh…

TALLEST GENE POOL
For tall, blonde and handsome look no further than the Netherlands, where the average height for a man is 1.8 metres.

BRAVEST MENU CHOICE
Hákarl (rotten shark meat) served with a welcome shot of potent brennivín (schnapps) is one of Iceland's more curious snacks, and a bold choice in any language.

LONGEST RIVER
Europe's longest river, the Volga, flows a mighty 3700 kilometres from the Valdai Hills, northwest of Moscow, south to the Caspian Sea.

MOST MULTICULTURAL CITY
With over 300 languages spoken every day in London, the English capital buzzes with multiculturalism.

MOST UNASSUMING NATURAL BEAUTY
According to local legend, when God was creating the world he saved the best bits for Georgia. With snowcapped mountains, raging rivers, lush fauna and a medley of national parks, who's to argue?

A SIBERIAN TIGER'S MOTTO? WORK HARD, PLAY HARDER «

THE INTENSITY AND FLOURISH OF SPANISH FLAMENCO «

HILLTOP VISTAS FROM SANTORINI, GREECE «

GREAT JOURNEYS

Scandinavian Europe titillates the traveller with breathtaking fjords, the mystique of the Arctic Circle, reindeer and Santa Claus, volcanoes and Vikings. This journey starts in the grand imperialist Russian city of St Petersburg (spend a few days here if you have time), from where an overnight ferry leaves for the Finnish capital, Helsinki.

Explore the National Museum of Finland and the National Gallery before wandering around this intimate city's parks and markets, and taking a boat to the islands. An overnight train will whisk you to the Santa Claus Village in Rovaniemi, where you can meet the bearded one himself. While summer offers the midnight sun, a winter visit to Lapland promises the amazing aurora borealis (northern lights), reindeer-drawn sleigh rides, dogsledding, snowmobile trips and a generous dollop of the Christmas spirit. The more adventurous can continue to Nordkapp, Europe's most northerly point. Next head south for the snow castle at Kemi, where you can sup in the ice restaurant and sleep in an ice room before taking an incredible icebreaker cruise – the braver (or more stupid?) can swim in the freezing Arctic waters.

Take the Turku-to-Stockholm ferry, stopping off at the Åland Islands if your trip coincides with their lively midsummer celebrations. The Swedish capital is one of Europe's most beautiful cities; to best appreciate Stockholm, borrow a boat and potter among its islands before exploring the old town, Gamla Stan, and sampling the city's happening nightlife.

Catch a train to Copenhagen and don your horned helmet for the Viking part of the trip – take in Denmark's Viking Ship Museum in Roskilde, the Trelleborg Viking fortress and the Ladbyskibet Viking ship. A ferry then takes you from Hanstholm to Iceland and the Viking village of Hafnarfjörður. Take some time to explore this extraordinary volcanic country and its gushing geysers, ensuring you visit the steamy Blue Lagoon and the vibrant capital, Reykjavík.

For the last part of your journey take a ferry to Bergen and witness Norway's fjords. This attractive university town boasts a lovely mountain backdrop, a strong cultural scene, and, less appealingly perhaps, a lot of rain. The Flåm railway is spectacular: it winds its way through sheer slopes washed by waterfalls and rivers that cleave through the rock. From Flåm hop on a boat to cruise through the dramatic Sognefjorden, Norway's longest and deepest fjord. Impressive as it is, prettier views can be had in the smaller channels such as Nærøyfjord to Gudvangen. If you're missing your horns, finish your Scandinavian sojourn in the Viking museum at Balestrand.

≫ LIE BACK AND PUT YOUR FEET UP IN ICELAND'S BLUE LAGOON

It may not be as long as some of the other journeys, but the Camino de Santiago (Way of St James) is no less epic. For Catholics undertaking this pilgrimage in a Holy Year (which occurs when Santiago's feast day, 25 July, falls on a Sunday), there's the chance to absolve themselves of all the sins they've ever committed – strong incentive indeed.

This famous pilgrimage started in the 9th century when a religious hermit followed a shining star to discover the bones of apostle James the Greater (Santiago, in Spanish). Confirmation of the relic created pandemonium and pilgrims far and wide beat a path to Santiago de Compostela. Benedictine monks founded monasteries along the way, and roads and towns sprang up. Between the 11th and 13th centuries, it was the hottest pilgrimage in Europe and, after a low spell during the Protestant Reformation, its star rose once again.

The most popular route is the Camino Francés, which cuts through the Pyrenees just north of Roncesvalles to enter Spain. If you're planning to walk the whole thing allow at least five weeks and stay in *albergues* (refuges) on the way. Blue and yellow road signs guide motorists along the route.

After the picturesque beech forests of the mountains, the trail reaches Pamplona, where you might see the Running of the Bulls festival in July. West of here a lush valley is home to Eunate, a 12th-century octagonal chapel and a Camino must-see. Puente la Reina has some Romanesque masterpieces, but the most impressive are in Estella: the portal of the Iglesia de San Miguel, the cloister of the Iglesia de San Pedro de la Rúa and the Palacio de los Reyes de Navarra (on which you can spot the symbols for lust, sloth and avarice).

Next you're in wine country, specifically the home of the red Rioja grapes. Take time to refresh, and enjoy the ecclesiastical art in Logroño (especially Michelangelo's crucifixion scene in the Catedral de Santa María la Redonda). The monastery in Nájera and cathedral of Santo Domingo de la Calzada are further standouts.

If you're travelling during the autumn or spring equinoxes, witness the Miracle of the Light at the monastery at San Juan de Ortega before heading into the open landscape of the *meseta* tableland. The Romanesque churches in this area culminate in the glorious Iglesia de San Isidoro in León.

Unwell pilgrims were pardoned at Villafranca's Iglesia de Santiago if they couldn't make the final destination. Further on, O Cebreiro is where the miracle of the Holy Grail is said to have occurred.

After the scenic landscapes of Galicia, end your pilgrimage watching the Botafumeiro incense burner swing in Santiago's cathedral, and luxuriate in your spiritual enlightenment.

≫ REACHING RELIGIOUS HEIGHTS IN BASQUE COUNTRY

SCANDINAVIAN SURPRISES

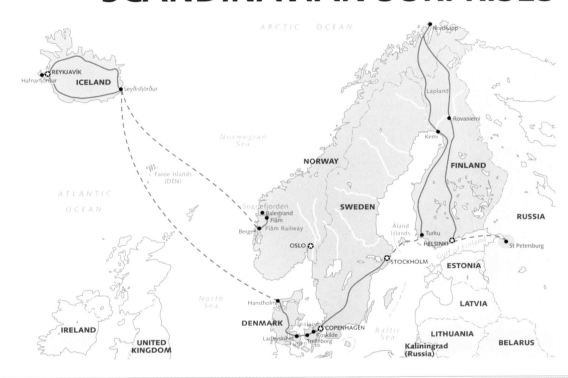

- Nordkapp
- REYKJAVÍK
- Hafnarfjörður
- ICELAND
- Seyðisfjörður
- ARCTIC OCEAN
- Lapland
- Rovaniemi
- Kemi
- NORWAY
- FINLAND
- Norwegian Sea
- ATLANTIC OCEAN
- Faroe Islands (DEN)
- Sognefjorden
- Balestrand
- Flåm
- Flåm Railway
- Bergen
- SWEDEN
- RUSSIA
- Åland Islands
- Turku
- HELSINKI
- St Petersburg
- OSLO
- Gulf of Finland
- ESTONIA
- STOCKHOLM
- LATVIA
- North Sea
- Hanstholm
- IRELAND
- UNITED KINGDOM
- DENMARK
- Zealand
- COPENHAGEN
- Roskilde
- Ladbyskibet
- Trelleborg
- Baltic Sea
- LITHUANIA
- Kaliningrad (Russia)
- BELARUS

PILGRIMS' PROGRESS

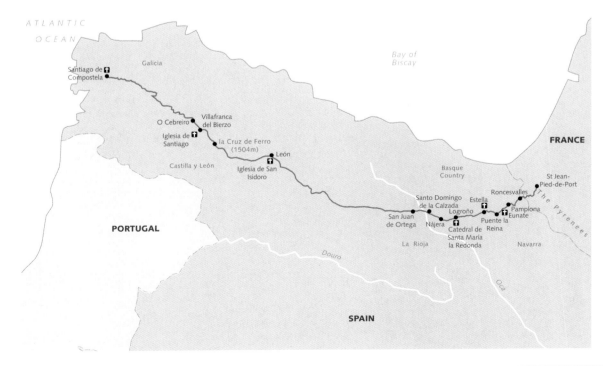

- ATLANTIC OCEAN
- Galicia
- Bay of Biscay
- Santiago de Compostela
- O Cebreiro
- Villafranca del Bierzo
- Iglesia de Santiago
- la Cruz de Ferro (1504m)
- León
- FRANCE
- Castilla y León
- Iglesia de San Isidoro
- Basque Country
- St Jean-Pied-de-Port
- Roncesvalles
- Santo Domingo de la Calzada
- Estella
- Pamplona
- Logroño
- Eunate
- Puente la Reina
- The Pyrenees
- San Juan de Ortega
- Nájera
- Catedral de Santa María la Redonda
- La Rioja
- Navarra
- PORTUGAL
- Douro
- Oca
- SPAIN

THE GRAND TOUR

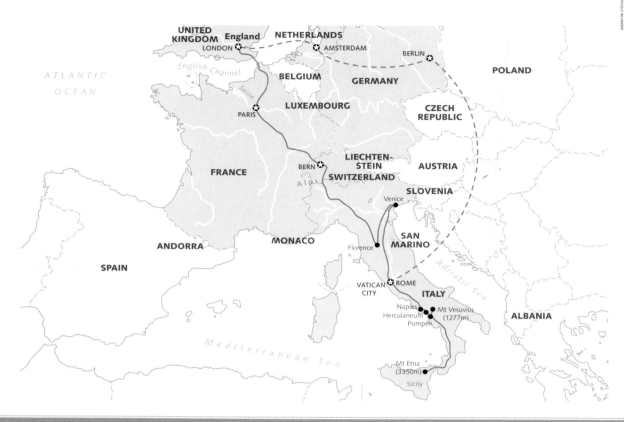

BEHIND THE IRON CURTAIN

The Grand Tour was a rite of passage for young, privileged men between the 16th and 18th centuries (women, such as Lucy Honeychurch in EM Forster's *A Room with a View,* caught on later). The icing on the cake of a classical education, the tour promised a study of Renaissance art, antiquity and fashionable high society – although the famous Venetian courtesans were undeniably a drawcard. In the days before rail travel, these youthful aristos and their tutors journeyed by foot, coach, ship and the occasional sedan chair, but you might prefer more modern forms of transport.

Starting in London, dine in an elegant Piccadilly restaurant to fuel for the journey ahead. First stop is Paris, where a round of upper-class dinner parties will help prepare you for a leadership position on your return home. French classes at the Sorbonne and visits to the *haute couture* boutiques of rue du Faubourg Saint-Honoré, avenue Montaigne and to the Sentier garment district round off your Parisian education. En route to the tour's most important destination, Italy, wind your way through Switzerland and over the Alps (this is where the sedan chair and your fleet of servants come in).

In Florence, the birthplace of the Renaissance, head to Galleria degli Uffizi to see why Botticelli's *Allegoria della Primavera* (Allegory of Spring) and *La Nascita di Venere* (The Birth of Venus) are such blinding examples of Renaissance art. In the Galleria dell'Accademia, wonder at Michelangelo's towering *David,* muscular and proud, as he prepares to face Goliath (a replica stands in its original position in Piazza della Signoria). Explore the Ponte Vecchio, the Palazzo Vecchio, the Palazzo della Signora, the *campanile* (bell tower) and, of course, the Duomo.

Sated by art, you'll be ready for some R&R in Venice. Take a gondola and glide down the small canals, sip a spritz apéritif on lively Campo Santa Margherita, soak up the grandeur of Piazza San Marco and see where too much of the good life got Casanova in the Palazzo Ducale. For insight into 18th-century life visit Ca' Rezzonico; for another art fix tick off the Galleria dell'Accademia and the Collezione Peggy Guggenheim.

The antiquities of Rome beckon at this point, with visits to the Colosseum, the Pantheon and Ostia Antica. Seek spiritual guidance at the Vatican, and throw a coin into the Trevi Fountain to ensure your return to Rome. To explore ancient Roman cities preserved at their demise, head down to Pompeii and Herculaneum, just south of Naples. Finish your Italian odyssey hiking Mount Vesuvius, and if you've still got steam (the volcanoes certainly do) continue south to Sicily's Mount Etna.

Those seeking further edification could travel through Germany and the Netherlands back to London. Or you might prefer to return to Venice in search of those courtesans…

MARVELLING AT BOTTICELLI'S *THE BIRTH OF VENUS* IN FLORENCE'S GALLERIA DEGLI UFFIZI »

Between 1946 and 1989 a physical, ideological and economic divide called the 'Iron Curtain' split Europe in two, with the Soviet-run and communist states to the east and the democratic countries to the west. Travel was heavily restricted between the two areas. From a Western perspective, the divide kept information out of the East and its people in.

A journey along the curtain's length reveals vestiges of Soviet rule and offers a glimpse of an earlier Europe. This itinerary focuses on the northern stretch, but you could choose to follow the whole route. If you're feeling energetic, you can walk or cycle the dividing line – travelling by car or train will allow you to make side trips to the sights.

Your journey starts in the Baltic States, which threw off the USSR with bloody battles in 1991. In Estonia, head for Tallinn to see the former KGB headquarters; the TV Tower, built for the 1980 Olympic Games; the Maarjamäe war memorial; and the Museum of Occupation and Fight for Freedom. See what's left of the Soviet military bases in Naissaar and Paldiski. In Latvia, imagine people laying flowers around Riga's Freedom Monument (and earning themselves a one-way ticket to Siberia), before you head to the Bastion Hill memorials, Victory Park's Soviet war memorial, communist graves at Pokrov Cemetery and the Soviet Aviation Museum. When you reach Lithuania, stop outside Vilnius' Museum of Genocide Victims to ponder the names scratched on the stone wall in remembrance of those murdered in the former KGB prison.

The fall of the Iron Curtain was precipitated by the Solidarity trade union in the 1980s, whose birthplace is Gdańsk in Poland. The country's tallest building, and one of Stalin's favourite examples of Soviet Realist architecture (ironically inspired by the Empire State Building), is the Palace of Culture and Science in Warsaw. Over 5000 Soviet workers were ferried in to work around the clock on its construction – and took just three years to complete it.

Berlin is the highlight of this journey. Follow the path of the Berlin Wall, touch the remaining sections, witness the extant swathes of no-man's-land yet to be built upon, and visit the Haus am Checkpoint Charlie for tales of daring escapes from East to West Germany. Climb the Fernsehturm (TV tower) for a giddy view, drive down the grand Karl-Marx Allee, take in the Stasi Museum and the Stasi Prison and consider that one in five of the East German population were allegedly Stasi informants. Reflect on the atmosphere of fear and suspicion that East Berliners lived in, only metres away from the affluence of the West.

The Iron Curtain continued past the Czech Republic and on through Slovakia, Hungary, Romania and Bulgaria. If you have the time, keep exploring.

SOVIET RELICS PINNED UP FOR SALE AT A MARKET IN TALLINN, ESTONIA »

The height of glamorous European rail travel in the 1930s, the Orient Express spluttered and died in the late 20th to early 21st centuries. The Venice Simplon Orient Express, comprising restored 1920s, '30s and '50s train remnants, now chugs a truncated route from London to Paris and Venice. For the full journey, why not trace the tracks of the original Orient Express on modern trains? Imagine wood-panelled sleeper compartments that converted to snug sitting rooms by day…

Your journey starts in Turkey's exotic İstanbul. Studded with domes and minarets, the city boasts Byzantine beauty, magical mosques and tantalising markets. Dine at the Pera Palas Hotel, built in 1892 by the Compagnie Internationale des Wagons-Lits to accommodate guests riding the Orient Express.

In Bulgaria, pass through Sofia, where a visit to the huge gold-domed Aleksander Nevski Church and a meander around the city are precursors to the main attraction – Mount Vitosha. During the ski season you can don poles and planks to test its metal.

The original Orient Express divided at Belgrade. Take advantage of this historic halt to ponder the city's war-ravaged history and drown your sorrows in its energetic nightlife. You'll need to relax afterwards in Budapest's thermal baths – try the Gellért Baths in Buda or the Széchenyi Baths in Pest. For a trip back in time, visit the 2nd-century Roman ruins at Aquincumi Múzeum.

Vienna is a dream for those who hunger for a bit of culture, and it's a suitably glamorous stop on the Orient Express route. Take in a performance at the Staatsoper, watch the famous Lipizzaner stallions prance at the Spanish Riding School and wander around the gardens of the Hapsburgs' enormous summer palace, Schloss Schönbrunn.

If you time your trip well, your next break will be Munich's Oktoberfest, a world-famous orgy of beer drinking. If this doesn't appeal, the Bavarian capital also has palaces, museums and stunning parks to keep you amused.

A city that ping-ponged between French and German rule during the heyday of the Express, Strasbourg is now one of Europe's political pivots and host to the Council of Europe, the European Court of Human Rights and the European Parliament. Hopefully, you won't need to square up to any of these, although you might want to take a peep as a visitor. Other attractions include the sandstone Gothic cathedral, the medieval timber-framed buildings and beautiful bridges, including the stunning Ponts Couverts.

Unless you're connecting to Calais for an onward ride to London, your last moments on this surrogate Orient Express will be spent trundling into Paris' Gare de Lyon. For total authenticity, you'll have taken three days to get there from İstanbul, but we suggest you dawdle and see the sights.

⌃ RETRACE THE ULTIMATE ROMANTIC JOURNEY ON THE MODERN-DAY ORIENT EXPRESS

With around 1200 islands and 5835 kilometres of coastline, Croatia is the jewel of the Adriatic, and the starting point for this trip. Part of the former Yugoslavia until 1991, the country has put its war-torn past firmly behind it, and its beautiful walled cities, fishing villages and unspoilt beaches are proving a worthy magnet for travellers. You can explore the coast from any point, but the most scenic route starts in Split, Dalmatia.

The largest city on Croatia's Adriatic shore, Split is bustling and picturesque with its impressive Roman ruins of Diocletian's Palace and a charming Old Town. Dip your toes into the crystal-blue waters of the Adriatic on a boat ride to Hvar Island, where beaches beckon and the marble streets of the medieval town glint in the almost ever-present sun. Nearby Korčula Island's lure, in addition to its stunning walled town, is the local produce. Drink your fill of wine and drench your dishes in olive oil. Then set sail by ferry for delicious Dubrovnik, and see why it has been lauded by poets and travellers alike.

From Dubrovnik, venture into Montenegro, which has enjoyed independence since 2006. In Kotor, a climb up the town's fortifications will reward you with a breath-sapping view of the biggest fjord in southern Europe. From Kotor, the ferry continues to Bari, in Italy's southeastern Puglia region – take a peek at the area's famous conical-roofed stone houses, known as *trulli*.

You'll need a rest when you reach lush, green Corfu. Park yourself on a beach for a bit, then stroll around the Venetian buildings of Corfu Town before flying to Athens. Here in the Greek capital you can spy the amazing Acropolis and other ancient sights, and board a ferry for the Cyclades. Santorini's dramatic island setting is hard to beat – watch various vessels crisscross the caldera before bidding the scene-stealing sun goodnight. From Santorini's volcanic sand head to the fertile pastures of Naxos, where its relaxed capital, Naxos Town, and endless stretches of beach offer a different vibe. In the northeastern Aegean, captivating Ikaria and Samos attract travellers eager to stray off the beaten track.

Turkey's Kuşadası is just a short ferry ride from Samos. Before you go on to İstanbul, visit the country's best-preserved classical ruins at Ephesus. A former Byzantine capital and Ottoman Empire headquarters, İstanbul remains Turkey's premier city. After rambling around Sultanahmet, İstanbul's Old Town, and discovering the Blue Mosque, the Grand Bazaar, Aya Sofya (Church of Holy Wisdom), Topkapı Palace and various museums, take a ferry trip up the Bosphorus to regain your sea legs. You'll need them for the journey's last stretch – a ferry trip across the Black Sea to Odesa in Ukraine.

After a punishing climb up Odesa's 192 Potemkin Steps, you might fancy a deeper exploration of this fascinating country. Kyiv's Caves Monastery sounds intriguing…

⌃ ST JOHN'S FORTRESS KEEPS WATCH OVER DUBROVNIK'S COASTAL IDYLL, CROATIA

NOSTALGIA ON THE ORIENT EXPRESS

FLOAT THE ADRIATIC, AEGEAN & BLACK SEAS

BRITISH ISLES & THE LOW COUNTRIES

THEY MAY BE HANGING OFF THE NORTHWESTERN EDGE OF EUROPE, BUT THE BRITISH ISLES (ENGLAND, SCOTLAND, WALES AND IRELAND) AND THE LOW COUNTRIES (THE NETHERLANDS, BELGIUM AND LUXEMBOURG) ARE AT THE VERY CENTRE OF EUROPEAN POLITICS AND CULTURE.

At first glance, the countries of the British Isles may seem to have little connection to their Low Countries neighbours across the Channel, other than relative proximity and Eurostar train services, but historical links are strong. It was people from the northern Netherlands region of Frisia who settled in England during the 5th and 6th centuries. They brought with them a language that would eventually become English, which spread across the British Isles to become the predominant language. The lucrative medieval wool trade connected the south of England to the Flemish towns of what is now Belgium, producing enormous wealth that is reflected in the architecture of places such as Bruges and Ghent. In 1688 it was the Dutch ruler, William of Orange, who was invited by the English parliament to become king of England, and in the 20th century, the UK entered World War I to protect Belgian neutrality. Today, as members of the European Union (founder members in the case of Belgium, the Netherlands and Luxembourg), the various nations

work together to shape the economic and political landscape of the continent. London is the powerhouse of the European economy, as well as a cultural reference point for the world; Brussels is home to the European Parliament; and Luxembourg hosts the European Court of Justice.

Within the British Isles, England has historically dominated its neighbours, imposing political unions but never completely destroying the strong, Gaelic-speaking cultures in Scotland, Ireland and Wales that have maintained a distinctly non-English world view. These cultures saw a revival in the late 20th century, particularly in Ireland, which has prospered both culturally and economically in recent years, though a repercussion of former English dominance is still to be seen in the divisions between Catholics and Protestants in Northern Ireland.

Similarly, across La Manche ('The Sleeve' as the Channel is called in French), the Netherlands controlled modern Belgium and Luxembourg for hundreds of years, the two countries only becoming

independent in 1830 and 1890 respectively. Even today, however, the Dutch legacy in Belgium is felt in the tense relationship, tenuously resolved by a federal system of government, between the Dutch-speaking Flemish in the north and the French-speaking Walloons in the south.

Historically, conflicts have played a part in forging these countries, and contributes to often uncomfortable intercommunal relationships today, but for the visitor this generally goes unobserved. All across the British Isles and the Low Countries, the mix of cathedrals, palaces and medieval towns with dynamic, fascinating cities and strong cultural identities provides enough variety to occupy a lifetime of exploration.

TEXT CLIFTON WILKINSON

Orkney
Islands

Thurso

The Hebrides

Inverness

Aberdeen

Scotland

Oban   Perth

⚙ EDINBURGH

Glasgow

ATLANTIC
OCEAN

North Sea

Derry

Northern
Ireland

Sligo

BELFAST ⚙

Isle
of Man

Irish
Sea

Liverpool

UNITED
KINGDOM

York
Leeds

Manchester

IRELAND

Wales

DUBLIN ⚙

Kilkenny

Birmingham
England

Cork

Swansea   CARDIFF ⚙

Oxford

LONDON

Exmoor
National
Park

Thames

Plymouth

English Channel

Groningen

NETHERLANDS

⚙ AMSTERDAM

Rotterdam

Bruges   Eindhoven

Antwerp

⚙ BRUSSELS

BELGIUM

LUXEMBOURG

⚙ LUXEMBOURG CITY

FRANCE

SWEDEN

DENMARK

GERMANY

POLAND

CZECH
REPUBLIC

TEXT FRAN PARNELL

IRELAND

IRELAND HAS EMERGED FROM A TROUBLED HISTORY AND INGRAINED POVERTY TO BECOME A COSMOPOLITAN POWERHOUSE, WITH BELFAST, DUBLIN AND CORK THE COUNTERPOINTS TO A RURAL OASIS.

CAPITAL CITIES DUBLIN (REPUBLIC OF IRELAND), BELFAST (NORTHERN IRELAND)   **POPULATION** 6 MILLION (INCLUDING NORTHERN IRELAND)   **AREA** 84,130 SQ KM
OFFICIAL LANGUAGES ENGLISH, IRISH GAELIC

⌃ A FARMER AND HIS COLT CHECK OUT THE COMPETITION AT A HORSE SHOW FROM THE STABLES

LANDSCAPE

Ireland is famous for its 40 shades of green – and in spite of a rash of bungalow building, its gently rolling hills and hedgerows still exert a lush grassy calm. Craggy sea cliffs plunge into the ocean on the west coast, and jagged islands are scattered offshore. Many of the country's windswept, sandy beaches are both unpolluted (81 of them reach Blue-Flag standards) and delightfully empty. Low-lying wetlands shelter huge numbers of waterfowl and waders.

HISTORY IN A NUTSHELL

Prehistoric Ireland gave us monuments to rival any in the ancient world. But since 300 BC, when the Celts arrived, Irish history has been a tempestuous human drama. The Christian Irish were ravaged by Vikings, then by Anglo-Norman barons, and finally succumbed to the English Crown after massacres and near cultural annihilation. Nationalism gained momentum in fits and starts from the 18th century, through the tragedy of the 19th-century Great Famine, when millions died or were forced to emigrate, to the Easter Rising of 1916. After the Irish Free State was founded in 1922, later to become the Republic of Ireland in 1949, a legacy of bitterness persisted in the British-governed North, exploding into violence through the Troubles of the 1970s. With the 2007 agreement between Catholic and Protestant parties to share power in the North as the British bowed out, a new era of peace looks set to begin.

PEOPLE

English is the most commonly spoken language, although Irish Gaelic predominates in towns and villages along the west coast. Although 88 per cent of the population is Roman Catholic, the church is gradually losing its grip on the country, and is dogged by falling attendance and persistent child-abuse scandals. Recently, immigrants and refugees from all over Europe, Africa and Asia have added a huge range of nationalities to Ireland's traditionally homogeneous society.

MARKETPLACE

Joining the European Union transformed Ireland from a scrawny pussycat into today's roaring 'Celtic tiger' that is pouncing on prosperity – one third of all Ireland's houses were built in the last 10 years. Once a nation of small farmers, Ireland now creates most of its wealth through manufacturing and services. Inevitably, the booming economy has widened the gap between rich and poor, causing an increase in social problems; but a strong community spirit still prevails, with Irish people giving more to charity than any other nation.

TRADEMARKS

○ Guinness
○ Potatoes (with everything)
○ Plastic leprechauns
○ The gift of the gab
○ TV comedy show *Father Ted*

URBAN SCENE

Dublin has changed beyond recognition in the last 10 years. With its museums, castles, classy cafés, world-class restaurants and the lively Temple Bar district, the port city can hold up its head alongside the best of Europe's capitals. A contender for liveliest city, Cork is still on a roll from its year as European Capital of Culture 2005. The winding River Lee, thriving university, cosmopolitan market, pubs and clubs all contribute to its upbeat atmosphere.

NATURAL BEAUTY

The country is preserved by five national parks, ranging from the Burren's limestone cliffs, rocky hills and ancient burial chambers to Connemara's lonely mountains and glittering black lakes. With numerous strolls and 31 long-distance 'waymarked ways' to try out, walkers will be in heaven. The longest is the 214-kilometre Kerry Way, which threads through one of

VIBRANT TERRACE HOUSES BRIGHTEN THE STREETS OF CORK ⤢

THE VAST GALLERY OF TRINITY COLLEGE'S OLD LIBRARY IS A BIBLIOPHILE'S PARADISE IN DUBLIN ⤢

Ireland's most picturesque counties and tiptoes past the foot of the country's highest mountain, Carrantuohil (1041 metres).

IN STONE
- Newgrange (County Meath) Prehistoric tomb predating the pyramids.
- Clonmacnoise (County Offaly) Tenth-century monastic city on the banks of the River Shannon.
- Kilkenny Castle (County Kilkenny) Magnificent fortress filled with Celtic and Pre-Raphaelite motifs.
- Skellig Michael (County Kerry) Unesco World Heritage–listed jagged rock island with 6th-century monastery ruins.
- Trim Castle (County Meath) Impressive motte-and-bailey castle that starred in the film *Braveheart*.

TRADITIONS
Traditional music is the essence of Ireland; it flows like water at the slightest encouragement. Jigs, reels and tear-jerking ballads cascade from pubs and street corners. The most traditional instruments are the harp, which is the symbol of Ireland; the uilleann pipes ('elbow pipes'), which evolved from an early battle instrument; and the bodhrán, a goatskin drum sounded with the hand or a short stick (although piper Séamus Ennis recommended a penknife).

RANDOM FACTS
- The first Irish divorce to ever be granted was in January 1997.
- 'Slogan' comes from the Irish word *sluagh-ghairm*, meaning 'battle cry'.
- The average house price in Dublin is 10 times the average annual wage.

CUISINE
Ireland's naturally moist climate and lush green grass produce famously creamy milk, butter and cheese. Potatoes are still an important staple, and you'll come across uniquely Irish recipes that use them, such as boxty (potato pancake) and champ (mashed potato with spring onions). The west coast is fabulous for seafood – try Baltimore in County Cork for lobster, prawns and oysters.

MYTHS & LEGENDS
This nation of storytellers has myths and legends stretching right back to its early Celtic past. Many tales are linked to the landscape, including the story of the Giant's Causeway, an amazing clustering of hexagonal basalt columns in Northern Ireland. The story goes that the Irish giant Finn MacCool built the causeway so that he and his Scottish rival, Benandonner, could fight each other. Construction was tiring work; so when Benandonner came striding over the sea, the exhausted MacCool fell back on trickery. Disguising himself as a baby, he lay in a giant-sized cot. When Benandonner saw the size of MacCool's 'child', he scurried back to Scotland, tearing up the causeway as he went.

TOP FESTIVAL
Exported by Irish emigrants, St Patrick's Day is celebrated by millions of people all over the world. The biggest parade is in New York, where foaming green beer, plastic shamrocks and leprechaun hats take a tacky precedence. In Ireland, church services traditionally played a much larger role in celebrations, and a subtle sprig of shamrock was usually the only green in evidence. Happily, nowadays pubs are allowed to open and big parades are also held in Irish cities on 17 March – Dublin's parade attracts up to half a million people.

⌃ STUNNING AERIAL VIEW OF INISHEER, SMALLEST OF THE ARAN ISLANDS

ESSENTIAL EXPERIENCES

- **Supping a pint of Guinness in a cosy old pub**
- **Wandering the ruins of ancient monasteries and stone circles**
- **Watching racehorses at the Curragh**
- **Setting sail for the Aran Islands off the west coast**
- **Learning more about Ireland's disastrous yet defining Great Famine in the 1840s**

MAP REF // F7

BEST TIME TO VISIT **MAY TO SEPTEMBER**

⌃ TRINITY COLLEGE STUDENT CATCHES UP ON SOME READING

CATHERINE KARNOW // CORBIS

FRANK WHITNEY // GETTY

≫ PADDY'S DISTILLERY LORRY IS PACKED FULL OF THE GOOD STUFF – PADDY IRISH WHISKEY, MADE IN CORK SINCE 1779

STAIRS STRETCH TO THE GIANT'S CAUSEWAY, NORTHERN IRELAND ≫

DUBLIN'S TEMPLE BAR DISTRICT TAKES ON A GOLDEN GLOW AFTER A PINT OR TWO OF GUINNESS ≫

TEXT CLIFTON WILKINSON

ENGLAND

FROM THE MYRIAD ATTRACTIONS OF LONDON AND THE REGENERATED PROVINCIAL CITIES OF MANCHESTER, LEEDS AND NEWCASTLE, TO THE RURAL IDYLLS OF THE LAKE DISTRICT AND ANCIENT SITES SUCH AS STONEHENGE, ENGLAND RARELY FALLS SHORT OF EXPECTATIONS.

CAPITAL CITY LONDON   **POPULATION** 51 MILLION   **AREA** 129,720 SQ KM   **OFFICIAL LANGUAGE** ENGLISH

LANDSCAPE

For a small country, England has a diverse landscape. The mountains of the Lake District and the Pennines in the north contrast with the flat, open spaces of East Anglia, and while much of the countryside is taken up by agriculture and the ever-expanding suburbs, there is enough woodland, moorland and rugged coastline (often part of national parks) to satisfy the fussiest of rural enthusiasts. The weather is equally variable, though it's warmer and drier than most visitors imagine, especially the further east and south you go.

HISTORY IN A NUTSHELL

Although hundreds of sites give a tantalising glimpse of a highly advanced prehistoric society, the first recorded English history begins with the Roman invasion in AD 43. After the Romans withdrew in AD 410, some 600 years of squabbling ensued between Britons, Angles, Saxons and Vikings. When the tensions were finally resolved, it was just in time for the appearance of William of Normandy (later to be named the Conqueror), who in 1066 imposed a French-speaking elite on an English-speaking people. The 16th century saw England emerge as a major European power under Henry VIII and Elizabeth I. The monarchy was temporarily abolished in the mid-17th century, while the 18th and 19th centuries saw the country consolidate its control over the rest of the British Isles, and gradually over the rest of the globe, with the building of the massive British Empire. England's apogee was reached during Queen Victoria's long reign (1837–1901), but the 20th century's two world wars drained the country and indirectly led to the break-up of the empire. After a couple of soul-searching decades, and a spot of swinging in the 1960s, England has since enjoyed an economic and cultural revival that continues in the new millennium.

PEOPLE

Having always been a nation of immigrants – from ancient Romans, Anglo-Saxons and Vikings, to more recent arrivals from Ireland, other parts of Europe and the former countries of the empire – England has long been a multicultural society. Newcomers have generally settled in the cities – in particular London, where today more than 300 languages are spoken – and each group has contributed to the richness of English life by adding aspects of their own culture to the already vibrant mix.

MARKETPLACE

After being the workshop of the world during the 19th-century Industrial Revolution, England's economic decline in the 20th century was relentless, with worker unrest going hand in hand with the closure of many of the country's key industries. Since the early 1990s, however, the economy has seen unprecedented growth, fuelled by a buoyant service-industries sector, which employs 70 per cent of the working population. Unemployment and inflation are low, and average annual incomes are relatively high (£23,000) compared to other European nations. Foreign aid contribution stands at around £4 billion per year.

TRADEMARKS

- Fish and chips
- Warm beer
- Rain
- Football
- Afternoon tea
- History
- Pop music

TESSELLATED GLASS ROOF OF THE GREAT COURT CASTS CROSSHATCHED SHADOWS IN THE BRITISH MUSEUM, LONDON »

⌃ ROLL UP, ROLL UP: LADY LUCK IS IN THE HOUSE AT THE BLACKPOOL GOLDEN MILE, LANCASHIRE

⌃ NATURALLY ERODED CHALK CLIFFS CHARACTERISE THE COASTLINE AT HANDFAST POINT, DORSET

⌃ BLACKPOOL BEACH-GOERS SHELTER AMID BRIGHT WINDBREAKERS

WESTMINSTER BRIDGE LIGHTS THE WAY ACROSS A BURNISHED LONDON »

THE ANCIENT ROMAN FORTIFICATION OF HADRIAN'S WALL CUTS THROUGH A WINTER LANDSCAPE »

ON DISC

English pop music came of age in the 1960s when Beatlemania spread across the planet and, along with the Rolling Stones and the Kinks, the Beatles defined a decade. The arrival of punk in the mid-'70s shook up the prog-rock bands that had preceded it, but it had disappeared by the '80s to be replaced by New Romantics such as Duran Duran and other classic popmeisters, including Wham and Culture Club. By the mid-1990s, Oasis was reviving guitar rock, a genre that has gone from strength to strength in the 21st century, with bands such as the Kaiser Chiefs and Razorlight.

URBAN SCENE

London's appeal is unmistakable. More than just the capital, it's a city of the world, and you'd be forgiven for thinking the rest of England's cities were a little dull in comparison. But you'd be wrong. Recent years have seen a resurgence in the former industrial centres of Birmingham, Manchester and Liverpool, which have shaken off grim pasts and are now abuzz with bars, restaurants, pubs and attractions. Liverpool was named European Capital of Culture 2008. Perhaps the biggest success stories, however, are Leeds and Newcastle, two cities that were down and almost out until new cultural and retail development put them at the top of the regenerated-provincial-cities pile.

ON PAPER

- The Canterbury Tales by Geoffrey Chaucer
- King Lear by William Shakespeare
- The Life and Opinions of Tristram Shandy, Gentleman by Laurence Sterne
- Pride and Prejudice by Jane Austen
- Wuthering Heights by Emily Brontë
- Oliver Twist by Charles Dickens
- Mrs Dalloway by Virginia Woolf
- White Teeth by Zadie Smith

ON FILM

- Brief Encounter (1945)
- Great Expectations (1946)
- The Ladykillers (1955)
- A Clockwork Orange (1971)
- Four Weddings and a Funeral (1994)
- The Full Monty (1997)
- East is East (1999)

RANDOM FACTS

- Over 80 per cent of the UK population lives in England.
- The English drink 10 times more tea than anyone else in the world.
- Lincoln Cathedral was the tallest building on earth for almost 250 years, before the central tower's spire was destroyed in 1549 during a storm.

CUISINE

Contrary to popular belief, the English *do* have a cuisine, and a rich one at that, based on hearty meals followed by even heartier desserts. Roast beef and Yorkshire pudding, fish and chips, Cumberland sausage and Cornish pasties have all been reinvented in recent years by celebrity chefs, while traditional puddings – spotted dick, trifle, crumbles and banoffee pie – are perennial favourites.

TOP FESTIVAL

The first Glastonbury Festival of Contemporary Performing Arts took place in September 1970, when farmer Michael Eavis moved his cows and opened his fields to music lovers. Entry cost £1 and the event attracted just 1500 people. Today, the festival takes place annually in June and attracts up to 150,000 people, for many of whom the headline bands play second fiddle to getting a henna tattoo, enjoying a tofu burger and, if the cider takes control and the weather obliges, enjoying a bit of impromptu mudsliding.

WILD THINGS

When it comes to wildlife, foxes, badgers and deer are common across the country. Ornithologists twitch excitedly at the variety of birds in England; however, heavy pesticide use has caused a decrease in both the number and variety of insects, which has in turn had a devastating effect on many bird species, including the formerly ubiquitous sparrow.

IMPORT

- ↗ Tea
- ↗ Curry
- ↗ Madonna
- ↗ Australian sitcoms
- ↗ Polish builders
- ↗ Potatoes

EXPORT

- ↖ David Beckham
- ↖ Punk
- ↖ The Ashes
- ↖ Miniskirts
- ↖ Harry Potter
- ↖ Rugby
- ↖ Monty Python

ESSENTIAL EXPERIENCES

- Sailing through historical London on a cruise along the Thames
- Taking in the view on a hike through the Lake District
- Straining your neck to get a better look at the superb vaulting in Canterbury Cathedral
- Savouring the food at the Fat Duck, one of the world's best restaurants, while in Bray
- Joining the Geordies for an unforgettable night on the toon in Newcastle
- Finding your Caribbean rhythm at the Notting Hill Carnival
- Imagining you're lord or lady of the manor as you explore a stately home
- Satisfying your shopping needs in Leeds' Victorian-era arcades
- Getting to know the locals over a pint in a traditional pub

IT'S NOT ALL ENGLISH ROSES AT COLUMBIA ROAD'S SUNDAY FLOWER MARKET, LONDON

JULIET COOMBE // LONELY PLANET IMAGES

HAMMERSMITH BRIDGE ON THE THAMES AT DUSK

ADAM WOOLFITT // CORBIS

FROM THE TRAVELLER

Europe goes beyond landscapes and beautiful architecture – it's also about the people who live there. One of my favourite cities, London, is one of the most amazing, not least because it's one of the most multicultural. Brixton has long had a bad reputation, but I was instantly captivated. I was particularly drawn to the outdoor market and, as the light faded in the late afternoon, the lurid glow of a butcher's shop caught my eye. Where else in the world can you buy halal goat from guys wearing Nike beanies because it's the middle of winter and it's bloody freezing?

SHEILA PHAM // AUSTRALIA

MAP REF // H8

BEST TIME TO VISIT **MARCH TO OCTOBER**

ON THE LOOKOUT: AN ANCIENT KEEP WATCHES OVER A FIELD OF GREEN «

« PERFECT FOR A SPOT OF WORDSWORTH: DAWN AT BUTTERMERE IN THE LAKE DISTRICT

BENEATH LONDON'S LANDMARK DOME IN ST PAUL'S CATHEDRAL «

TEXT ANDY SYMINGTON

SCOTLAND

ONE OF EUROPE'S MOST SPECTACULAR COUNTRIES, HOSPITABLE SCOTLAND IS A WILD, MAGICAL PLACE WITH NEVER-TO-BE-FORGOTTEN SCENERY, LIVELY CITIES AND REMOTE ISLAND RETREATS.

CAPITAL CITY EDINBURGH   POPULATION 5.1 MILLION   AREA 78,770 SQ KM   OFFICIAL LANGUAGES ENGLISH, SCOTTISH GAELIC, SCOTS

≪ THE ROMANTIC RUINS OF 15TH-CENTURY KILCHURN CASTLE CONJURE UP *MACBETH* ON PLACID LOCH AWE, ARGYLL

LANDSCAPE

The jagged outline of Scotland occupies the northern portion of the island of Britain and has three distinct mainland geographical zones: the rolling hills in the south; the fertile Lowlands, home to most of the population; and the northern Highlands, a wild, majestic, barren zone of mountains and glens that has a lonely feel and irresistible appeal. Scotland also includes hundreds of islands, most of which lie off the west coast. Although Scotland deserves its reputation for having wet, cold winters, its climate, thanks to the Gulf Stream, is actually far milder than you'd expect at these latitudes.

HISTORY IN A NUTSHELL

In the 9th century AD, the Picts and the Scotti were united under one king, Kenneth MacAlpin, and by 1034 Scotland had roughly established its modern boundaries. In the late 13th century the English king, Edward I, invaded Scotland, sparking off a national resistance led by such figures as William Wallace and Robert the Bruce. In 1603 James VI of Scotland acceded to the English throne, and in 1707 the Act of Union joined the two kingdoms. A turbulent period followed: Jacobite revolts in support of the descendants of the exiled King James VII culminated in the defeat of his grandson, 'Bonnie' Prince Charlie, at Culloden in 1746; then in the aftermath the cruel Highland Clearances evicted tens of thousands from their homes and led to the great Scottish diaspora. Nationalist feeling never evaporated, however, and in 1999, following a referendum on devolution, a new Scottish parliament was elected, giving Scotland substantial autonomy from the Westminster government.

PEOPLE

Scotland's population is mostly urban and white, with a less multicultural profile than England. Protestants (of various church affiliations) are in the majority, with the Catholic minority making up some 15 to 20 per cent of the population.

MARKETPLACE

The decline in Scotland's traditional heavy industries has been compensated for by a rise in the service and financial sectors, with Edinburgh becoming an important European banking centre. Average annual income is comparable with the rest of the UK. Fishing remains an important industry in the north of the country, and the North Sea oilfields remain Western Europe's most significant petroleum source.

TRADEMARKS

- Kilts
- Bagpipes
- Edinburgh Festival
- Haggis
- Tossing the caber
- Castles
- Whisky
- Loch Ness Monster
- Golf

URBAN SCENE

Just 45 miles apart, Edinburgh and Glasgow are the two great Scottish cities and wholly different in feel. With a magnificent castle dominating the atmospheric streets of its Old Town, and elegant terraces lining the classy streets of its New Town, Edinburgh wins in the looks and history stakes. But down-to-earth Glasgow can feel more vibrant, is a powerhouse of arts and culture, and has a truly Scottish energy to it, exemplified by its passionate 'Old Firm' football derbies between Celtic and Rangers.

NATURAL BEAUTY

Nearly all of Scotland is remarkably and memorably attractive, and every Scot will name a different corner of the country that makes their heart swell.

STOP HORSING AROUND! RUM PONY, ISLE OF RUM

The dramatic, jagged west coast has spectacular sea lochs, brooding hills and, offshore, the pastoral charms of Islay and the dramatic mountainscapes of Skye. Off the north coast, the Orkney and Shetland Islands have prehistoric sites and strong echoes of a Viking past. In the heart of the country, Perthshire's noble forests and achingly pretty lochs are another stunning highlight of a nation blessed with uncommonly good looks.

RANDOM FACTS

- Scotland has the highest proportion of natural redheads in the world – some 13 per cent of the population.
- Scots are responsible for inventing the television, penicillin, the steam engine, the pneumatic tyre, tarmac and (although Italians dispute this) the telephone.
- A haggis is the minced heart, liver and lungs of a sheep mixed with oatmeal and suet and boiled inside the sheep's stomach. It's traditionally served with 'neeps and tatties' (mashed swede and potatoes) and tastes much better than it sounds.

ON PAPER

- *Selected Poems* by Robert Burns
- *Trainspotting* by Irvine Welsh
- *Fleshmarket Close* by Ian Rankin
- *Kidnapped* by Robert Louis Stevenson
- *The Silver Darlings* by Neil M Gunn
- *The Prime of Miss Jean Brodie* by Muriel Spark
- *Waverley* by Sir Walter Scott
- *Indelible Acts* by AL Kennedy
- *The Crow Road* by Iain Banks

FROM THE TRAVELLER

At the end of Edinburgh's Royal Mile, the Scottish parliament building rises up among the city's tourist-geared tearooms and wool shops. Its modern cement and metal sides contrast with the distinctive wickerlike façade that faces Edinburgh's ornate and distinguished royal palace, Holyrood House. Frequent rain lends a distinctly Scottish atmosphere to the architectural juxtaposition.

SHAMUS BRENNAN // USA

ON DISC

Scotland has a vigorous folk-music scene, with bands such as Runrig, Wolfstone and Capercaillie having achieved worldwide success. But it's in the field of rock and pop that the country really punches above its weight. Numerous famous groups of the 1980s, '90s and noughties have hailed from Scotland, including Travis, Franz Ferdinand, the Eurythmics, Belle and Sebastian, Idlewild, the Jesus & Mary Chain, Texas, the Waterboys, Teenage Fanclub, Simple Minds, Wet Wet Wet, the Proclaimers and KT Tunstall.

SURPRISES

- Some of Scotland's west coast towns are warmed by the Gulf Stream to such an extent that palm trees line the streets.
- Scotland has some of Europe's most beautiful beaches, particularly on the islands of Lewis and Harris.
- The idea that every clan or family has their own traditional tartan is an idealised view and historically inaccurate.

TOP FESTIVAL

The Edinburgh International Festival brings some of the world's finest theatre, opera, music and dance to the Scottish capital every August. But it is the Edinburgh Festival Fringe that has outgrown its big brother and fills the city with everything from old-fashioned street performances to cutting-edge performance art, student revues to high-class comedy. There are dozens of daily performances at all hours, and worrying about what to see is less important than accepting the hit-or-miss nature of the event and then dissecting the performance with friends in the heaving festival bars afterwards!

ESSENTIAL EXPERIENCES

- **Nosing your way through the peaty local whiskies on the welcoming Isle of Islay**
- **Probing Scotland's prehistoric past on the Orkney Islands**
- **Revelling in the glorious hit-or-miss fun of the Edinburgh Festival Fringe**
- **Puffing your way up a hill in light drizzle on spectacular Isle of Skye**
- **Listening to the comforting Scots burr in the warmth of a traditional Aberdeen pub**

MAP REF // G6

BEST TIME TO VISIT **MAY TO SEPTEMBER**

⌃ AN ASPIRING BAGPIPER TAKES UP THE NATIONAL INSTRUMENT

MACDUFF EVERTON // CORBIS

⌃ WORLD-RENOWNED EDINBURGH FESTIVAL FRINGE TAKES TO THE STREETS EACH YEAR FOR A LITTLE ART, CULTURE AND MAYHEM

A LIGHTHOUSE MARKS THE JOINING OF ROCK, SEA AND SKYE ⌃

EARNING A WEE DRAM: BARLEY IS RAKED IN SPRINGBANK DISTILLERY'S MALT ROOM IN PREPARATION FOR SOME FINE SINGLE-MALT SCOTCH WHISKY, ARGYLL ⌃

TEXT DAVID ATKINSON

WALES

SMALL BUT PERFECTLY FORMED, WALES IS MORE THAN THE SUM OF ITS SHEEP AND DAFFODIL POPULATIONS: WITH A NATIONAL (WELSH) ASSEMBLY AND AN UPSURGE IN NATIONAL PRIDE, IT'S AN OLD COUNTRY WITH A YOUNG PERSPECTIVE AND EYES FIXED FIRMLY ON THE FUTURE.

CAPITAL CITY **CARDIFF** POPULATION **3 MILLION** AREA **20,760 SQ KM** OFFICIAL LANGUAGES **WELSH, ENGLISH**

≈ THE VIBRANT ANNUAL MAS CARNIVAL PARADE THROUGH SWANSEA HAS EVERYONE SMILING

LANDSCAPE

Believe the hype: the Welsh landscape is every bit as impressive as people say, from the rolling hills of Mid-Wales to the craggy peaks of the Brecon Beacons. With three national parks and five Areas of Outstanding Natural Beauty (AONBs), almost one quarter of Wales is protected. The Snowdonia National Park is the jewel in Wales' scenic crown, with Mount Snowdon (1085 metres) at its heart. The Snowdonia Society, a charity working to protect the the park, estimates that the Snowdonia National Park attracts an average of 10 million visitors per year.

HISTORY IN A NUTSHELL

It was King Edward I of England who shaped Wales' history by constructing his 13th-century 'Iron Ring' of four imposing castles to stem Welsh revolt. Of these, Caernarfon Castle is the ultimate expression of royal bravado, and the birthplace of Edward II, who went on to be crowned the first ever Prince of Wales. Political devolution has dominated Wales ever since, but these days legislation, not warfare, is the new battleground. The National Assembly took a historic first step towards a full parliament when the Queen signed into law the Government of Wales Act 2006.

PEOPLE

Since the expansion of the European Union, an influx of Eastern European workers has significantly boosted the Welsh populace, which is now numbered around 3 million. Nevertheless, Wales retains just a small foreign-born minority, about two per cent of the population, with the majority based in Cardiff and Newport.

MARKETPLACE

The age-old problems of rural poverty and manufacturing decline still make the headlines, but there's a sense that Wales today is moving forward. In fact, the economy is in good shape with inflation at about three per cent and the GDP per capita riding high at £13,800. House-price inflation is beginning to slow, making Wales a more afforable place to live. The redevelopment of Cardiff Bay and Swansea's waterfront are both testimony to the resurgence of the Celtic economy. South Wales has also attracted investments from the Asian technology sector.

TRADEMARKS

- Leeks and daffodils
- Poet Dylan Thomas
- Lovespoons
- Manic Street Preachers
- Sheep
- Actor Rhys Ifans
- Bara Brith (spicy fruit loaf)
- Singer Charlotte Church
- Male voice choirs
- Singer Tom Jones

ON DISC

The late-1990s post-Britpop days saw the Welsh sound riding high on the rabble-rousing rock of Manic Street Preachers and Catatonia, whose 1998 album *International Velvet* included the call to arms, 'Every day when I wake up I thank the Lord I'm Welsh.' But it was bilingual cult band Super Furry Animals that produced *Mwng*, the biggest-selling Welsh-language album of all time. Today, the Welsh music scene has lost the hype but found substance. Young pop scamps the Automatic are blazing a trail, Funeral for a Friend are heading the fertile metal scene, and the decadent pop of the Hot Puppies proves Wales still rocks.

CUISINE

The rise of the gastropub has seen Welsh chefs embrace country produce, adapting traditional recipes to modern gastronomy. Foods such as Welsh

DON'T MISTAKE THE CASUAL STANCE: FIERCE COMPETITION BREWS ON THE GREEN DURING LAWN BOWLS »

ANY WHICH WAY YOU TURN, WALES' NATIONAL HERITAGE ABOUNDS ON EVERY CORNER »

lamb, Welsh black beef, laver bread and farmhouse cheeses all now have their place in the best eateries. In the last decade there has also been a huge increase in the number of local farmers markets and food festivals. To wash it all down, microbrewery beers are enjoying a renaissance and the first Welsh whiskies are attracting fans.

MYTHS & LEGENDS

Wales' rich and dramatic history has inspired stories of giants and fairies, but most famous of all is the legend of King Arthur and Merlin the magician. The 12th-century Benedictine monk Geoffrey of Monmouth popularised the Arthurian legend in his *Historia Regum Britanniae* (History of the Kings of Britian), and clues still litter the Welsh landscape – from Carmarthen, Merlin's alleged birthplace, to Blaenau Ffestiniog, where Arthur is said to have fought the Battle of Camlan. Most of all, the fabled quest for the Holy Grail leads to Llangollen: legend says the treasured Christian relic is contained within the ruined Castell Dinas Brân.

TOP FESTIVAL

Quintessentially Welsh, the Royal National Eisteddfod is one of Europe's strongest cultural traditions. The descendant of ancient tournaments in which poets and musicians competed for acclaim, the eisteddfod was reinvented by Edward Williams as a modern festival in the late 18th century. Today it's a barometer of Welsh culture with aspiring bands and emerging artists making their debut here. The festival is held during the first week of August, alternately in North and South Wales.

RANDOM FACTS

○ Until the mid-1800s, husbands would bring their spouses to the square in Knighton, Mid-Wales, on the end of a rope to 'sell' them and obtain a divorce; the last wife was 'sold' in 1842.
○ Sheep outnumber people in Wales by almost four to one.
○ The late Sir Edmund Hillary and his team trained in the Snowdonia National Park before tackling their successful ascent of Mount Everest.

ECOTOURISM

The National Assembly has declared Wales one of only three countries with a commitment to sustainable development built into its constitution. The Centre for Alternative Technology (CAT), a pioneering environmental centre, has been the main catalyst for re-branding Mid-Wales as the 'green capital of Wales'. Founded in 1974 to test alternative technologies, the centre has blossomed as an ecologically driven laboratory and information source.

∧ DON'T FORGET TO STOP FOR TEA AND SCONES

∧ STEAMING ALONG CROSS-COUNTRY

∧ GRASS ENCROACHES ON A ROMAN AMPHITHEATRE, CAERLEON

ESSENTIAL EXPERIENCES

○ Stopping for a pint of traditional ale in a cosy pub and watching the local male voice choir rehearse

○ Blowing away the cobwebs with a stroll along the Anglesey or Pembrokeshire Coastal Paths

○ Marvelling at the national heritage with a visit to fairy-tale castles Beaumaris and Conwy

○ Indulging your tastebuds at one of Wales' new breed of gastropubs or country-hotel dining rooms

○ Sparking off the electric atmosphere at a major sporting event in Cardiff's Millennium Stadium

MAP REF // G8

BEST TIME TO VISIT **MAY TO SEPTEMBER**

≫ WELSH PRIDE IS AT STAKE WHEN THE NATIONAL RUGBY TEAM TAKES TO THE FIELD

FESTIVAL TIME CAN BE A WILD RIDE IN CARDIFF ≫

SEARCHING FOR MERLIN AMID THE SLATE RUBBLE AT BLAENAU FFESTINIOG AS A STORM GATHERS IN THE DISTANCE ≫

TEXT SIMON SELLARS

NETHERLANDS

THE NETHERLANDS IS LIKE DR WHO'S TARDIS: WITH ONE OF EUROPE'S MOST BEAUTIFUL AND ECCENTRIC CITIES, A CLASSY COLLECTION OF MUSEUMS AND GALLERIES, AND A POPULATION THAT'S UP FOR A GOOD TIME, MOST OF THE TIME, THERE'S MORE TO IT THAN MEETS THE EYE.

CAPITAL CITY **AMSTERDAM**   POPULATION **16.5 MILLION**   AREA **41,520 SQ KM**   OFFICIAL LANGUAGES **DUTCH, FRISIAN**

≈ MAKING FRIENDS: A MAN COMMUNES WITH THE UNESCO-PROTECTED WINDMILLS OF KINDERDIJK

LANDSCAPE

'What landscape?', you might ask. 'The Netherlands is as flat as a tack!' The highest point is just 321 metres above sea level, and half the country lies at or below sea level, most of it reclaimed. An incredible 2400 kilometres of dykes and dunes protect the cities from inundation, while complex engineering – pumping stations, dams and sluices – drains off excess water 24/7. Still, the Netherlands is not completely one-dimensional: the north has windswept islands, and there are forest and marshlands in the national parks.

HISTORY IN A NUTSHELL

The tiny Netherlands punches well above its weight. During the 17th-century Golden Age, vast wealth was generated through the Dutch East India Company, which sailed to the Far East for exotic goods, colonised Indonesia, and established Asian trading posts. The wealthy merchant class supported many artists, notably Vermeer and Rembrandt, and enabled the sciences to thrive – astronomer Christiaan Huygens discovered Saturn's rings at this time. These days, some observers might think the country is looking through the wrong end of the telescope. The Dutch, with a long history of social tolerance, have embraced the European Union, but immigration policy has proven controversial. In 2002, right-wing politician Pim Fortuyn, an advocate of zero immigration, was assassinated and, in 2004, filmmaker and columnist Theo van Gogh was murdered in retaliation for inflammatory statements about Muslims.

PEOPLE

Ninety per cent of the population are Dutch. Immigrants from the former Dutch colonies of Indonesia and Surinam began arriving in the mid-20th century, and a second wave of immigration since the 1960s included people from Morocco and Turkey. The Islamic community has almost doubled in size over the last decade to 920,000, and there are more than 300 mosques around the country. In the northern Fryslân province, around 400,000 people speak the Frisian language. It's apparently the closest language to English, although English speakers won't understand it – according to Frisians, 'As milk is to cheese are English and Frise.'

MARKETPLACE

Do the brand names Philips and Polygram ring a bell? Besides electronics and multimedia, banking's another heavyweight industry (ING will be familiar), and there's an advanced horticultural scene, a result of tulip mania. Agriculture is big, especially dairy farming, and the country provides a third of Europe's shipping and trucking. But there was a recent recession: Dutch business, dependent on exports, was caught in the larger downturn across Europe and the USA.

TRADEMARKS

- o 'Magic Centre' Amsterdam
- o Tulips
- o Cheese
- o Dutch ovens
- o Volatile, gifted footballers (Johan Cruyff is the exemplar)
- o Bicycles
- o Windmills
- o Dykes
- o Clogs

URBAN SCENE

Spanning the Maas River, Maastricht is a stunner with its pavement cafés, classy restaurants and lovely cobblestoned streets. The Netherlands can feel a bit 'samey', but here you'll find Spanish and Roman ruins, cosmopolitan food, French and Belgian twists in the

INDULGING IN A LITTLE GLOOP: THE BELOVED ACTIVITY OF WADLOPEN (MUD WALKING) AT LOW TIDE ON THE WADDENZEE

A SHADOWY FIGURE EXPLORES PETER STRUYCKEN'S LIGHT INSTALLATION IN ROTTERDAM'S NATIONAL ARCHITECTURE INSTITUTE ⌄

architecture – there are even hilly streets and what passes for mountains ringing the centre. Many Maastricht locals see themselves as a sophisticated breed apart from the north; by contrast, earthy northerners see posh Maastricht as having an identity crisis – 'Are these people Dutch, or what?'

ON CANVAS

○ Hieronymus Bosch (1450–1516) Proto-surrealist work.
○ Rembrandt van Rijn (1606–69) Shimmering portraits, landscapes and religious scenes.
○ Jan Vermeer (1632–75) Proto-cinematographic compositions.
○ Vincent van Gogh (1853–90) Revolutionary colour, coarse brushwork and layered contours.
○ Piet Mondrian (1872–1944) Abstract, rectangular compositions.
○ MC Escher (1902–72) Uncanny graphic art.

IMPORT

↗ Drunken British tourists
↗ Princess Máxima (born in Argentina)
↗ Linguistic dexterity
↗ Indonesian and Surinamese cuisine
↗ Disaffected celebrities during 'key' moments in their lives (Quentin Tarantino, Irvine Welsh)

EXPORT

↖ Mata Hari
↖ Miffy (the picture-book rabbit)
↖ Pilgrims
↖ Eddie van Halen
↖ Slang: Dutch oven, Dutch treat, Dutch courage, Double Dutch…

RANDOM FACTS

○ The late-19th-century sport of 'eel pulling' was very popular. Dutch loons in boats would scramble over each other and attempt to grab live eels attached to ropes suspended over canals – without falling in the water.
○ Rotterdam's harbour is the world's second largest.
○ The Netherlands was the first country to legalise prostitution (1815), decriminalise cannabis (1976), regulate doctor-assisted euthanasia (1993) and legalise same-sex marriage (2000).

TOP FESTIVAL

Koninginnedag (Queen's Day, or Orange Day), which is held on 30 April each year in celebration of Queen Beatrix's birthday, sees a million revellers descending on Amsterdam. It's basically an excuse for a gigantic drunken orgy and the wearing of ridiculous outfits all in orange, the national colour. Orange fake afros, orange balloon animals, orange leather boys, orange roller coasters, orange clogs, orange grannies, orange dope, orange beer (and the inevitable orange vomit), even orange Nazi helmets – it's all here. There's also a free market throughout the city, where anyone can sell anything they like, as well as street parties and live music. By day's end, you'll be afflicted with the *oranjeziekte* (orange sickness).

SURPRISES

○ The Dutch people probably speak better English than you do.
○ The successful reality-TV franchise *Big Brother* is a Dutch invention.

⌃ KONINGINNEDAG CELEBRATIONS HAVE THIS DANCER SEEING ORANGE

FROM THE TRAVELLER

Every year on 30 April in the Netherlands it's Koninginnedag, when the Queen's birthday is celebrated. The party is most prominent in Amsterdam. The Dutch are known as down-to-earth, almost stoic people, but on Koninginnedag everybody goes wild. Orange is everywhere (the royal family's name is Van Oranje), there are street parties, games, markets, costumes and silliness, and people ride boats in the canals (oops, Amsterdam wasn't the first city to have that idea).

CÉCILE OBERTOP // NETHERLANDS

ESSENTIAL EXPERIENCES

○ **Walking, biking or boating around Amsterdam's beautiful canal belt**

○ **Gazing at the architecture in Rotterdam – the future-forward skyline that dominates this unique city**

○ **Falling in love with sumptuous Maastricht, as far from windmills, clogs and tulips as you could want**

○ **Absorbing world-class art in superb museums across Amsterdam, Rotterdam and Den Haag**

○ **Pursuing good times in Amsterdam's coffeeshops, clubs and bars**

MAP REF // 18

BEST TIME TO VISIT **MAY TO SEPTEMBER**

STALLS SELLING DELICIOUS HOT PASTRIES MAKE AN APPEARANCE FOR NEW YEAR'S IN DECEMBER

AMSTERDAM LOCAL MAKES A POINT

PARK YOUR CYCLE AND ADMIRE AMSTERDAM'S STUNNING SINGEL CANAL LINED WITH DUTCH GOLDEN AGE ARCHITECTURE

BELGIUM

ONE OF WESTERN EUROPE'S LEAST-KNOWN COUNTRIES, BELGIUM HAS TURNED THE SPOTLIGHT ON ITSELF, AND VISITORS LOVE WHAT THEY ARE FINDING.

CAPITAL CITY **BRUSSELS**   POPULATION **10.4 MILLION**   AREA **30,530 SQ KM**   OFFICIAL LANGUAGES **DUTCH (FLEMISH), FRENCH, GERMAN**

JOERN SACKERMANN // ALAMY

⌃ BRUSSELS' RENOVATED ATOMIUM IS SET TO RIVAL MANNEKEN PIS FOR MOST POPULAR MONUMENT

LANDSCAPE

Belgium's landscape mirrors its linguistic divide. The northern half is flat ol' Flanders, where only grazing cattle, church steeples and age-old belfries break the monotonous horizon. Here, famous art cities such as Bruges, Ghent and Antwerp sit side by side, making this one of Europe's most densely populated corners. In stark contrast is southern Wallonia's hilly Ardennes – a region of wooded plateaus, deep river valleys and snoozy villages.

HISTORY IN A NUTSHELL

Ruled for centuries by ever-changing European powers, Belgium's tumultuous history of invasions began with the Romans. By the Middle Ages, Flemish cities such as Bruges were thriving, and Ghent, birthplace of powerful Charles V, had outstripped all European rivals, Paris aside. Under the reign of Infanta Isabella and Hapsburg archduke Albert in the 17th century, the arts flourished. Napoleon met his Waterloo near Brussels in 1815. Fifteen years later, an opera performance at Brussels' La Monnaie sparked a revolution: incited by the riotous scenes in *La Mouette de Portici* (The Dumb Girl of Portici), a performance about the 1647 Naples uprising against the Spanish, the Belgians took to the streets and ousted their Dutch rulers. The country's darkest period came at the end of the 19th century, when millions of Congolese died due to King Léopold II's rule of central Africa. Under occupying German forces, World Wars I and II were also bleak. In 1962 the linguistic divide, an invisible line between northern Flemish and southern Walloons, officially cut the country in half. Since then, the question of separatism simmers – should Flanders go it alone?

PEOPLE

Belgium's population is divided between northern Dutch-speaking Flemish (60 per cent), southern French-speaking Walloons (39.5 per cent) and German speakers (less than one per cent) to the east. About 75 per cent of Belgians are Roman Catholic, with the remaining population split between Protestant, Islamic, Jewish and other beliefs.

MARKETPLACE

Financial services, engineering, textiles and diamonds are Belgium's main industries. The economy struggles with one of the highest public-debt levels in the European Union. Flanders is the powerhouse, a position it regained following Wallonia's steel-industry collapse. The economic disparity between the two regions is a factor that drives the calls for Flanders' independence.

TRADEMARKS

○ Comic-strip character Tintin
○ Chocolate
○ Little boy peeing, aka Manneken Pis fountain
○ Tennis stars Justine Henin-Hardenne and Kim Clijsters
○ Beer!

URBAN SCENE

Fairy lights flicker in the growing darkness. Little boys (illegally) cast fishing lines into willow-lined canals. Bells ring out from the illuminated belfry on the market square. Night is calling in Bruges, Belgium's most visited town, and this is the moment to be here. Forget the midday crowds when queues of people await canal boats and the cobbled streets resound with horses and carts skidding close by your arse. Peak hour is perfect for a long lunch or a beer in a linger-as-long-as-you-like café, but definitely not the time to be strolling streets or reflecting on past centuries. Leave that to the evening, when a wander past gabled houses beneath a sky of crushed blue will reveal Bruges' medieval magic.

AT HOME IN HIS COLLECTOR'S CORNER, YPRES LOCAL EUGENE 'BILL' VAN OUDENDYKE IS A MAGNET FOR WARTIME SCRAP METAL ≫

ON CANVAS

Belgium's art history is saturated with big names. It began with Jan Van Eyck (c 1390–1441), the Flemish Primitive artist widely credited with inventing oil painting. A century later, Pieter Breugel the Elder (c 1525–67) got right into quirky peasant scenes. Next up came Pieter Paul Rubens (1577–1640), whose enormous canvases are baroque masterpieces. Expressionist pioneer James Ensor (1860–1949) abandoned traditional for carnivalesque. And last on the roll call is Mr Magritte (1898–1967) – René to his surrealist mates – forever associated with the man in the bowler hat.

RANDOM FACTS

- A world leader in gay rights, both marriage and adoption by gay couples are legal in Belgium.
- The literal translation of the Dutch word for 'cobblestones', *kinderkopkes*, is 'the heads of little children'.
- Belgium's dense motorway system – lit like a Christmas tree every night – is the only manmade structure, besides China's Great Wall, visible from space.

CUISINE

Belgians are passionate foodies. They're reputed to dine out more than any other people in the world, and their cuisine ranks among Europe's best. But it can be quirky. One national dish to watch out for is *filet américain*. It's not America's most succulent steak, but rather minced beef, served raw. *Breugel Kop* translates to Breugel's Head, but it's doubtful the great artist would consider chunks of beef and tongue set in gelatine a compliment. *Paling in 't groen* is basically eel in spinach sauce – not the most visually appetising of dishes, but a good entrée nonetheless. If all this is a tad daring, there's always the country's so-called national dish – *moules et frites* – mussels cooked in white wine and served with a mountain of chips.

IMPORT

- ↗ First monarch King Léopold I (born in Germany)
- ↗ Eurocrats and expats
- ↗ Mussels
- ↗ Artist Hans Memling
- ↗ Large Turkish and Moroccan communities

EXPORT

- ↖ Spa (Belgian town synonymous with health resorts worldwide)
- ↖ Hollywood muscle man Jean-Claude Van Damme
- ↖ Godiva chocolates
- ↖ French singer Jacques Brel
- ↖ Trappist beers
- ↖ Antwerp Six's avant-garde fashions

TOP FESTIVAL

Locals in the town of Binche batten down the hatches, and visitors come prepared for a bruising, at Belgium's most bizarre carnival celebration, recently World Heritage–listed. On Shrove Tuesday local men, known as *gilles*, stomp around to the ominous beat of drums, while wearing strange green-eyed masks and shaking sticks to ward off evil spirits. After lunch, the *gilles* slow-dance through town, decked out in all their finery, including enormous ostrich-feather headdresses, and accompanied by local lads laden with baskets of oranges. From here things get messy as the crowd is pelted with oranges to bless the forthcoming summer. No matter how tempting, don't hurl one back – it's a gift!

≫ BINCHE CARNIVAL KIDS: CUTE UNTIL THEY HIT YOU WITH ORANGES

ESSENTIAL EXPERIENCES

- Rounding the corner of Harengs Street to reveal Brussels' breathtaking Grand Place
- Choosing *praline* (filled chocolates) from exquisite arrays at exclusive *chocolaterie* (chocolate shops) on Brussels' Grand Sablon square
- Risking a hangover at specialist beer cafés in Antwerp or Brussels
- Cycling yourself silly in the quaint, medieval city of Bruges
- Timing a visit for Ghent's Gentse Feesten, one big, happy street party

MAP REF // 19

BEST TIME TO VISIT **MAY TO SEPTEMBER**

≫ NEUHAUS CHOCOLATE BOXES REVEAL A BELGIAN SPECIALITY

⌃ PEACE, QUIET AND POPLAR TREES CREATE AN ENCHANTING BELGIAN LANDSCAPE

BRUGES' MEDIEVAL ROOTS ARE APPARENT CANALSIDE AT NIGHT ⌃

IT'S FINGERS CROSSED FOR A WHITE CHRISTMAS AS MIDWINTER SNOWFALL BLANKETS THE STREETS OF FLANDERS ⌃

LUXEMBOURG

LET YOUR IMAGINATION RUN LOOSE AMONG FEUDAL CASTLES, ENCHANTED FORESTS AND WINE-MAKING VILLAGES…
THE GRAND DUCHY OF LUXEMBOURG IS FAIRY-TALE STUFF.

CAPITAL CITY LUXEMBOURG **POPULATION** 480,000 **AREA** 2590 SQ KM **OFFICIAL LANGUAGES** LUXEMBOURGISH, GERMAN, FRENCH

LANDSCAPE

Though too small for its name to fit on most maps of Europe, pint-sized Luxembourg is wonderfully diverse. Lush highlands and valleys in the northern Ardennes merge effortlessly with the Müllerthal's ancient landscape to the east. In the south, the Moselle Valley snakes along with its steep vineyards and riverside hamlets.

HISTORY IN A NUTSHELL

Listen to the story of this land's tumultuous history and be drawn into a tale of counts and dynasties, wars and victories, fortresses and promontories. Only the dragon is missing. Luxembourg stems from the loins of Count Sigefroid of the Ardennes, who raised a castle here in AD 963. Besieged, devastated and rebuilt 20 times in 400 years, it became the strongest fortress in Europe after Gibraltar. The borders of the Grand Duchy as we know it were finally drawn in 1830. As an active European Union member, Luxembourg today enjoys affluence, stability, and an ever-popular royal family led by Grand Duke Henri.

PEOPLE

Luxembourg's population comprises 30 per cent foreign-born residents – the European Union's highest ratio. Multilingual Luxembourgers are used to their country being held up as a successful multicultural model, though they're also quick to point out that combining a couple of European cultures, in this case Italian and Portuguese, is radically easier than melding different ethnic backgrounds. About 87 per cent of the population are Roman Catholic.

MARKETPLACE

Many nations aspire to an economy such as Luxembourg's. With per capita GDP among the world's highest, it boasts low unemployment and a consistently high standard of living. Iron ore discoveries around 1850 got things rolling. Following the 1970s steel slump, Luxembourg wooed foreigners with its favourable banking and taxation laws.

TRADEMARKS

○ Tax breaks
○ Medieval castles
○ World War II's Battle of the Ardennes
○ Grand Ducal family
○ Cheap petrol

URBAN SCENE

It says something when a city's gardeners get around in suits and ties. Proud, poised and confident, Luxembourg City clearly grew from noble seed. Take in the views over deep gorges that for centuries defended the city's elite; or the vista of old working-class quarters and market gardens below the sheer rock walls of the beautiful Corniche; a skyline studded with slender black steeples (and hard-working cranes); and long, arched bridges that go on forever. Cross Pont Adolphe, and notice it spans more than space… it also spans centuries.

NATURAL BEAUTY

The Müllerthal is distinguished by an almost primeval landscape of ancient gorges scoured by crystal streams through sandstone plateaus. Step silently here to witness deer or fox, or wander deeper into this storybook world to wait for Snow White, or the like, to appear. It feels almost possible.

MYTHS & LEGENDS

Once upon a time, a count called Sigefroid built a castle high on a promontory in the forested heart of Europe. In so doing, he laid the Grand Duchy's foundation and spawned a dynasty that would rule far and wide. By the Middle Ages, Sigefroid's castle was a highly sought-after fortified city – the Burgundians, Spanish, French, Austrians and Prussians all waged bloody battles to secure it. But it was Luxembourg that had the final say. Following independence, the Grand Duchy declared itself neutral and torched its much-contested fort.

RANDOM FACTS

○ Famous US World War II general George S Patton is buried here.
○ Edward Steichen's *Family of Man* exhibition, collated for New York's Museum of Modern Art, resides in Clervaux.
○ Luxembourg's claim to sporting fame is cyclist Charles Gaul, Tour de France winner in 1958.

TOP FESTIVAL

June 23 is Luxembourg National Day. Things kick off the night before with fireworks, dancing and drinking at bars open until dawn. The next day celebrates the birth of the Grand Duke, with a military parade and festivities countrywide.

ESSENTIAL EXPERIENCES

○ **Strolling along 'Europe's most beautiful balcony', Luxembourg City's Chemin de la Corniche**

○ **Allowing fantasy to reign as you hike the Müllerthal's mysterious forests**

○ **Sampling fruity white wines on the bank of the Moselle**

○ **Awaiting your prince or princess from the lofty heights of Château de Bourscheid**

○ **Awaking in a medieval tower in the charming town of Echternach**

MAP REF // I9

BEST TIME TO VISIT MAY TO SEPTEMBER

HISTORIC LUXEMBOURG'S MYTHS, LEGENDS AND FAIRY TALES ARE HOUSED IN THE MAGNIFICENT MEDIEVAL STONE OF VIANDEN CASTLE »

EAMS, FOREST AND CRAGGY ROCKS EARN THE MÜLLERTHAL REGION ITS LITTLE SWITZERLAND MONIKER »

A LUXEMBOURGER WONDERS WHO LET THE DOGS OUT AT HIS LOCAL COFFEE JOINT »

WESTERN MEDITERRANEAN

GATHERED AROUND THE SHIMMERING BASIN OF THE MEDITERRANEAN, THESE LANDS FORM A CRADLE OF ANCIENT AND MODERN CIVILISATION; ALL SHARE COMMON ROOTS IN THE DAYS OF THE PAX ROMANA AND A HEALTHY OBSESSION WITH FINE WINE, BUT ARE OTHERWISE DELIGHTFULLY DIFFERENT.

To stretch the analogy a trifle, the Iberian and Italian Peninsulas could be two prongs of a giant magnet, with France as the handle. And what a magnet! These three pillars of Western European civilisation are among the world's top five tourist destinations and together account for a fifth of world tourism revenues.

With millennia of history behind it, this part of Europe gave us the three 'Rs': Rome, the Renaissance and Revolution. For centuries, the Pax Romana reigned over this most stable and prosperous part of the Roman Empire. The stamp of Rome remains imprinted on the region's character today. From Malta to Portugal, nearly all of the languages spoken (French, Italian, Spanish, Catalan, Portuguese and myriad dialects) are descendants of Latin, which for centuries was the *lingua franca* of empire and learning. Many of the motorways that traverse Italy, southern France and Spain still follow roads laid out by the Romans.

As the Middle Ages drew to a close, the whirlwind revolution in art, architecture, literature and the sciences that is known as the Renaissance exploded

forth from Italy and burst across Europe. An indirect but logical result of this was the French Revolution, which provided a model for the rise of the modern nation-state and, eventually, continental European democracy. The Roman Empire, Renaissance and Revolution shaped the way the West views the world today.

The sheer beauty of these countries doesn't begin and end with the Renaissance. The first Gothic cathedrals were built in France, and Italy's Venice is like a medieval mirage hovering on water. Alongside the splendour of ancient Rome burns the elegant Renaissance light of St Peter's Basilica in the Vatican. Southern Spain and Portugal were home for centuries to a flourishing Muslim culture that left incomparable testaments of Eastern architecture such as Granada's Alhambra. This stretch of Western Europe offers the greatest concentration of beautiful historic towns, soaring cathedrals and splendid art, and accounts for more than 120 Unesco World Heritage Sites.

Not all the beauty spots are the work of human genius. The majesty of the French Alps, Pyrenees and

Italy's Dolomites is a divine spectacle. The sparkling Mediterranean caresses the coasts of island gems such as Corsica, Sardinia and Mallorca. On the western edge, Portugal faces out to the Atlantic, with golden beaches and the faded glory of the port capital, Lisbon.

Good things come in threes: in France, Italy and Spain we have three of the world's greatest cuisines and three of the world's most sybaritic peoples. Whole holidays could be organised just around eating! And drinking. These countries are the world's top wine producers, together making half the annual global output. And it's not just about quantity. In recent decades, Italian and Spanish tipples have joined the French among the greatest drops on the planet.

Western Europe has known good times and dark. The last great conflagration, World War II, spurred some of these countries to create a union, and in 1957 the founding treaty of what today is the European Union was signed… in Rome.

TEXT DAMIEN SIMONIS

ATLANTIC
OCEAN

English Channel

BELGIUM

GERMANY

LUXEMBOURG

CZECH
REPUBLIC

SLOVAKIA

• Rouen

PARIS ✪

Seine

• Brest

Rennes •

FRANCE

AUSTRIA

LIECHTENSTEIN

HUNGARY

Loire

SWITZERLAND

SLOVENIA

ROMANIA

• Nantes

Bay of
Biscay

La Rochelle •

Lyon •

Massif
Central

Rhône

Venice •

CROATIA

• Bordeaux

La Coruña •

Florence •

SAN MARINO
✪ SAN
MARINO

BOSNIA &
HERCEGOVINA

SERBIA

Marseille

MONACO
✪ VILLE
MONACO

Bilbao •

Pyrenées

Golfe
du Lion

Adriatic Sea

MONTENEGRO

Ebro

✪ ANDORRA
ANDORRA
LA VELLA

Corsica
(France)

✪ ROME

KOSOVO

SPAIN

• Barcelona

ITALY

MACEDONIA

Porto •

MADRID
✪

Sardinia
(Italy)

Naples •

ALBANIA

PORTUGAL

Tajo

Valencia •

Golfo de
Valencia

Mallorca
(Spain)

Palma •

Menorca
(Spain)

Tyrrhenian
Sea

GREECE

LISBON ✪

• Ibiza
Ibiza
(Spain)

• Murcia

Mediterranean Sea

Palermo •

• Seville

Sicily
(Italy)

Gibraltar (UK)

• Málaga

MALTA ✪ VALLETTA

TEXT NICOLA WILLIAMS

FRANCE

HIDDEN LANDSCAPES AND WORLD-RENOWNED LANDMARKS STUD FRANCE, EUROPE'S FABLED LAND OF GOOD FOOD
AND WINE, ART AND ROMANCE, JOIE DE VIVRE AND SAVOIR-FAIRE.

CAPITAL CITY PARIS   POPULATION 63.7 MILLION   AREA 643,430 SQ KM   OFFICIAL LANGUAGE FRENCH

LANDSCAPE

Europe's third-largest country, through which five
major rivers run, is hugged on every side, bar one, by
mountains or water. France's 4670-kilometre-long
coastline embraces white chalk cliffs, treacherous
promontories, sand and pebbles. Its mountains – the
Pyrenees, Jura, ski-happy Alps and the ancient Massif
Central with its extinct volcanoes – peak with Mont
Blanc (4807 metres). France's climate is temperate.

HISTORY IN A NUTSHELL

The Celtic Gauls arrived in France between 1500 and
500 BC, Julius Caesar took charge in 52 BC, and by the
2nd century AD the region was partly Christianised. In
the 5th century the Franks (hence 'France') and other
Germanic groups overran the country. Under the 'Sun
King', Louis XIV (reigned 1643–1715), the first
centralised French state was created and in 1789 the
French Revolution stormed the Bastille and kicked out
the monarchy for good. Napoleon Bonaparte's
promulgation of the Napoleonic Code (the basis of the
French legal system) and the separation of church and
state marked the 19th century. World War I, World War
II and the Algerian War (1954–62) were brutal
moments in French history. Postwar presidents include
Charles de Gaulle (1958–69), François Mitterrand
(1981–95), Jacques Chirac (1995–2007) and Nicolas
Sarkozy (2007–), known for his eagerness to reform and
for his glamourous love life.

PEOPLE

France is not densely populated: 107 people inhabit
every square kilometre, although 20 per cent of the
national population is in the greater metropolitan area
of Paris. Some 83 per cent (around 53 million) of French
class themselves as Roman Catholic and one million as
Protestant. Of France's 4.9-million-strong foreign-born
community, 13 per cent are Algerian, 13 per cent
Portuguese, 12 per cent Moroccan and nine per cent
Italian. Only one-third has French citizenship. Muslims
number six million and France's Jewish population is
Europe's largest at 600,000.

MARKETPLACE

France is the European Union's largest agricultural
producer and is heavily dependent on the global
marketplace: imports include machinery, chemical
products, crude oil and plastics; and exports cover iron,
steel, pharmaceutical products and aircraft (Airbus is
headquartered in southern France). The French
economy has long been slack, with unemployment
stuck at around eight per cent proving an ongoing
thorn in the government's side. The average French
employee working in the industry and services sector
earns around €28,800 per year (before tax) – €10,000-
odd less than counterparts in Germany and the UK.

TRADEMARKS

○ The Eiffel Tower and Arc de Triomphe
○ Garlic
○ Bloody blue steaks
○ Chic, petite, well-dressed women
○ Gérard Depardieu and Juliette Binoche
○ Cannes Film Festival
○ Tour de France

NATURAL BEAUTY

Skiing, snowboarding, hiking and paragliding provide
inspirational views in the Alps and the Pyrenees. At
lower altitudes, the cliffs and rock formations at Étretat
in Normandy, the Grande Corniche with its sweeping
panoramas of the Mediterranean coast, Brittany's sea-
swept islands and the Côte d'Opale in far northern
France are all naturally stunning. In Corsica, the GR20
hiking route is both soul stirring and heart stopping.

⩕ ROWING BOATS PAVE THE WAY TO THE CHÂTEAU DE CHAMBORD, SET IN THE BEAUTIFUL LOIRE VALLEY

⩕ THE EUROPEAN PARLIAMENT BUILDING IN STRASBOURG REFLECTS MODERN CITY LIFE

⩕ FIRE – AN UNUSUAL ITEM ON THE PARISIAN MENU

MAGNIFICENT BUILDINGS ON THE NORMANDY HARBOUR OF HONFLEUR RISE FROM THE BANKS OF THE SEINE »

TUTUS GLOW IN THE GHOSTLY LIGHT INSIDE THE MAGNIFICENT OPÉRA BASTILLE »

A MOUNTAIN BIKER NEGOTIATES A ROCKY STEEP IN RUSTREL, PROVENCE »

URBAN SCENE

Chic capital aside, the silk-weaving city of Lyon surprises with its duo of rivers, Renaissance and baroque architecture and buzzing bar life. Nancy, with its gilded wrought-iron work and Art Nouveau masterpieces, is another must for art lovers. There's also wine-rich Bordeaux, and Strasbourg, the Alsatian capital with a pink sandstone cathedral and treasure trove of museums. Sizable populations spice Spanish-inspired Toulouse, Montpellier and Lille. Must-see magical Marseille on the Mediterranean is France's rough-cut diamond.

SURPRISES

○ The French are staunchly conservative, suckers for tradition and snail-slow at embracing new technologies.
○ Leave the beret and blue-and-white striped T-shirt at home: no-one wears them.
○ Only now are French feminists saying they want to be *madame* from birth – rather than the discriminative *mademoiselle* bestowed upon anyone unmarried.

TOP FESTIVAL

Paris is *the* place to be on Bastille Day, France's national day celebrated each year on 14 July. Late on the night of the 13th, *bals des sapeurs-pompiers* (dances sponsored by Paris' fire brigades – who are considered sex symbols in France) are held at fire stations around the city. At 10am on the 14th there's a military and fire-brigade parade along the Champs Élysées, accompanied by an aircraft flyover. Around 11pm fireworks light up the Champ de Mars with a sensational crash, bang and wallop.

ON PAPER

○ *Gargantua et Pantagruel* (Gargantua and Pantagruel) by François Rabelais
○ *Le Rouge et le Noire* (The Red and the Black) by Stendhal
○ *Notre Dame de Paris* (The Hunchback of Notre Dame) by Victor Hugo
○ *Madame Bovary* by Gustave Flaubert
○ *Nana* by Émile Zola
○ *Eugénie Grandet* by Honoré de Balzac
○ *The Complete Claudine* by Colette
○ *Les Chemins de la Liberté* (The Roads to Freedom) by Jean-Paul Sartre
○ *L'Invitée* (She Came to Stay) by Simone de Beauvoir
○ *L'Étranger* (The Outsider) by Albert Camus
○ *Histoire d'O* (Story of O) by Dominique Aury

ON CANVAS

Impressionism had its field day in 19th-century France where Claude Monet (1840–1926) experimented with light and colour. He excited critics in 1874 with *Impression: Soleil Levant* (Impression: Sunrise), a painting of the sun rising over the harbour at Le Havre, which they instantly slammed as 'impressionism'. The name stuck. Monet went on to paint subjects such as *Rouen Cathedral* (1891–95) multiple times in different light and later moved to Normandy where he zoomed in on water lilies.

ON FILM

○ *La Règle du Jeu* (The Rules of the Game, 1939)
○ *Les Enfants du Paradis* (Children of Paradise, 1945)
○ *Et Dieu Créa la Femme* (And God Created Woman, 1956)

○ *À Bout de Souffle* (Breathless, 1960)
○ *37°2 Le Matin* (Betty Blue, 1986)
○ *Le Grand Bleu* (The Big Blue, 1988)
○ *Nikita* (1990)
○ *Jeanne d'Arc* (Joan of Arc, 1999)
○ *Asterix and the Vikings* (2005)

CUISINE

Hands down the most important and influential style of cooking in the West. French cuisine stands apart for its fabulous use of a great variety of foods – beef, lamb, pork, poultry, fish and shellfish, cereals, vegetables and fruit – and its holy trinity of humble staples – bread, cheese and *charcuterie* (cured, smoked or processed meat products) which, married with a decent glass of red, transports foodies straight to gastronomic heaven.

RANDOM FACTS

○ In France, Époisses is known as the pongiest of its 500-odd cheeses; in the UK 19 humans and an electronic nose voted Vieux-Boulogne the world's smelliest cheese.
○ The expression 'French kissing' doesn't exist in French, although cheek-skimming kisses are the quintessential greeting.

ESSENTIAL EXPERIENCES

○ **Marvelling at Mont Blanc from the world's highest cable car in Chamonix**
○ **Meandering the Paris of story, song and myth in Montmartre**
○ **Absorbing exceptional art in the world's most romantic city**
○ **Living the high life on the French Riviera**
○ **Playing royalty in the chateau-studded Loire Valley**
○ **Scouring farms in Cancale for the perfect Breton oyster**
○ **Touring vineyards to taste full-bodied reds in Bordeaux and bubbly in Champagne**
○ **Discovering medieval and Renaissance France in beautiful old towns such as Lille, Strasbourg and Avignon**
○ **Café hopping and lounging over *un café* in Paris and Lyon**

THE MAJESTIC MONT BLANC MASSIF GAZES AT ITS STUNNING REFLECTION IN AN ALPINE LAKE ≫

FROM THE TRAVELLER

The coastline of Ouistreham, Normandy, was the setting for Allied landings on D-day, 1944. These days, the beaches are far removed from the scenes experienced in World War II. On this particular cold, windswept day, the beach was almost deserted, except for two brave girls rugged up against the elements. This winter scene is in stark contrast to the summer months, when the owners of beach huts flock to the seaside in search of sun and relaxation.

JUSTIN HANNAFORD // AUSTRALIA

MAP REF // H10

BEST TIME TO VISIT DECEMBER TO JUNE & SEPTEMBER

THE SLOW TRAIN SLIPS OUT OF THE PRETTY CORSICAN FISHING VILLAGE OF ALGAJOLA »

OLLIES AND KICK FLIPS AT THE SKATE PARK WIN OUT OVER A GAME OF BOULES »

A POPCORN-YELLOW FIELD IN BURGUNDY STEALS A STEEPLE'S THUNDER »

MICHAEL GEBICKI / LONELY PLANET IMAGES

LANDSCAPE

People, skyscrapers and *belle époque* beauties leave little room for much else in this sliver of urban land that is wedged between the brilliant deep-blue Mediterranean Sea and neighbouring France. Cliffs, beach, the world's largest floating dyke and a palace-crowned rock lace its coastline. Monaco's climate is distinctly Mediterranean, bringing mild winters and hot summers.

HISTORY IN A NUTSHELL

The Genoese from northern Italy built a fortress here in 1215, which was later snagged by the Grimaldis in 1297. France seized Monaco in 1793 during the French Revolution and the Grimaldis did not assume the throne again until 1814 – only to quickly lose most of its territory back to the French again. When France finally recognised its independence in 1860, Monaco slumped to became Europe's poorest country. Five years later, however, the famous Monte Carlo Casino opened its doors for the first time and the country transformed itself into a millionaire. In the time of Rainier III, who reigned from 1949 to 2005, Monaco's area grew in size by 20 per cent with land reclaimed from the sea. Albert II, Rainier's playboy son, acceded to the throne upon his father's death in 2005.

MONACO

WHAT THE WORLD'S SECOND-SMALLEST COUNTRY LACKS IN SIZE, IT MAKES UP FOR IN ATTITUDE: GLITZY, GLAM AND SCREAMING HEDONISM, THIS FAIRY-TALE KINGDOM COMPELS YOU TO LET RIP.

CAPITAL CITY **MONACO VILLE**   POPULATION **32,670**   AREA **1.95 SQ KM**   OFFICIAL LANGUAGE **FRENCH**

⌃ THE CIRCUS BEATS THE CASINO HANDS DOWN: BEAUTIFUL WHITE STEEDS PERFORM AT MONTE CARLO'S INTERNATIONAL CIRCUS FESTIVAL

PEOPLE

Monaco is the world's most densely populated country, where 16,000 people squash into each square kilometre. Monégasques (citizens of Monaco) comprise just 16 per cent of the population; French nationals form the majority (47 per cent), followed by Italians (16 per cent) and a colourful cocktail of 125 other nationalities (21 per cent) that lend Monaco its enticing international bite. Practically no-one speaks the traditional dialect, Monégasque (a French-Italian mix), and almost everyone (90 per cent) is Roman Catholic.

MARKETPLACE

With zero natural resources to rely on, this confetti state has made pampering the super-rich its speciality. Residents do not pay income tax and the standard of living is exceptionally high. Monaco is not a European Union member, but it does use the euro as its currency and has no border formalities with France. Since World War I, Monaco has aligned its economic and military policies with those of France.

TRADEMARKS

- ○ Tax haven
- ○ Millionaires
- ○ Actress and princess Grace Kelly
- ○ Formula One racing
- ○ The world's most eligible bachelor (Prince Albert)
- ○ Paparazzi-plagued princesses

TRADITIONS

It's illegal to rollerblade, or walk around barechested, barefooted or bikini-clad. Oh, and littering, smoking and crossing the road at any point other than at a zebra crossing are disliked by the whistle-blowing police officers who monitor the streets alongside CCTV cameras. Key phrase: *tenue de ville* (jacket and tie required).

MYTHS & LEGENDS

Monarch of 56 years, Rainier III won the heart of a nation with his fairy-tale marriage to Grace Kelly in 1956. The legendary Hollywood actress made 11 films in the 1950s, including Hitchcock's *To Catch a Thief* (1955), in which she played the cool blonde on the French Riviera, meeting Rainier in Monaco during a photo shoot. In 1982 Kelly died in a car crash, leaving behind three children, Albert, Caroline and Stephanie.

RANDOM FACTS

- ○ There are more millionaires per capita in Monaco than anywhere else in the world.
- ○ Businesses are required by law to display an official portrait of the reigning prince.

TOP FESTIVAL

Ste Dévote, a young Corsican woman, was martyred in AD 312. After her torturous death, her body was laid in a boat and left to drift at sea. Miraculously, a dove flew from the dead woman's mouth and blew the boat safely to Monaco, where locals snapped her up as their patron saint. Her feast day is celebrated on 27 January with a torchlight procession, ceremonial burning of a boat, and Mass in Monégasque.

FUTURE DIRECTIONS

Monaco's future is at all sea: with no room for expansion on land, it is looking to its 19 kilometres of territorial waters to make more space. Extending the ward of Fontvieille is one idea, although the sudden falling away of the seabed is problematic. A second proposal is to build three offshore islands, each mounted by one leg of a futuristic 390-metre-tall tower.

ESSENTIAL EXPERIENCES

- ○ **Watching the changing of the guard at the Palais du Prince**
- ○ **Risking a little or a lot on the tables at Monte Carlo Casino**
- ○ **Sipping champagne with the international jet set in a designer bar**
- ○ **Razzing round the Formula One Grand Prix circuit in a red Ferrari**
- ○ **Strolling the coastal path into neighbouring France**

MAP REF // 112

BEST TIME TO VISIT **APRIL TO SEPTEMBER**

≫ SPEED AND DARING AT MONACO'S GRAND PRIX FORMULA ONE

≫ APPEARANCES ARE EVERYTHING IN THE LOUIS XV RESTAURANT, HÔTEL DE PARIS, MONTE CARLO

SPAIN

IN THIS CAULDRON OF EXTREMES, GOTHIC CATHEDRALS COMPETE FOR ATTENTION WITH AVANT-GARDE WONDERS; MADRID AND BARCELONA BURST WITH URBAN ENERGY, WHILE MEDIEVAL VILLAGES STAND STILL; AND LIVE-FOR-TODAY SPANIARDS DEVOTE QUALITY TIME TO GOOD GRUB, DRINK AND THE ODD SIESTA.

CAPITAL CITY MADRID **POPULATION** 40.5 MILLION **AREA** 504,780 SQ KM **OFFICIAL LANGUAGES** SPANISH (CASTILIAN), CATALAN, GALICIAN, BASQUE

LANDSCAPE

At the country's heart stretch the high plains and rolling hills of the *meseta* tableland. It is cut in two by the Cordillera Central mountain chain and traversed by three of the country's main rivers, the Duero, Tajo and Guadiana. While much of the interior is dry (it is blistering in summer and icy in winter), the north coast is a softer emerald green strip, hilly in the Basque country, more mountainous in Cantabria and Asturias, and dotted with endless pretty coves and beaches. Marking the frontier with France, the Pyrenees are scattered with glacial lakes and peaks that attract skiers, walkers and mountaineers. Many holidaymakers head for the Mediterranean, whose beaches range from hidden inlets on the craggy Costa Brava to broad strands in Murcia. Of the Balearic Islands, Mallorca is characterised by a stunningly mountainous northwest coast, while Menorca's beaches are picturesque and idyllic.

HISTORY IN A NUTSHELL

When the Romans arrived in 218 BC, the peninsula had already seen thousands of years of human activity, as evidenced by the 12,000 BC cave paintings of Altamira, in Cantabria. Six centuries of Pax Romana gave way to a brilliant Arabo-Berber Muslim culture that flourished until the Catholic monarchs, Isabel and Fernando, completed the Christian Reconquista in 1492, the year Columbus bumped into America. Defeat of the Spanish Armada off England in 1588 was the symbolic turning point and Spain gradually subsided into poor, provincial backwater status. Bloody civil war tore the country apart from 1936 to 1939, followed by almost 40 years of dictatorship under General Franco, who died in 1975. The transition to democracy and European Union membership catapulted the country to the forefront of prosperous Western nations. Led by the progressive socialist José Luis Rodríguez Zapatero, Spain entered the vanguard, passing laws allowing gay marriages, easing divorce and abortion restrictions and promoting greater employment equality for women.

PEOPLE

The Spanish people have become largely homogeneous through the centuries, but three separate cultures enliven the mix: the Basques, Catalans and Gallegos (people from Galicia), each with their own language and traditions. Some consider Spain's *gitanós* (Roma people) to be the country's only true long-standing ethnic minority. Immigration has skyrocketed, however, and 11 per cent of the population are estimated to be foreigners.

MARKETPLACE

Some years ago, former president José María Aznar proclaimed that '*España va bien*' ('Spain is doing well') and, by most appearances, one would have to agree. Annual growth is high at around four per cent and unemployment, at around seven per cent, is lower than in some European Union giants such as Germany.

TRADEMARKS

- Fiery flamenco
- The Running of the Bulls
- Sipping sangria
- Sand, sea and sex
- Hemingway
- Paella
- Throaty red Rioja
- Tapas
- The siesta

EVOKING SAND DUNES, OR PERHAPS SOMETHING LUNAR, MODERNISTA ARCHITECT ANTONI GAUDÍ'S LA PEDRERA, BARCELONA »

⌃ BRAVERY IN WAITING: WHETHER ART, SPORT OR CRUELTY, THE TRADITION OF BULLFIGHTING IS A SERIOUS BUSINESS

COLIN MCPHERSON // CORBIS

⌃ SURREALIST VISION INSIDE THE DALÍ THEATRE-MUSEUM, FIGUERES

⌃ SUN, SAND AND MATADORS ON THE COSTA DEL SOL

JOSE FUSTE RAGA // CORBIS

MATIAS COSTA // PANOS PICTURES

AND THEY ALL FALL DOWN… HUMAN CASTLE BUILDERS AT THE CASTELLERS FESTIVAL IN TARRAGONA «

GLOWIMAGES // PHOTOLIBRARY

GUY MOBERLY // LONELY PLANET IMAGES

PEACE AND QUIET BENEATH SPECTACULAR ARCHWAYS INSIDE A CÓRDOBA MOSQUE «   STEPPING OUT ON THE GRAN VÍA, ONE OF MADRID'S MAIN DRAGS «

RANDOM FACTS

○ Spain is the world's second-noisiest country after Japan.
○ With an average altitude of 660 metres, Spain is the second-highest country in Europe after Switzerland.
○ Madrid only became capital of Spain in 1561.

URBAN SCENE

Madrid is Spain's political and party capital, with traffic jams of clubbers at 5am on the weekends. Hedonistic Barcelona combines chill-out music scenes on the beach with sophisticated dining and discos. Valencia has a rock-and-roll reputation and Seville exudes a sunny, sherry-tinged bonhomie by day and night.

NATURAL BEAUTY

Spain is blessed with a mantle of magical coves and beaches, from the tiny island of Formentera to the fjord-like rias of Galicia. Aside from the mighty Pyrenees, walkers exalt in the Picos de Europa, the Sierra de Gredos and Sierra Nevada (Europe's most southerly ski resort) ranges.

ON FILM

○ *Jamón, Jamón* (Ham, Ham, 1992)
○ *Todo Sobre mi Madre* (All About My Mother, 1999)
○ *Mar Adentro* (Out to Sea, 2004)
○ *La Vida Secreta de las Palabras* (The Sea Inside, 2005)
○ *Volver* (Return, 2006)

ON CANVAS

Spain's golden age in art came midway through the 16th century and was dominated by masters such as Diego Velázquez, Francisco de Zurbarán, José de Ribera and Bartolomé Murillo. In a class of his own was Francisco de Goya, who dominated the late 18th and early 19th centuries. The first half of the 20th century brought the extraordinary trio of Pablo Picasso, Joan Miró and Salvador Dalí.

IN STONE

Spain's architectural heritage ranges from Celtiberian hamlets and Roman ruins (such as those at Mérida and Segovia) to 21st-century wonders such as Frank Gehry's Guggenheim Museum in Bilbao and Jean Nouvel's Torre Agbar in Barcelona. In between are ranged a plethora of pre-Romanesque (in Asturias) and Romanesque churches, grand Gothic cathedrals (such as in Burgos and Toledo), and extraordinary jewels of Muslim architecture, led by the Alhambra (Granada) and Mezquita (Córdoba). A brief and manic spurt around the turn of the 20th century saw Antoni Gaudí and co at work on their madcap *modernista* fantasies in Barcelona.

CUISINE

Dining in Spain is a way of life. This is the land of the long lunch, sitting down – or standing up! Munching on tapas over beer, wine or sherry is a favourite pastime. Spaniards love their ham and sausages, and are spoiled for choice with wine, especially from the Rioja. Catalonia and Valencia offer various rice-based seafood dishes, best known of which is paella. Seafood predominates around the coast, from octopus in Galicia to whitebait in Andalucía. In the interior expect heartier meat fare. Chefs such as Ferran Adrià, Juan Mari Arzak and their acolytes have revolutionised Spanish cooking and have their French colleagues trembling before the new-wave *nueva cocina española*.

SURPRISES

○ Central Spain is freezing in winter while the north is akin to rain-soaked Ireland.
○ Per capita, Spaniards drink more beer than wine.
○ The Basque language, spoken in parts of Spain, is one of Europe's oldest tongues.

TOP FESTIVAL

Crackling, spitting flames roar into the night sky from an extraordinary 30-metre-high *falla*, a fantastical sculpture in wood, papier-mâché and polystyrene. This spectacle in mid-March is the culmination of five days' round-the-clock partying in the streets of Valencia. Throughout the city, some 400 *falla* of all shapes and sizes burn in this wild ritual to mark the end of winter.

WILD THINGS

Almost 200 brown bears wander the Cordillera Cantábrica and Pyrenees mountain ranges, accompanied in the northwest by about 2500 wolves. Only a handful of the feline Iberian lynx survive, mostly in Andalucía. Spain has the biggest and most varied bird population in Europe, including 25 species of birds of prey, among them the golden eagle and griffon vulture.

ESSENTIAL EXPERIENCES

○ **Meandering the winding medieval lanes of old Toledo**
○ **Skiing the slopes of Baqueira-Beret in the Pyrenees**
○ **Sampling hearty reds in the wine cellars of the Rioja**
○ **Immersing yourself in the crystal waters of Menorca**
○ **Gawping at Gaudí's La Sagrada Família in Barcelona**
○ **Sipping tea in Granada's Albayzín district after a visit to the Alhambra**
○ **Exploring the villages of Las Alpujarras**
○ **Hiking the remote trails of the Sierra de Gredos**
○ **Marching the Camino de Santiago pilgrimage to Santiago de Compostela**
○ **Hopping the *pintxo* (tapas) bars on a lively night out in San Sebastián**

JEAN-PIERRE LESCOURRET // PHOTOLIBRARY

THE ANCIENT ALHAMBRA PALACE IN GRANADA WAS ONCE HOME TO SPAIN'S MUSLIM KINGS ⬆

SIMON GREENWOOD // LONELY PLANET IMAGES

MAP REF // E12

⬆ THERE MUST BE AN EASIER WAY TO MAKE TOMATO SAUCE: TOMATO FIGHT AT LA TOMATINA FESTIVAL IN BUÑOL

BEST TIME TO VISIT **MARCH TO JUNE & SEPTEMBER**

FLAMENCO DANCERS PERFORM SOME FANCY FOOTWORK »

JEAN-PIERRE LESCOURRET // CORBIS

THE ART AND SCIENCE OF ARCHITECTURAL ASTONISHMENT: VALENCIA'S CIUDAD DE LAS ARTES Y LAS CIENCAS »

FROM FIELD TO SUMMIT: SPAIN SHOWS THERE'S BEAUTY IN CONTRAST »

ANDORRA

THE PRINCIPALITY OF ANDORRA IS WEDGED BETWEEN SPAIN AND FRANCE. IT MAY BE TINY, BUT IT OFFERS BY FAR THE BEST SKIING IN THE PYRENEES, SPECTACULAR SUMMERTIME MOUNTAIN WALKING – AND YEAR-ROUND DUTY-FREE SHOPPING.

CAPITAL CITY ANDORRA LA VELLA **POPULATION** 71,820 **AREA** 468 SQ KM **OFFICIAL LANGUAGE** CATALAN

LANDSCAPE

Rucked and buckled, with scarcely a flat patch to its name, Andorra is a land of rugged mountains sliced right through by tight valleys. This small country has just one main road, plus a couple of secondary highways.

HISTORY IN A NUTSHELL

Tradition has it that Andorra was created in AD 803 by the emperor Charlemagne, who is also considered the founding father of France and Germany. From the 13th century until as recently as 1993, Andorra was ruled jointly by the president of France and the bishop of Urgell, just over the frontier in Spain. Nowadays, Andorra is independent and defined as a parliamentary co-princedom, although the princes' powers are in fact merely symbolic.

PEOPLE

Andorrans are a minority in their own country, comprising just 33 per cent of the total population, outnumbered by Spanish-born residents (43 per cent). At 83.5 years, Andorran life expectancy is the world's highest – could it be the fresh mountain air, perhaps?

MARKETPLACE

Some 11 million visitors, most of them on day trips, pour into Andorra every year. As such, the tourism industry accounts for more than 80 per cent of the country's gross GDP, while banking is also making an increasing, if less evident, contribution to the national economy. The residual agricultural sector (tobacco growing and cattle raising, in the main) these days represents only around one per cent of economic activity.

TRADEMARKS

- Duty-free shopping
- Skiing
- Mountain walking
- Smuggling
- Banking
- Stamps

IN STONE

The oldest and most attractive building to be found in many Andorran villages will be its church: slate roofed, simple and built of shaped stone in soft browns and greys. Other architectural jewels include the Església de Santa Coloma, with its 12th-century freestanding bell tower; the Romanesque churches of Sant Martí, in La Cortinada, and Sant Joan de Caselles, near Canillo; and the contemporary Santuari de Nostra Senyora de Meritxell, a replacement of the original 12th-century shrine that was destroyed by fire in 1972.

RANDOM FACTS

- Andorra is the only country in the world whose official national language is Catalan.
- Of Andorra's seven *parròquie* (parishes), six have existed since at least the 9th century.
- The country isn't *completely* tax-free. A modest service tax of four per cent was introduced in 2006 (and oh, the protests and palaver!).

MYTHS & LEGENDS

One day, villagers from Meritxell stumbled across a statue of the Virgin Mary beside a rose bush. The local priest took the statue and placed it in his church, but the next day it had gone, only to reappear beside the rose bush. They tried again and put the Virgin in the church of a nearby parish, but once again she mysteriously appeared back by the rose bush. The villagers got the message, and chose that spot to construct a shrine to Nostra Senyora de Meritxell, today the patron saint of Andorra.

SURPRISES

- Fresh milk is imported by the hectolitre, then sold on to day-trippers from France, who buy it by the bucketful.
- Although Andorra is famous for its postage stamps, it has no postal service of its own. France and Spain each issues its own Andorran stamps.
- Scarcely 50 years ago, before the advent of skiing and shopping, Andorra's population hovered around just 6000.

FUTURE DIRECTIONS

Andorra is constructing at an alarming pace. There's a real risk that greed and uncontrolled development will continue to seep into its valleys and destroy the high mountain tranquillity that entices many visitors.

ESSENTIAL EXPERIENCES

- **Hauling yourself up Pic de Coma Pedrosa (2942 metres), Andorra's highest summit**
- **Swishing along the cross-country ski trails from La Rabassa**
- **Steeping yourself in the naturally warm waters of La Caldea spa**
- **Whizzing down Grandvalira's Gall de Bosc blue-rated ski run (total altitude loss is 760 metres)**
- **Dancing away the ski bruises in the bars and clubs of Soldeu**
- **Browsing the Museu del Tabac, a museum that recalls the pleasurable sins of tobacco and smuggling**

MAP REF // G12

BEST TIME TO VISIT DECEMBER TO APRIL, JULY TO SEPTEMBER

TAKING THE SLIPPERY SLOPE TO PAS DE LA CASA SKI RESORT IN THE BREATHTAKING PYRENEES »

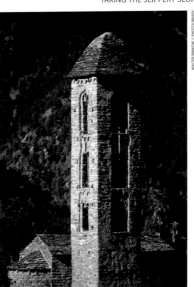

LA CALDEA SPA'S DYNAMIC ARCHITECTURE MIMICS ITS PYRENEAN SETTING »

BELL TOWER, SANT MIGUEL D'ENGOLASTERS »

LAW AND ORDER, ANDORRAN STYLE »

TEXT REGIS ST LOUIS

PORTUGAL

ONE OF THE WORLD'S SUPERPOWERS OF THE 16TH CENTURY, PORTUGAL TODAY IS A COUNTRY OF SLEEPY VILLAGES, DRAMATIC COASTLINE AND HISTORIC CITIES THAT HAVE UNDERGONE A DRAMATIC RENAISSANCE.

CAPITAL CITY LISBON   POPULATION 10.6 MILLION   AREA 92,390 SQ KM   OFFICIAL LANGUAGES PORTUGUESE, MIRANDESE

⌃ PONTE 25 DE ABRIL SUSPENDS ITSELF ACROSS THE RIO TEJO TO LISBON, WATCHED OVER BY CHRIST THE KING

LANDSCAPE

Portugal has an impressive coastline: 830 kilometres of Atlantic-fronting beaches, cliffs and coves, along with Lisbon's magnificent natural harbour. The Rio Tejo, which flows past the capital, effectively divides the country in two. The northern half is a land of rugged mountains, river-filled gorges and fertile valleys. South of the Rio Tejo lies the arid Alentejo, with vineyards, cork plantations and olive groves covering the rolling hillsides. Further south, and divided by small mountain chains, is the Algarve, Portugal's dramatic southern coast.

HISTORY IN A NUTSHELL

Neolithic tribes, Romans and Visigoths all left their mark on Portugal before the arrival of the Moors (North African Muslims) in the 8th century, who introduced new crops such as oranges, sugarcane and rice. Portugal came into its own in the 1500s, when seafaring discoveries filled the royal coffers and transformed the state into a world power. Later conflicts subjected Portugal to foreign rule – including the dastardly Spanish for much of the 17th century. Dominating the 1900s was António de Oliveira Salazar, a demagogue who brutalised the populace. When Portugal emerged from the shadows of dictatorship in 1975, the country was an economic ruin. Despite the obstacles, it's developed considerably in recent decades, transforming itself from one of Europe's backwaters into a modern, forward-looking European Union member.

PEOPLE

The country that practically invented the notion of long-distance travel has an estimated four million Portuguese living abroad. Portugal's largest immigrant population hails from former African colonies, although there are large numbers of Brazilians and Eastern Europeans. Portugal is almost exclusively Roman Catholic (around 94 per cent of the population).

MARKETPLACE

Portugal's economy is still based on traditional industries such as textiles, clothing and footwear, cork and paper products, wine and glassware. Agriculture accounts for three per cent of GDP, although it employs 12 per cent of Portugal's workforce, an indication of Portugal's old-fashioned tendency towards manpower over machinery. While economic growth remained above the European Union average for much of the 1990s, it hit a speed bump in 2001 and has been in a slump ever since.

TRADEMARKS

- Wild beaches backed by red-streaked cliffs
- The scent of freshly grilled sardines
- Black-garbed widows guarding village squares
- The plaintive voice of a soulful *fado* singer
- Imposing castles atop craggy peaks

URBAN SCENE

Draped across riverside bluffs, Porto is a city of Roman ramparts, medieval alleyways, baroque churches and Parisian-style squares. In recent years, it has undergone a remarkable renaissance, with Siza Vieira's Museu de Arte Contemporânea and Rem Koolhaas' Casa da Música its latest stars. Across the river lies Vila Nova de Gaia, where historic port wine lodges clamber up the slopes.

ON DISC

Portugal's most famous style of music is *fado* (meaning 'fate'). These melancholic chants probably have their roots in troubadour songs (although African slave songs have also had an influence). Traditionally sung by one performer accompanied by a 12-string Portuguese guitar, *fado* emerged in the 18th century in Lisbon's working-class districts of Alfama and Mouraria. The greatest modern *fadista* was Amália Rodrigues (1920–99), who brought international recognition to the art.

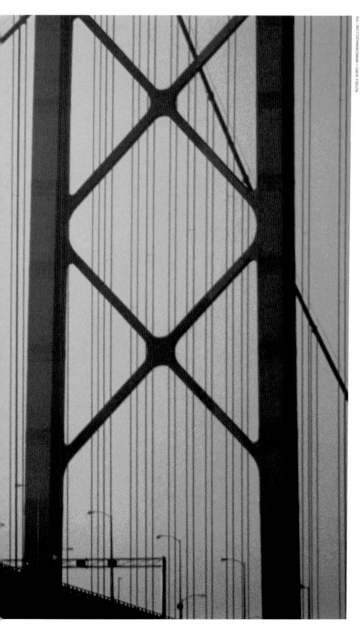

SPINDLY SYMMETRY OF EUCALYPTUS TREES CREATES A MYSTICAL BACKDROP ON A PLANTATION NEAR COIMBRA ≫

A WATCHED FISH NEVER CURES ≫

ON PAPER

The grandfather of Portuguese literature is Luís Vaz de Camões (1524–80), whose epic poem *The Lusiads*, describes Vasco da Gama's sea voyage to India. The great poet of the early 20th century was Fernando Pessoa (1888–1935), whose masterwork, *The Book of Disquietude*, was published long after his death. Today's literary scene is dominated by José Saramago, a discursive and brilliantly inventive writer, who won the Nobel Prize for Literature in 1998. Saramago's *The Gospel According to Jesus Christ* retells the famous story from a radically different perspective. Another superb contemporary writer is António Lobo Antunes. His novel *The Return of the Caravels* features a time warp where 15th-century navigators meet 1970s soldiers.

MYTHS & LEGENDS

The most violent earthquake in Europe's recorded history struck Lisbon on All Saints' Day, 1 November, in 1755. It happened around 9.30am, when half the city was attending the holy day Mass. Many churches collapsed outright, while others burned in the ensuing fires. Lisboetas who survived the initial tremor fled to the sea, only to be drowned by a tsunami set off by the quake. As many as 90,000 (out of a population of 270,000) perished. To some, the earthquake was the wrath of God – though why the brothel district and prison survived was difficult for fire-and-brimstone-preaching friars to explain. The French philosopher Voltaire, who felt the quake in Switzerland, immortalised the catastrophic event in his satirical novel *Candide*.

RANDOM FACTS

○ Portuguese explorers introduced the mosquito net, guns, tempura and bread to the Japanese.

○ During World War II, numerous spies lingered in Portugal, including Dusko Popov, Ian Fleming's inspiration for James Bond.

○ Over the 15 years following the monarchy's collapse in 1910, Portugal went through 45 changes of government, the shortest lasting less than a day.

CUISINE

In coastal towns, fresh fish, octopus and prawns are cooked on sizzling hot coals outside restaurants. Rich seafood stews such as *arroz de tamboril* (monkfish rice) and *caldeirada*, a kind of Portuguese bouillabaisse, are other coastal specialities. In the north, *cabrito assado* (roast kid) is a crowd pleaser, as is *posta de barrosã*, a tasty rare beef. Portugal produces much wine, with the best reds coming from the Douro. Decadent desserts such as *pastel de nata* (custard tarts) are highly addictive.

TOP FESTIVAL

The Festa de Santo António, celebrated from 12 to 13 June in Lisbon, is the climax of three weeks of partying known as the Festas de Lisboa. This lively festival is celebrated with particular fervour in Alfama by some 50 *arraiais* (street parties). The highlight is the Marchas Populares, on the evening of 12 June, when dozens of communities march along Avenida da Liberdade.

⌃ SHELTERING BY DEGREES FROM THE SEARING PORTUGUESE SUN

ESSENTIAL EXPERIENCES

○ Catching a melancholic, traditional *fado* performance, sung in Lisbon's Alfama district

○ Watching the sunset from the dramatic cliffs near Sagres

○ Exploring the whitewashed villages of the Alentejo

○ Savouring a glass of port in the Douro valley

○ Taking in the sun and surf of the Algarve

MAP REF // D12

BEST TIME TO VISIT **MAY TO OCTOBER**

≫ THE LUMINOUS MODERNITY OF ESTAÇÃO DO ORIENTE METRO STATION AT LISBON'S PARQUE DAS NAÇÕES

BRIGHT IMPÉRIO (CHAPELS) DECORATE TERCEIRA ISLAND IN THE AZORES ≫

THE SIMPLICITY OF PRIMARY COLOURS MARKS A BOLD PALETTE ≫

TEXT PAULA HARDY

ITALY

ITALY BOASTS INTERNATIONALLY FAMOUS ART AND ARCHITECTURE, UNESCO HERITAGE SITES, SUNNY ISLES AND ELECTRIC-BLUE SURF, SNOW-COATED ALPINE PEAKS AND ROLLING GREEN COUNTRYSIDE – STILL THE *BELLEZZA* (BEAUTY) OF THIS COUNTRY DEFIES DESCRIPTION.

CAPITAL CITY ROME   **POPULATION** 58.1 MILLION   **AREA** 301,230 SQ KM   **OFFICIAL LANGUAGE** ITALIAN

LANDSCAPE

More than 75 per cent of Italy is mountainous and two chief ranges dominate the landscape. The Alps stretch 966 kilometres from east to west across the northern edge of the country; their foothills are ringed by a string of grand lakes, the largest including Lago di Garda, Lago di Como and Lago Maggiore. The Apennines run north to south for more than 1350 kilometres from Genoa to Calabria. Beyond these mountain peaks, just one quarter of Italy's landmass can be described as lowland. One of the largest areas is the Po valley, divided by the Po River, the longest in Italy at 628 kilometres. For many, however, Italy's 7600 kilometres of coastline remains the real drawcard, from the translucent waters of Sardinia to the sandy beaches of the Adriatic seaboard.

HISTORY IN A NUTSHELL

Italy has been a geographic entity for thousands of years, but it was the Romans who subdued the Italian tribes during the 2nd century and unified the country. Another important legacy of the Roman period was the establishment of the Catholic Church with the pope at its head; it was the medieval papacy that set in motion the modern era. For centuries popes and emperors fought to control Italy's disparate city-states, many of which grew fabulously rich on trade and commerce. Venice, Florence, Milan, Genoa, Pisa and Siena all had their heyday; their wealth and new-found curiosity brought an end to the Dark Ages and ushered in the Renaissance in the 14th century. Finally, in 1861, after hundreds of years of foreign interference, the country was reunited under a single monarchy, which was abandoned in 1946 in favour of today's republic.

PEOPLE

Although Italy has one of the oldest and most homogeneous populations in Europe, regional affiliations still rule the day. It's hardly surprising that since the fall of the Roman Empire until reunification in 1870, the Italian peninsula was divided into city-states, imperial territories belonging to one foreign nation or another. These days Italy is facing a population crisis. With more than 10 million people over 65, Italians are dying more quickly than they're arriving. An average of 2.1 children per woman is required to keep the population stable. The average is currently just 1.3.

MARKETPLACE

Italy is currently plagued by a deep-rooted economic malaise, largely caused by corrupt governance and vested interests that have made modernising the economy a near impossible task. In 2006 Italy was the only economy in the European Union that actually shrank (annual growth for the year was just 0.1 per cent), and prospects for the future are anaemic at best. Furthermore, Romano Prodi's coalition government does not bode well for any radical change. The *Economist* has gloomily concluded that Italy is 'slipping inexorably back into the past'.

TRADEMARKS

o Michelangelo
o The pope and Easter festivals
o Pizza
o The Colosseum (and Russell Crowe as the archetypal gladiator)
o Fiat and Ferrari
o Campari Rosso
o The Mafia
o Sophia Loren
o Sex in parked cars

≫ ROME'S COLOSSEUM STOPS TRAFFIC

≫ CAFFEINE CONNOISSEURS RELAX IN ROME'S PIAZZA NAVONA

≫ HAVING A BALL IN PIAZZA DEL PLEBISCITO, NAPLES

MAURO FERMARIELLO // PHOTOLIBRARY

MARTIN CHILD // GETTY

TAKING A MODERN APPROACH TO THE TRADITION OF ITALIAN SCULPTURE ⌃

SIME / GIOVANNI SIMEONE // 4CORNERS IMAGES

GARY YEOWELL // GETTY

THE WHITEWASHED COAST OF THE SORRENTINE PENINSULA, CAMPANIA ⌃

FLORENCE'S RUST-COLOURED ROOFTOPS SPRAWL FOR MILES ⌃

RANDOM FACTS

○ Alessandro Volta invented the electric battery in 1800 and gave his name to the measurement of electric power.
○ The annual pasta consumption is 28 kilograms per person.
○ Estimated Mafia profits amount to 10 per cent of Italy's GDP.

NATURAL BEAUTY

Italy's cultural riches are matched by stunning natural beauty: from the rolling hills of Tuscany, Umbria and Emilia-Romagna to the dramatic peaks of the Alps and Apennines, the brooding volcanoes of Campania and Sicily, and fragrant maquis-covered coastal cliffs of the Cinque Terre, the Tuscan riviera and the Amalfi Coast.

ON CANVAS

The story of Italian art from the 13th to the 15th century illuminates one of the richest periods in European art history. It was a period that saw the reinvention of the fresco technique by the likes of Duccio di Buoninsegna and the brilliant Giotto di Bondone. Their work laid the foundations for the High Renaissance, which was dominated by luminaries such as Leonardo da Vinci, Michelangelo Buonarotti, Raphael, Titian and Correggio, culminating in the work of *l'enfant terrible,* Caravaggio.

ON FILM

○ *La Dolce Vita* (The Sweet Life, 1960)
○ *Il Gattopardo* (The Leopard, 1963)
○ *Death in Venice* (1971)
○ *A Room with a View* (1986)
○ *Buongiorno, Notte* (Good Morning, Night; 2004)

IN STONE

Classical ruins are scattered across the country, from the Roman Forum to the ashes of Pompeii in Campania. From such monumental beginnings Italian architecture runs the gamut of styles: Pisa's Piazza dei Miracoli, with its concentration of Romanesque splendour; Brunelleschi's picture-perfect dome on Florence's Duomo; the soaring Gothic steeples of Milan's Duomo; and the madcap baroque excesses of the Basilica di Santa Croce in Lecce. For modern architecture, Milan is at the vanguard with an urban regeneration programme involving architects Massimiliano Fuksas, Zaha Hadid, Norman Foster and Daniel Libeskind.

URBAN SCENE

Contemporary Rome more than stands up to its past, with festivals, outdoor summer cinema, squatter arts venues and sexy clubs. For cool, cutting-edge culture Milan leads the way; for a shot of high-voltage street life anarchic Naples is hard to beat; but the party capital of Italy has to be Bologna with its 90,000-strong student population.

CUISINE

Italians are rightly proud of their food. It is invested with all the ritual significance that a rich culinary tradition attracts. Although bread, pasta and rice are the staples of any Italian table, in keeping with the microcultures and geography of the peninsula, regional variations show great diversity. The northern Lombardy style is creamy, cheesy and meat-obsessed, while the palate of the south is lighter and fruitier with peppery olive oils and sweet tomatoes. What all regional cuisines have in common, however, is a respect for quality seasonal ingredients and strong, simple flavours.

TOP FESTIVAL

With its solemn supplicants, writhing snakes, and jewel-bedecked effigy, the Processione dei Serpari (Snake-Charmers' Procession) is like a scene from some otherworldly pagan past. Held in the village of Cocullo (Arbruzzo), on the first Thursday in May, this bizarre ritual celebrates the miraculous healing powers of San Domenico, a Benedictine friar who allegedly purged the fields of the slithery menace back in the 11th century.

SURPRISES

○ Italy is the largest consumer of concrete in the world.
○ Spectacles were invented in Venice in the 13th century.
○ Milan is considered the third-wealthiest city in Europe after London and Paris.

ECOTOURISM

One of the best features of Italian tourism is the *agriturismo* (farmstay), a tradition that began roughly 20 years ago when small farmsteads found themselves under pressure to compete with larger producers. With their livelihood at risk, farmers began to offer accommodation to tourists. A key ingredient of Italy's magic, *agriturismi* are rapidly growing in popularity and do much to preserve an ancient way of life.

ESSENTIAL EXPERIENCES

○ **Exhausting yourself in the museums of Rome, Venice and Florence**
○ **Bobbing between opulent *palazzi* on the Venetian lagoon**
○ **Indulging your penchant for fine food in Bologna**
○ **Walking coastal cliffs at the Cinque Terre**
○ **Seeing how the Romans lived and died in Pompeii**
○ **Witnessing the evening pyrotechnics of Stromboli**
○ **Exploring the medieval alleys of Tuscany's hilltop towns**
○ **Diving in the sun-split waters of Sardinia**
○ **Skiing the Milky Way in alpine Piedmont**
○ **Shopping with high-rollers in Milan's Golden Square**

STATUES OF THE VIRGIN MARY STAND GRACEFULLY IN THIS SHOP WINDOW NEAR VATICAN CITY ≫

FROM THE TRAVELLER

After a long day wandering through the narrow streets of Florence, taking in the city's wondrous treasures at every step, I was drawn back to the Duomo and its *campanile* (bell tower). Their stunning neogothic marble façades were painted a pinkish orange by the setting sun. I snapped this picture in front of the baptistry, which cast a shadow over the Duomo. I then climbed to the top of the terracotta-orange *cupola,* which offered spectacular panoramic views of the city.

PH YANG // HONG KONG

MAP REF // K12

BEST TIME TO VISIT **JULY & SEPTEMBER TO OCTOBER**

HOLD YOUR HORSES – HORSEMEN PERFORM AT THE SA SARTIGLIA CARNIVAL IN ORISTANO, SARDINIA ≫

KEVIN COZAD // CORBIS

TRADERS HAGGLING AT A MARKET IN FLORENCE ≫

A GONDOLA SNAKES UP A VENICE CANAL IN EERIE HALF-LIGHT ≫

VATICAN CITY

CAPITAL OF THE CATHOLIC WORLD, THE VATICAN IS A SPIRITUAL SUPERPOWER, A GILDED ENCLAVE OF PRICELESS ART AND ARCHITECTURAL EXCESS.

CAPITAL CITY VATICAN CITY   **POPULATION** 930   **AREA** 0.44 SQ KM   **OFFICIAL LANGUAGES** LATIN, ITALIAN

LANDSCAPE

To the northwest of Rome's historic centre, the Vatican City, or Holy See, sits atop the low-lying Vatican Hill, just a few hundred metres west of the River Tiber. A tiny urban pocket, the Vatican's cityscape is dominated by the domed bulk of St Peter's Basilica and Piazza San Pietro. Beyond its 3.2-kilometre borders, the Holy See also has extraterritorial authority over a further 28 sites in and around Rome. These include the basilicas of San Giovanni in Laterano, Santa Maria Maggiore and San Paolo Fuori-le-Mura; the catacombs; and the pope's summer residence at Castel Gandolfo.

HISTORY IN A NUTSHELL

Established under the terms of the 1929 Lateran Treaty, the State of the Vatican City is the modern vestige of the Papal States. For more than a thousand years, the Papal States had encompassed Rome and much of central Italy, but when Italy was unified in 1861 and Rome fell to Italian troops in 1870, Pope Pius IX was forced to give up the last of his territorial possessions. Relations between Italy and the landless papacy remained strained until Mussolini and Pius XI agreed to form the Vatican State in 1929. More than 75 years on, the pope is still fighting in the Vatican's corner, this time to ensure a place for Catholic morality in an increasingly secular world.

PEOPLE

The Vatican's resident population is almost entirely made up of Catholic clergy and the Swiss Guard. During the day, about 3000 people work in the Holy See, but most are nonresident lay-workers. Latin is the Vatican's official language, although Italian is used for everyday business. Not at all surprisingly, Roman Catholicism is the state religion.

MARKETPLACE

Catholic contributions (known as Peter's Pence), tourism (sales of souvenirs and museum fees) and the Holy See's vast property portfolio are the mainstays of the Vatican economy. Further revenue is generated from sales of postage stamps, coins and medals, as well as various media enterprises. The Vatican has reported an annual profit of €9.7 million.

TRADEMARKS

o The pope
o St Peter's Basilica
o The Sistine Chapel
o The Swiss Guard
o Overpriced tourist tat

TRADITIONS

Of the Vatican's traditions, none is as dramatic as the papal conclave, the process by which a new pope is elected. Dating back to 1274, give or take a few modifications, the rules are explicit: between 15 and 20 days after the death of a pope, the entire College of Cardinals (comprising all cardinals under the age of 80) is locked in the Sistine Chapel to elect the new pontiff. Four secret ballots are held each day until a two-thirds majority has been secured. News of the election is then communicated by the emission of white smoke through a specially erected chimney.

RANDOM FACTS

o The world's smallest country, the Vatican is the only entire nation on Unesco's World Heritage List.
o The Holy See has one of the world's highest crime rates.
o In Piazza San Pietro you'll find 284 columns, 88 pillars and, on top of the colonnade, 140 statues.

IN STONE

The Vatican's current look owes much to the architects and artists of the 16th and 17th centuries. The original 4th-century St Peter's Basilica was almost entirely rebuilt in the 16th century by a phalanx of Renaissance greats – Bramante, Raphael, Antonio da Sangallo and Michelangelo. Later, Giacomo della Porta and Carlo Maderno added further contributions. Piazza San Pietro was designed by the baroque genius Gian Lorenzo Bernini.

SURPRISES

o St Peter's is not the world's largest church: the cathedral in Yamoussoukro, Côte d'Ivoire, is bigger.
o The Swiss Guards are actually Swiss.

MYTHS & LEGENDS

Legends abound regarding St Peter, Christianity's first pope. Tradition holds that he was crucified head down in Nero's stadium, the Ager Vaticanus, in AD 64 or 67, and buried on the site where the main altar of St Peter's Basilica now stands.

ESSENTIAL EXPERIENCES

- ○ **Feasting your eyes on centuries of artistic genius in St Peter's Basilica**
- ○ **Climbing St Peter's dome to clock one of Rome's great rooftop views**
- ○ **Trying to avoid art overload in the vast Vatican Museums**
- ○ **Elbowing your way through the crowds in the Sistine Chapel**
- ○ **Taking a breather in Piazza San Pietro and counting the columns**
- ○ **Exploring the Vatican Grottoes, last resting place of Pope John Paul II and many of his predecessors**
- ○ **Snapping a po-faced Swiss Guard for that unavoidable holiday photo**

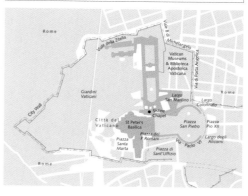

MAP REF // K12

BEST TIME TO VISIT APRIL TO JUNE, SEPTEMBER TO OCTOBER

LONG TIME STANDING: THE PAPAL SWISS GUARD HAS BEEN SERVING THE VATICAN SINCE 1506 »

ARCHITECTURAL ASCENDENCY IS REACHED THROUGH THIS SUBLIME VATICAN DOME »

NUNS GATHER IN PRAYER UPON THE DEATH OF POPE JOHN PAUL II, PIAZZA SAN PIETRO »

SAN MARINO

THIS TINY MOUNTAIN FASTNESS MAY BE EUROPE'S THIRD-SMALLEST STATE BUT ROOTS GROW DEEP HERE IN THE CONTINENT'S OLDEST REPUBLIC.

LANDSCAPE

You can walk all that is of interest in the state of San Marino from end to end in less than half an hour. Its only town perches atop a rocky outcrop, rearing from the surrounding pancake-flat plain that stretches as far as the Adriatic Sea. The town is essentially one long street bordered by shops and cafés, clinging for dear life to the crest's northern limit. Above it looms Monte Titano, the state's highest point at 775 metres. To the south, outside the old city walls, is a craggy and relatively unspoilt area, clad in typical Apennine vegetation of pine and oak.

HISTORY IN A NUTSHELL

According to tradition, the city-state was founded in AD 301 by the eponymous St Marino. Thanks to a near-impregnable position lording it over the surrounding plains, some smart acts of diplomacy over the centuries, and perhaps too because no-one else coveted it enough, San Marino has been pretty much independent ever since. There have been just three brief occupations in its history: the first by Cesare Borgia, of the infamous papal Borgia family, in 1503; the second by the papal governor of coastal Ravenna a couple of centuries later in 1739; and the final one by beleagured Nazi forces in 1944.

CAPITAL CITY **SAN MARINO**   POPULATION **29,600**   AREA **61.2 SQ KM**   OFFICIAL LANGUAGE **ITALIAN**

≫ SAN MARINO'S ANCIENT CRENELLATED FORTIFICATIONS HOLD FAST TO THE ROCKS

PEOPLE

Among the country's 29,000 inhabitants, around one thousand are foreign-born, the majority of whom are Italian. Ninety-five per cent of the population are adherents of the Roman Catholic faith, and the spoken language is Italian.

MARKETPLACE

Tourism represents well in excess of 50 per cent of San Marino's GDP. The per capita output of the Sammarinese, as citizens of the country are called, hovers around €26,000. The economic envy of many a larger country, San Marino sustains a regular annual state budget surplus and hasn't a cent of national debt.

TRADEMARKS

- Stamps
- Formula One Grand Prix
- Chocolate-box soldiers on guard
- Crossbows
- Shopping

RANDOM FACTS

- The San Marino Formula One Grand Prix doesn't roar around the republic's narrow streets; it's held at Imola, in Italy's Emilia-Romagna region, 100 kilometres away.
- To deter gold-diggers, a regulation forbids the employment of female domestic staff under the age of 50.
- San Marino has an honorary consul in Honolulu.
- Darryl Zanuck rented the entire republic for his 1949 film *Prince of Foxes*.

MYTHS & LEGENDS

Marino was a stone mason and a particularly ardent early Christian believer. According to legend, he escaped persecution by the Roman emperor Diocletian, who objected to his inflammatory sermons in nearby Rimini, by retreating to Monte Titano. Here the stone mason built himself a small church and founded the tiny city-state that today bears his name.

IMPORT

- ↗ Visitors – more than three million every year
- ↗ Nearly all its foodstuffs and consumer goods
- ↗ Bank deposits from overseas (few questions asked)
- ↗ All its electricity
- ↗ Tacky souvenirs made in Asia

EXPORT

- ↖ Commemorative stamps, a regular contribution to state coffers since 1894
- ↖ Coins, both San Marino euro issues and its own legal-tender gold coins
- ↖ A plucky, if unlucky, international football team, scorer of the World Cup's fastest goal (after eight seconds, against England)
- ↖ Ceramics
- ↖ Tacky souvenirs made in Asia

TOP FESTIVAL

San Marino's Giornate Medioevali are four days and nights of medieval merriment at the end of July. Flags are twirled and hurled high, drums thump and roll, and arrows fly from crossbows, traditionally the local weapon of choice.

- **Exploring the crenellated battlements and the fortified Guaita and Cesta towers**
- **Browsing for back issues in the Uffizio Filatelico-Numismatico, official outlet for San Marino's colourful stamps, coins and, for the seriously nerdy, telephone cards**
- **Savouring the vast hilltop panorama of the plain below**
- **Enjoying the cable-car ride up to San Marino from Borgo Maggiore at the foot of the mountain**
- **Competing with friends for who can spot the tackiest souvenir**
- **Leaving the heaving shopping streets to seek peace and spectacular, plunging views along the narrow footpath following the crest southward**

MAP REF // K12

BEST TIME TO VISIT **APRIL TO JUNE, SEPTEMBER & OCTOBER**

⌃ FENDER AND FORTRESS: A WELL-LOVED DUO DRAWS A CROWD

⌃ VERANDAS STRETCH OUT ALONG NARROW STREETS TO OFFER SHOPPERS REPRIEVE FROM THE SUN

TEXT CAROLYN BAIN

MALTA

FROM MYSTERIOUS, PREHISTORIC TEMPLES TO MAGNIFICENT BAROQUE ARCHITECTURE, CELEBRATORY FEASTS TO A *FESTA* OF NOISY FIREWORKS, ANTIQUE YELLOW BUSES TO COLOURFUL FISHING BOATS, THIS LILLIPUTIAN COUNTRY OFFERS SURPRISING DRAWCARDS OUT OF ALL PROPORTION TO ITS SIZE.

CAPITAL CITY **VALLETTA**   POPULATION **401,880**   AREA **316 SQ KM**   OFFICIAL LANGUAGES **MALTESE, ENGLISH**

⌃ A SALT HARVESTER WORKS THE SALT FLATS UNDER THE MIDDAY SUN, GOZO ISLAND

LANDSCAPE

Malta is made up of three inhabited islands: Malta, Gozo and Comino. They lie in the middle of the Mediterranean, directly south of Sicily, and enjoy agreeably warm weather year-round, rising to uncomfortably hot in summer. Malta's small surface area hosts one of the world's highest population densities and is heavily built-up; there are no major hills or watercourses, and little greenery to soften the sun-bleached landscape.

HISTORY IN A NUTSHELL

There's been an eclectic mix of influences and a roll call of rulers over the centuries. After the mysterious era of the temple-builders, Malta was colonised by the Phoenicians and Carthaginians, then became part of the Roman Empire. According to folklore, St Paul was shipwrecked here around AD 60 and brought Christianity to the population. The Arabs came next, and afterwards a succession of foreign rulers. In 1530 the islands were given to the Knights of the Order of St John, a religious crusader organisation, who built the capital and left an indelible mark on the country. Napoleon was the next to plant his flag here, in 1798, but the British quickly helped liberate the country from the French.

The Brits began to develop Malta into a major naval base, and it suffered hugely from bombing during World War II. The country gained independence from Britain in 1964, became a republic in 1974, and joined the European Union in 2004.

PEOPLE

Malta's population is just over 400,000, of which 97 per cent is Maltese-born. Despite an easy blend of Mediterranean and British culture, there's still a strong feeling of tradition. Around 98 per cent of Maltese are Roman Catholic, and the Church wields considerable influence. The vast majority of the population is bilingual, speaking English alongside Maltese (a fascinating language with Arabic grammar and construction).

MARKETPLACE

Statistically, the Maltese people enjoy a good standard of living, low inflation and a relatively low level of unemployment. Malta produces only about 20 per cent of its total food needs, has limited fresh water supplies, and has no domestic energy sources. Tourism is the most vital component of the country's economy, generating around a quarter of its GDP.

TRADEMARKS

o The Maltese Cross
o Catholicism
o World War II heroism
o The Knights of the Order of St John
o Scuba diving
o Rabbit feasts
o British tourists

URBAN SCENE

Valletta is one of Europe's tiniest capitals. When the city was built in the 16th and 17th centuries, it was decreed it should be 'a city built by gentlemen for gentlemen', and it retains much of its elegance to this day. There's much to admire in the history-filled streets, squares and alleys, and in its idiosyncratic quirks – a colourful row of overhanging first-floor balconies, a hulking bastion as a reminder of a turbulent past, a shop front that could be a relic of 1930s Britain. When you tire of the history lessons, there are the treats you'd expect of most European capitals, albeit on a tiny scale.

NATURAL BEAUTY

You don't expect a small, densely populated country to offer too much in the way of natural beauty, but the occasionally dramatic coastline and slow-paced rural

COASTAL HUGGING, MEDITERRANEAN STYLE, LEAVES ROOM FOR QUILTED FIELDS TO SPRAWL OUTSIDE OF TOWN »

THROWING A BEACH BALL ISN'T NEARLY AS MUCH FUN AS THROWING A BEACH BOY AT MELLIEHA BAY »

areas (particularly of Gozo) provide relief when you've overdosed on Malta's urban sprawl. Dwejra on Gozo's west coast showcases Malta's nature at its rawest – bays, a lagoon, a natural arch and other oddly shaped rock formations. Clifftop walks at Dingli and Ta'Ċenċ provide dramatic views, while pristine water beckons at beaches such as Golden Bay (Malta), Ramla Bay (Gozo) and the ever-photogenic Blue Lagoon (Comino).

CUISINE

Like the local language, Maltese cuisine demonstrates multicultural influences. The food is quite rustic, and meals are generally based on seasonal produce and the fisherman's catch. *Fenek* (rabbit) is *the* favourite Maltese dish, whether fried in olive oil, roasted, stewed, served with spaghetti or baked in a pie. A *fenkata* is a big, communal meal of rabbit; it supposedly originated as a gesture of rebellion against the occupying Knights, who hunted rabbits and denied them to the local population.

RANDOM FACTS

- The most common name for males in Malta is Joseph, and for women it's Mary (spot the trend?).
- Malta has one of the highest number of cars in the European Union on a per-capita basis, and the least amount of land on which to drive them.
- Malta's fortresses are something of a magnet for film crews and have been the setting for swords-and-sandals blockbusters, including *Gladiator* (2000) and *Troy* (2004).

MYTHS & LEGENDS

Malta's oldest monuments are megalithic temples built between 3600 and 2500 BC, the oldest surviving freestanding structures in the world. Well before the construction of the Egyptian pyramids, the people of Malta were manipulating megaliths weighing up to 20 tonnes and creating buildings that appear to be oriented in relation to the winter solstice sunrise. Little is known about these temple-builders, but they appear to have worshipped a cult of fertility; archaeologists have found large numbers of figurines and statues of wide-hipped, well-endowed female figures – the so-called 'fat ladies' of Malta (no offence, girls) – that have been interpreted as fertility goddesses.

IMPORT

- ↗ St Paul and Catholicism
- ↗ The Maltese language (a melting pot of influences)
- ↗ Oh-so-British red telephone boxes
- ↗ The George Cross, awarded to the entire population of Malta for bravery during World War II
- ↗ Masterful 16th-century Italian painter Caravaggio
- ↗ British expats and tourists

EXPORT

- ↖ A huge diaspora
- ↖ Edward de Bono, world authority on the study of thinking and creativity
- ↖ *Very* enthusiastic Eurovision Song Contest entrants
- ↖ Sunburnt holidaymakers
- ↖ Scuba-diving qualifications

↗ WINE IS BECOMING A SERIOUS BUSINESS IN MALTA

ESSENTIAL EXPERIENCES

- Immersing yourself in the historical architecture of the pint-sized capital of Valletta

- Experiencing first-hand Malta's reputation for bucket-and-spade holidays at its beckoning beaches

- Toasting a town's patron saint at a *festa*, with an infectious mix of music, food and fireworks

- Stepping back through time in the silent streets of Mdina, an oasis of loveliness

- Basking in the charms of greener, more peaceful Gozo, and some of Europe's best scuba diving off its shores

↗ COMPACT TERRACES LINE ST PAUL'S STREET, VALLETTA

MAP REF // K15

BEST TIME TO VISIT **APRIL TO JUNE, SEPTEMBER TO OCTOBER**

↗ A GOZO GRANDMOTHER EMBRACES HER GRANDDAUGHTER

≫ SCHOOL GIRLS ENJOY A BREAK FROM THE CLASSROOM

CUBIST'S DELIGHT: LIMESTONE BLOCKS CHISELLED IN A QUARRY ≫

TRADITIONAL FISHING BOATS MOORED AT DUSK CREATE A QUINTESSENTIALLY MALTESE SCENE ≫

CENTRAL EUROPE

INTRIGUE AND BEAUTY ARE ON A COLLISION COURSE IN THE CENTRAL PIECE OF EUROPE'S PUZZLE, A PLACE WHERE EAST MEETS WEST AND THE GHOSTS OF COMMUNISM STILL LINGER, WHERE THE SPY-NOVEL HISTORY IS AS RICH AND MEATY AS A POLISH POTATO STEW.

From folklore to the Cold War, Central Europe's plot has always been thick. This is where Heidi falls in love with James Bond while skiing down the face of a glacier in the Swiss Alps, then follows him to a smoky coffee house in Prague for a little pre-fall-of-the-Iron-Curtain-style spy speak over a glass of schnapps. Behind the pastel-hued façade of spindly old steeples, cobbled streets and medieval castles, Central Europe is a place that is full of secrets, heady with mystery and burdened with a less-than-nice historical legacy. Even squeaky-clean Switzerland has a darker side. Beyond the mask of rosy-faced goat herders yodelling to a melody of clinking cowbells is a country that created absinthe and LSD, a place known as much for secret bank accounts as it is for chocolate and cheese.

More than anything, Central Europe stimulates its visitors with an enhanced version of the continent. This is the region where Europe's quirks and contrasts, colourful (sometimes clashing) cultural kaleidoscope, and geographical (as well as ideological) peaks and valleys collide.

Speaking of peaks, Central Europe has plenty of them; there's good reason why 'It's a little Switzerland' has become a travel-writing cliché. Sightseers, hikers, cyclists, canoeists – none can go wrong in this part of the continent. Whatever your passion, the legendary Mittleuropa beckons. Soaring mountains, regal rivers, verdant foliage, bucolic countryside, and cities and towns so picture perfect they seem as if they've been created especially for the silver screen are all found here. Adventurers can go from hopping atop a horse-drawn carriage in East Slovakia to skiing powder with the jet set in ritzy St Moritz, Switzerland. History buffs can walk in the footsteps of the Holy Roman, Hapsburg, Austro-Hungarian, Polish-Lithuanian, Ottoman and Prussian empires. Adrenaline addicts can tackle some of the world's highest mountain peaks, spelunk to their hearts' content or turn wrinkly as prunes in old-world thermal spas. Gourmands can compare the goulash in Hungary, Austria and Slovenia, while brew enthusiasts can sample the best of beers at Oktoberfests in Germany, the Czech Republic and Slovakia.

Not bad for a region that for most of the 20th century was split in two. In fact we'd have to say it's made a pretty damn fine comeback. What other bit of Europe has alternately been called a 'tragedy' (Milan Kundera), a 'myth' (countless Russian and European intellectuals), 'utopia' (European Union bureaucrats, of course) and 'Nothing but a meteorological concept' (Peter Handke)? Now that most of the countries in the region (except Switzerland and Liechtenstein) are under the same European Union umbrella, the differences of opinion about this political family reunion will add some spicy sauce to your holiday. Plus, it's super easy now to skip happily across the same borders that once kept Europe strictly divided.

TEXT BECCA BLOND

TEXT ANDREA SCHULTE-PEEVERS

GERMANY

DEEP IN THE HEART OF EUROPE, GERMANY IS AN ECONOMIC AND POLITICAL DYNAMO WITH BEWITCHING SCENERY, PULSATING CITIES, PROGRESSIVE CULTURE AND AN AWARENESS OF A LEGACY TEETERING BETWEEN HORROR AND GREATNESS.

CAPITAL CITY BERLIN   POPULATION 82.4 MILLION   AREA 357,020 SQ KM   OFFICIAL LANGUAGE GERMAN

LANDSCAPE

Europe's fourth-largest country is an intriguing patchwork of mountains, rivers and forests with pockets of moor and heath, mud flats and chalk cliffs, glacial lakes and wetlands. There's something undeniably artistic in the way the landscape unfolds from the flat, windswept north to the brooding forests, river valleys and vast vineyards of the central uplands, all the way south to the Bavarian Alps where Germany's highest peak, the Zugspitze, rises to a lofty 2962 metres.

HISTORY IN A NUTSHELL

No other country has shaped European history more than Germany. Not bad for a nation that only became a unified state in 1871, cobbled together from countless fiefdoms by the Iron Chancellor, Otto von Bismarck. Germanic influence, however, began a thousand years earlier with Charlemagne, whose alliance with the pope laid the foundation for the Holy Roman Empire. A German monk named Martin Luther gave the world the Reformation in 1517 and, a couple of centuries later, the Enlightenment turned Germany into a land of 'thinkers and poets'. This lofty legacy suffered tremendously in the 20th century, which heralded war, Nazism, genocide, division,

dictatorship and – finally – reunification. Modern Germany is solidly democratic and has taken a leading role in the integration of Europe.

PEOPLE

Germany packs over 82 million inhabitants into a pretty tight frame, making it the second most populous nation in Europe. Immigrants account for about nine per cent, or seven million people, with the largest group (1.8 million) hailing from Turkey. There are pockets of Slavonic Sorbs in the eastern part of the country and a Danish minority in the far north, as well as sizable numbers of Italians, Serbs, Greeks and Poles. Germany is a predominantly Christian country with roughly equal numbers of Protestants and Catholics (34 per cent). Muslims account for about four per cent. There are also about 100,000 Jews, many of them immigrants from the former Soviet republics.

MARKETPLACE

Germany has Europe's largest economy, and the third-largest in the world after the US and Japan, with a gross domestic product averaging €2.1 trillion. It is also the world's export champion, whose impressive export volume of €929 billion is fuelled mostly by the

automotive, electrical, chemical and engineering sectors. Income levels are comfortable, if not extravagant by European standards. Workers can expect to take home about €2,500 per month. Inflation runs steady at a low two per cent, but Germany's domestic economy remains hamstrung by low consumption and a high unemployment rate hovering around 11 per cent.

TRADEMARKS

o Autobahns
o Berlin Wall (or what's left of it)
o Boisterous beer halls
o Claudia Schiffer and Heidi Klum
o Dirndls and lederhosen
o Football mania
o Bratwurst and sauerkraut
o Christmas markets

RANDOM FACTS

o The title 'Kaiser' is a direct derivation of the Roman word 'Caesar'.
o The world's first youth hostel was founded by Richard Schirrmann in the medieval castle of Altena in 1912.

A BADEN-WÜRTTEMBERG VINEYARD IS STILLED BY A BLANKET OF WINTER »

≫ MAKING TRACKS THROUGH SEASON'S FIRST SNOWFALL IN MECKLENBURG-VORPOMMERN

≫ LUCKILY THIS PICTURESQUE GUESTHOUSE HAS A DOOR, AT STREET LEVEL

≫ YOUNG BOY ADDS A CANDLE IN TRIBUTE TO NEEDY CHILDREN, BERLIN

BERLIN'S POTSDAMER PLATZ HAS RISEN FROM THE ASHES TO BECOME A VIBRANT CULTURAL HUB ≫

TAKING A LEAP OF FAITH INTO THE FRESHWATER BODENSEE (LAKE CONSTANCE), FRIEDRICHSHAFEN ≫

- The ditty accompanying a bride walking down the aisle is taken from Richard Wagner's opera *Lohengrin*, while the classic post-ceremony song is Felix Mendelssohn's *Wedding March*.
- The north German state of Schleswig-Holstein generates 25 per cent of its power from wind turbines, making it a world leader.

URBAN SCENE

There can be little doubt that Berlin is one of the most red-hot capitals of Europe these days. 'Poor but sexy' is how the city's mayor summed up this cauldron of creativity, hedonism and 24/7 party scenes. From world-class opera to offbeat theatre to trashy dives – you'll find all of them here. Germany's other big cities may be less intense but are no less intriguing. For the full survey, visit elegant Hamburg, cosy Munich, earthy Cologne, lively Leipzig and dreamy Dresden.

ON FILM
- *Metropolis* (1927)
- *Das Boot* (The Boat, 1981)
- *Good Bye Lenin!* (2003)
- *Der Untergang* (Downfall, 2004)
- *The Lives of Others* (2006)

ON PAPER
- *Faust – Part I* by Johann Wolfgang von Goethe
- *Buddenbrooks* by Thomas Mann
- *All Quiet on the Western Front* by Erich Maria Remarque
- *Die Blechtrommel* (The Tin Drum) by Günter Grass
- *Russian Disco* by Wladimir Kaminer

IN STONE

Despite war and destruction, Germany offers a smorgasbord of great architecture with every style from Roman to postmodern represented. Prepare to be awed by the symmetry of Romanesque churches, the loftiness of Gothic cathedrals, the romance of medieval half-timbered villages, the exuberance of baroque palaces and the grandeur of neoclassical monuments. In the 20th century, the German-grown Bauhaus movement laid the groundwork for much of modern architecture.

NATURAL BEAUTY

Germany is a magical quilt of spirit-lifting scenery, a great deal of which is protected in national or nature parks. The jagged peaks of the big-shouldered Bavarian Alps unfold above flowering mountain pastures where cows graze lazily. Mighty rivers flow through romantic valleys, passing steep vineyards, thick fairy-tale forests and sandstone formations that have been chiselled into rugged splendour by the elements. Even the windswept north beckons with its dune-fringed coastline, dramatic white chalk cliffs and endless fields of golden wheat.

CUISINE

German food may not have the same crave-quotient as Italian, but these days foodies are finding lots more than meat, potatoes and cabbage on the average menu. Clever young chefs have given time-honoured dishes an adventurous new edge in a wave called New German Cuisine. Exotic ingredients, seasonal produce and healthful preparation are increasingly becoming the norm, and big cities are awash with a veritable UN of cuisines, from American to Zambian. But even waistline-watchers should not miss out on Germany's favourite snack food: a steamy roasted bratwurst – the ultimate guilty pleasure.

IMPORT
- Oil and natural gas
- Halloween
- A large Turkish community
- McDonald's
- Fitness studios

EXPORT
- BMW and Mercedes
- Aspirin
- Love Parade
- *Grimm's Fairy Tales*
- Christmas trees

TOP FESTIVAL

Rio has its Carnaval, Cannes has its film festival, and Indianapolis has its 500. But the world's biggest party is right here in Germany: Munich's Oktoberfest, an unapologetic assault on the senses and sensibility. For 16 wild days, beginning in late September, the city is ruled by lovers of beer and pretzels, food and foolishness, roller coasters, parties, oompah music and every other indulgence under the sun.

ESSENTIAL EXPERIENCES

- **Counting medieval castles on a lovely, leisurely boat trip through the romantic Rhine Valley**
- **Hoisting a perfect mug of beer while cheering on the oompah band in a Munich beer hall**
- **Admiring Dresden's painterly silhouette from an outdoor café along the Elbe River**
- **Losing track of time during a night of bar hopping and clubbing in sizzling Berlin**
- **'Walking on water' between islands in the Wattenmeer National Park**
- **Treating yourself to steamy mulled wine and bratwurst at Nuremberg's dazzling Christmas market**
- **Getting lost in the maze of crooked lanes in half-timbered Rothenburg ob der Tauber**
- **Catching your breath after climbing the spire of Cologne's colossal cathedral**
- **Rambling through the forest for your favourite view of Schloss Neuschwanstein**

⌃ MODERN-DAY BIG FOOT SNOWSHOES ACROSS NEBELHORN PEAK IN THE GERMAN ALPS

⌃ THE DREAMY SCHLOSS NEUSCHWANSTEIN

FROM THE TRAVELLER

German politicians and Jewish leaders have marked 60 years since the end of World War II by opening Berlin's vast Holocaust memorial, a sprawling field of 2700 stone slabs. The dark-grey, monolithic stones usually have a monochrome appearance. I had passed by it several times in different lighting and it was very stark and sterile. On this particular evening, however, the sun was at just the right angle to cause an interesting three-colour effect. The pedestrian passing through with his bright yellow jacket adds another nice contrast.

SCOTT STANTON // USA

MAP REF // K9

BEST TIME TO VISIT **MAY TO OCTOBER**

AN ELABORATE BEER HALL KEEPS A LID ON SOME RAUCOUS DRINKERS AT MUNICH'S OKTOBERFEST »

ALPHORN PLAYERS BLOW THEIR OWN HORN DURING THE ÄLPLERLETZE CEREMONY, A TRADITION OF ALPINE HERDSMEN TO MARK THE END OF SUMMER »

TEXT BECCA BLOND

SWITZERLAND

AS MELT-IN-YOUR-MOUTH AS THE RICH CHOCOLATES AND CREAMY CHEESES IT IS FAMOUS FOR, SWITZERLAND IS AN EASY COUNTRY TO GET ADDICTED TO.

CAPITAL CITY BERN   POPULATION 7.5 MILLION   AREA 41,290 SQ KM   OFFICIAL LANGUAGES GERMAN, FRENCH, ITALIAN

≫ LIFE'S NOT SO BAD, REALLY, GRAZING AND GAZING IN THE BERNESE ALPS

LANDSCAPE

Mountains comprise 70 per cent of the country's landscape. The famous Alps with their craggy, snowcapped peaks occupy the central and southern portions of Switzerland. The most famous is the 4478-metre Matterhorn. Farming of cultivated land in the mountain valleys is intensive and cows graze on the upper slopes in summer. Switzerland is home to Europe's largest valley glacier, the Aletsch, which encompasses a 169-square-kilometre area.

HISTORY IN A NUTSHELL

The Swiss Confederation was founded on 1 August 1291, and was followed by 200-odd years of military campaigns that expanded its borders. The neutrality for which the country is famous was not declared until 1515. Switzerland flourished after World War II. Zürich developed as an international banking and insurance centre, and many international bodies set up headquarters in Geneva. The country's neutrality led it to decline joining the United Nations until 2002, and it still has not joined the European Union. In recent times a series of scandals has rocked Switzerland's clean-cut image. In 1995 pressure from international Jewish groups led Swiss banks to announce they had discovered millions of dollars in dormant pre-1945 accounts belonging to Holocaust victims and survivors. Banks have since paid US$1.25 billion compensation to Holocaust survivors and their families.

PEOPLE

Switzerland's name may stand for everything from knives to watches, but don't expect this nation to take a stand for anyone other than itself. Militarily neutral for centuries, and armed to the teeth to make sure it stays that way, in Switzerland it's the Swiss way or the highway. Most people are of Germanic origin, as reflected in the breakdown of the four national languages: German (64 per cent), French (20 per cent), Italian (6.5 per cent) and Romansch (0.5 per cent). Around 20 per cent of the population are residents but not Swiss citizens.

MARKETPLACE

Switzerland has some of the highest standards of living in the world. The pharmaceuticals industry is a major contributor to the Swiss economy, giants of which are Novartis and Roche (the manufacturer of the much sought-after antiviral Tamiflu). Nestle, founded in Switzerland more than 100 years ago, remains the world's biggest consumer-food firm.

TRADEMARKS

- Chocolate
- Watches
- Fondue
- Chalets
- Clocks
- Cows

NATURAL BEAUTY

Switzerland dishes up the kind of salacious natural beauty Hollywood filmmakers swoon over. Its seductive Matterhorn country has endless panoramic vistas and breathtaking views to win over the toughest critics. The exquisite area also boasts the 10 highest mountains in Switzerland, all above 4000 metres. Mark Twain once wrote that no opiate could compare to walking through the Bernese Oberland, which is filled with snow-white, craggy, so-big-they'll-swallow-you mountains.

URBAN SCENE

Geneva, Zürich, Basel and Lausanne heave with heady artistic activity and, sometimes, incendiary nightlife. The grandeur of the finest churches, such as the cathedrals in Lausanne and Bern, contrasts with sparkling, lesser-known treasures such as the frescoes of Müstair or the abbey complex of St Gallen (both World Heritage Sites).

SIGHTSEEING INNOVATION: INTERNATIONAL BALLOON WEEK TAKES TO THE SKY ABOVE CHÂTEAUX D'OEX »

WINE ENTHUSIASTS LINE UP FOR A TASTE INSIDE KLEIN MATTERHORN'S GLACIAL CAVE, ZERMATT »

TRADITIONS

When drinking with Swiss, always wait until everyone has their drink in their hand and toast each of your companions, looking them in the eye and clinking glasses. Drinking before the toast is unforgivable, and will lead to seven years of bad sex… or so the superstition goes.

RANDOM FACTS

○ Albert Einstein came up with his special theory of relativity and the famous formula $E=MC^2$ in Bern in 1905.
○ Switzerland gave birth to the World Wide Web at the acclaimed CERN research institute outside Geneva.
○ Val de Travers, near Neuchâtel, claims to be the birthplace of absinthe.
○ Swiss chemist Albert Hofmann took the first acid trip in 1943; he was conducting tests for a migraine cure in Basel when he accidentally absorbed the LSD compound through his fingertips.

CUISINE

Chocolate and cheese are a way of life in Switzerland, and the country produces some of the world's finest varieties of both. The best-known Swiss dish is fondue, in which melted Emmental and Gruyère are combined with white wine, served in a large pot and eaten with bread cubes. Another popular artery hardener is *raclette,* melted cheese served with potatoes. *Rösti* (fried, buttery, shredded potatoes) is German Switzerland's national dish, and is served with everything.

ON FILM

Of the 800 or so films produced each year by India's huge movie-making industry, more are shot in Switzerland than in any other foreign country. 'For the Indian public, Switzerland is the land of their dreams,' filmmaker Raj Mukherjee has said. Favourite shoot destinations include the Bernese Oberland, Central Switzerland and Geneva.

MYTHS & LEGENDS

Switzerland's central Alpine region possesses one of Europe's richest traditions of myth and legend. Pontius Pilate is said to rise out of the lake on Mount Pilatus, near Lucerne, every Good Friday (the day he condemned Jesus Christ) to wash blood from his hands – and anybody who witnesses this event will allegedly die within the year.

‹ SCENIC STECHELBERG IN THE LAUTERBRUNNEN VALLEY

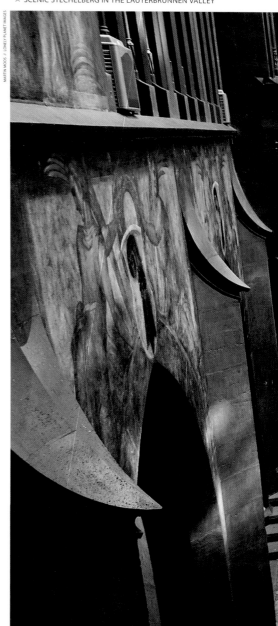

MARTIN MOOS // LONELY PLANET IMAGES

ESSENTIAL EXPERIENCES

○ **Gasping at gargantuan mountain vistas and partaking in white-knuckle adrenaline adventures in the Jungfrau region**

○ **Playing in the mighty Matterhorn's shadow in everyone's favourite Swiss ski town, Zermatt**

○ **Soaking up the seriously sexy ambience at a lakeside café in the sultry Italian canton, Ticino**

○ **Riding the cable car to the top of the Schilthorn then skiing down the mountain's gnarly front to the breathtaking mountain hamlet of Mürren**

○ **Getting clued in to Bern's medieval charm by day, then tasting its sophisticated art-house watering holes come dark**

○ **Joining Zürich's residents for a Sunday morning stroll around the lake then warming up in a cosy restaurant on a quiet, cobbled street with *rösti,* wine and fondue**

○ **Sleeping on straw in a splintery, old barn perched high in an alpine meadow in summer**

MAP REF // J11

BEST TIME TO VISIT **JUNE TO SEPTEMBER**

≫ FAMED AS RESCUE DOGS, ST BERNARDS ARE CARED FOR AS PUPS AT THE BARRY OF THE GREAT ST BERNARD FOUNDATION IN MARTIGNY

START THE CLOCK: WHICH SWISS CUCKOO WILL CHIME FIRST? ≫

LUCIUS MUNATIUS PLANCUS, FOUNDER OF BASEL, OVERSEES THE FRESCOED COURTYARD TO THE *RATHAUS* (TOWN HALL) ≫

LIECHTENSTEIN

IF YOU'RE VISITING THE POCKET-SIZED PRINCIPALITY OF LIECHTENSTEIN SOLELY FOR COCKTAIL-PARTY BRAGGING RIGHTS, KEEP THE OPERATION COVERT; THIS THEME-PARK MICRONATION TAKES INDEPENDENCE SERIOUSLY AND WOULD SHUDDER AT THE THOUGHT OF BEING CONSIDERED FOR NOVELTY ALONE.

CAPITAL CITY VADUZ **POPULATION** 34,250 **AREA** 160 SQ KM **OFFICIAL LANGUAGE** GERMAN

LANDSCAPE
Liechtenstein looks a lot like Switzerland, minus the big cities. It's a mix of towering mountains and cultivated farmland dotted with small villages. The Rhine River forms the entire western border of the country.

HISTORY IN A NUTSHELL
Liechtenstein was named after the powerful family that instigated its creation by merging the domain of Schellenberg and the county of Vaduz in 1712. A principality under the Holy Roman Empire from 1719 to 1806, it achieved full sovereign independence in 1866. A modern constitution was drawn up in 1921, but even today the prince retains the power to dissolve parliament and must approve every act before it becomes law. In 2000, Liechtenstein's financial and political institutions were rocked by allegations that money laundering was rife in the country. In response to international outrage, banks agreed to stop allowing customers to bank money anonymously. King Hans Adam stirred a healthy dose of controversy into the country's political mix in 2003, when he threatened to stomp back to Austria unless the people allowed him to dismiss the elected government, appoint new judges and veto proposed laws. Although opponents warned of dictatorship, the majority of the public stuck by their king and backed him in a referendum. The following year Hans Adam handed the day-to-day running of Liechtenstein to his son Alois, but kept his position as head of state.

PEOPLE
Liechtenstein is Europe's fourth-smallest country. Its residents are mostly Alemannic. Approximately 30 per cent of the resident population is foreign born, and comprises nearly 70 per cent of Liechtenstein's workforce. About 76 per cent of the population is Roman Catholic.

MARKETPLACE
Liechtenstein is a prosperous place with a high standard of living. It has numerous banks, low taxes and the wealthiest royal family in Europe. The unemployment rate, which hovers around 1.3 per cent, is enviable.

TRADEMARKS
○ Postage stamps
○ Mini-Switzerland
○ Expat retreat
○ Cute towns, castles and vineyards
○ Alps and meadows
○ Tax haven

NATURAL BEAUTY
Measuring just 25 kilometres in length and six kilometres in width, Liechtenstein is barely larger than Manhattan. It might not look like much on a map, but up close it's filled with numerous hiking and cycling trails offering spectacular views of rugged cliffs, quaint villages, friendly locals and lush green forests.

RANDOM FACTS
○ Liechtenstein is the only country in the world named after the people who purchased it.
○ In its last military engagement in 1866, none of its 80 soldiers was killed. In fact, 81 returned – the extra being a new Italian 'friend'.
○ Until 2005, Liechtenstein's cows were fed hemp to keep them happy and producing 'better' milk.
○ Liechtenstein is one of only two countries (the other is Uzbekistan) in the world that is doubly landlocked, meaning it's surrounded entirely by other landlocked countries.

ON PAPER
Get under Liechtenstein's historical skin and read *Secrets of the Seven Smallest States of Europe: Andorra, Liechtenstein, Luxembourg, Malta, Monaco, San Marino and Vatican City*, by Thomas Ecchardt. For an interesting take on the tiny country's modern culture, check out *Dots on the Map*, by Colin Leckey.

SURPRISES
○ Liechtenstein bites into a large chunk of the denture market – it's the world's largest exporter of the product.
○ There are 80,000 companies registered in the principality, which is nearly double the population of Vaduz.

○ If you ever meet the prince in the pub, make sure he buys a round. The royal family is estimated to be worth €4.8 billion.

TOP FESTIVAL
As small as it is, even Liechtenstein has its own international film festival. Visit in August and check out the Vaduz Film Festival, which pulls in crowds from across Europe. It features films that come from countries with less than 10 million inhabitants.

ESSENTIAL EXPERIENCES

○ **Snapping a picture of the royal castle in Vaduz with its stunning mountain backdrop**

○ **Sending a postcard home with a souvenir passport stamp**

○ **Hitting the slopes at Malbun for no other reason than to say you've skied the Liechtenstein Alps**

○ **Testing yourself with extreme hiking on the legendary Fürstensteig trail**

MAP REF // J10

BEST TIME TO VISIT DECEMBER TO APRIL, MAY TO OCTOBER

LIECHTENSTEIN CASTLE IN VADUZ IS SURROUNDED BY HIGH MOUNTAINS AND 'HAPPY' COWS »

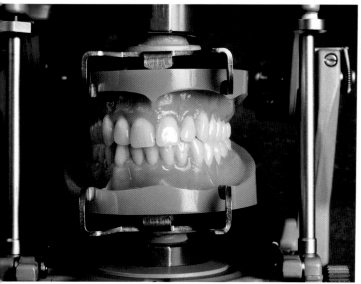

DENTURE EXPORTS HAVE LIECHTENSTEIN SMILING ALL THE WAY TO THE BANK »

GASTHAUS ZUR KRONE HAS BEEN HOUSING GUESTS SINCE THE 15TH CENTURY »

TEXT KERRY WALKER

AUSTRIA

ALPINE HIGHS, CULTURAL CLOUT AND GLORIOUS FOOD: YOU CAN GRAZE FOR WEEKS ON AUSTRIA'S RICHES AND STILL FIND SWEET SURPRISES.

CAPITAL CITY VIENNA   POPULATION 8.2 MILLION   AREA 83,870 SQ KM   OFFICIAL LANGUAGES GERMAN, SLOVENE, CROATIAN, HUNGARIAN

≫ ROYAL VIEWS ACROSS THE DANUBE RIVER FROM DÜRNSTEIN'S KUENRINGERBURG CASTLE, WACHAU VALLEY

LANDSCAPE

Take a map of Europe, try to pinpoint its navel and your finger will probably land on Austria – landlocked, smallish and straddling eight other countries. This chameleonlike nation is home to kaleidoscopic colours, from Tyrol's white slopes to the Wachau Valley's green vines and Styria's cobalt-blue lakes. The highs are the pointy Alps, which dominate most of the landscape, and the lows are the eastern flats, where the Danube slices its way through dense forests and castle-topped crags en route to Vienna.

HISTORY IN A NUTSHELL

The discovery of the buxom *Venus of Willendorf* statuette, one of the earliest examples of art, proves Austria's roots stretch back 25,000 years to Palaeolithic times. Around 500 BC the Celts settled in Hallstatt, centuries later the Romans built forts and named the capital Vindobona, and by 976 the Babenburg dukes ruled the roost. The Hapsburgs, kings of the castle for six centuries until 1918, witnessed two fruitless Turkish invasions, the Thirty Years' War and baroque in full bloom. Rising from the postwar ashes in 1945, Austria prospered and became a European Union member in 1995.

MARKETPLACE

The standard of living is high in Austria; it's the fourth-richest country in the European Union, with GDP per capita hovering around €$26,000. Underpinning the country's prosperous market economy, the service sector, particularly the tourism industry, flourishes thanks to the year-round appeal of the Alps. The rest of the pie is divided between the industrial and small (but significant) agricultural sector. Sound European Union relations and the availability of skilled labour have given the economy the kick it's needed to stay at the top.

PEOPLE

Most of the population are German-speaking Austrians (91 per cent), with former Yugoslavs and Germans making up the country's multiethnic fabric. German is the official language nationwide, but Slovene , Croatian and Hungarian spice up the linguistic mix in the regions. Almost 75 per cent of the population is Roman Catholic, while the rest is split between Protestantism, Islam and other beliefs.

TRADEMARKS
○ *The Sound of Music*
○ *Apfelstrüdel* (apple strudel)
○ Snow-topped mountains
○ Mozart and Strauss
○ Hapsburg palaces

URBAN SCENE

A whirl of colossal art collections and grand architecture, Vienna dishes up perennial favourites such as the imperial Hofburg, the Ringstrasse boulevard that twinkles by night, and *Sacher Torte* chocolate cake in sublime coffee houses. The MuseumsQuartier's avant-garde exhibitions put the cool into the capital. Going west, Salzburg strikes a chord with Mozart symphonies and giddy views atop Europe's largest fortress, Hohensalzburg. A Unesco World Heritage Site, Graz captivates with its lofty clock tower and bubble-shaped Kunsthaus gallery on the Mur River.

NATURAL BEAUTY

Deep powder that squeaks underfoot, thick fir forests and chocolate-box chalets give the Tyrolean Alps fairy-tale appeal. When the snow melts, nature lovers swap skis for sturdy boots to explore Bregenzerwald's limestone crags and green pastures, or the Wachau Valley's vineyards that tumble down to the Danube River. But if you're

BATTLE OF THE BLIMPS AT THE WORLD HOT AIR AIRSHIP CHAMPIONSHIP, STYRIA »

IT'S HARD TO CONCENTRATE ON YOUR FOOD AT CAFÉ LEOPOLD IN VIENNA'S LEOPOLD MUSEUM »

seeking superlatives, it has to be the Hohe Tauern National Park, where a spine of 3000-metre peaks, glacial valleys and the thundering Krimmler Falls look up to Austria's big daddy, the Grossglockner, rising like a vision from the frozen landscape.

ON DISC
Peerless in the classical music department, Austria's greats such as Mahler, Haydn and Schubert are names that trip effortlessly off the tongue. But when it comes to legends, it's a tale of two composers. Salzburg's greatest claim to fame is child prodigy Mozart, who wowed the world with more than 600 classical works, such as opera *The Magic Flute* and serenade *Eine kleine Nachtmusik*. In the 19th century, Strauss showed Vienna how to twirl, with a string of polkas, marches and waltzes, including belle of the ball *Blue Danube*.

RANDOM FACTS
- Austrians love wacky events. One not to be sniffed at is Altaussee's Big Nose Championship – may the best schnoz win…
- Ottoman Turks brought coffee to Vienna, leaving bags of the precious beans behind when they fled the city in the 16th century.
- Richard the Lionheart was imprisoned in Dürnstein's Kuenringerburg castle in the Wachau Valley until his faithful mistress, Blondel, rescued him.

ON CANVAS
Austrian Art Nouveau made waves at the turn of the 20th century. In 1897 Gustav Klimt swam away from the mainstream to found the Vienna Secession movement. His striking collection of femme fatale mosaics and murals includes *The Kiss*. Following in his footsteps, expressionist Egon Schiele shocked the world with erotic, highly charged paintings that explored human sexuality and reflected the rebellious nature of the tortured artist.

⌃ GROSSGLOCKNER LOOMS BEYOND HEILIGENBLUT, CARINTHIA

CUISINE
Schnitzel with noodles was one of Maria's favourite things in *The Sound of Music,* but there's more to Austrian cuisine than that. One of the greatest pleasures is slipping under each region's skin for home-grown flavours: from dairy hopping along the Bregenzerwald Käsestrasse (cheese route), to sipping cider on Lower Austria's Moststrasse route through Mostviertel and savouring fresh trout by Carinthia's lakes. Flavoursome specialities include *tafelspitz* (beef with horseradish), paprika-spiced *gulaschsuppe* (a version of Hungarian goulash), hearty *knödel* (dumplings) and *kaiserschmarrn* (raisin-stuffed pancakes) – the ultimate sugar fix.

SURPRISES
- Vienna's flashiest 21st-century kid is the MuseumsQuartier, one of the 10 biggest cultural complexes in the world.
- Austrians are mad about skinny dipping; Styria's Lake Grundlsee and the Donauinsel (Danube Island) beckon those who dare to bare.
- The drab Wallflower Ball and Ball of Bad Taste are quirky additions to Vienna's ball season.

MAP REF // L10

BEST TIME TO VISIT **MAY TO OCTOBER**

⌃ THE IMPERIAL HOFBURG PALACE ILLUMINATED AT DUSK, VIENNA

≫ TRAVERSING THE EXTRAORDINARY HOHE TAUERN NATIONAL PARK, CARINTHIA

THE BEER'S NOT BAD EITHER AT A MOUNTAIN MUSIC FESTIVAL ≫

UNDULATING LINES AND BRIGHT COLOURS TYPIFY RENOWNED ARCHITECT HUNDERTWASSER'S INNOVATIVE APPROACH, HUNDERTWASSERHAUS, VIENNA ≫

TEXT STEVE FALLON

HUNGARY

A KIDNEY-SHAPED COUNTRY WITH A UNIQUE CULTURE IN THE CENTRE OF EUROPE, HUNGARY'S IMPACT ON THE CONTINENT'S HISTORY HAS BEEN FAR GREATER THAN ITS PRESENT SIZE AND POPULATION WOULD SUGGEST.

CAPITAL CITY **BUDAPEST**   POPULATION **9.9 MILLION**   AREA **93,030 SQ KM**   OFFICIAL LANGUAGE **HUNGARIAN**

≫ THE ULTIMATE RELAXATION EXPERIENCE: LAPPING IN THE BLUE WATERS OF THE SUMPTUOUS SZÉCHENYI THERMAL BATHS, BUDAPEST

LANDSCAPE

Hungary occupies the Carpathian Basin in the very centre of Europe. About the size of Portugal, it shares borders with seven countries. It's not as flat as a pancake but close to it, with the highest peak 'soaring' to just over 1000 metres and the Great Plain, a prairie scarcely 200 metres above sea level, stretching for hundreds of kilometres east of the Danube River. Lake Balaton, the largest such body of water in continental Europe, is Hungary's 'inland sea'. The climate is temperate.

HISTORY IN A NUTSHELL

The Magyars occupied the Carpathian Basin in the late 9th century and were united under King Stephen around AD 1000. Hungary's golden age was under King Mátyás Corvinus in the late 15th century, but the nation was occupied by the Turks in the early 16th century, and then by the Austrian Hapsburgs. Hungary ruled jointly with Austria as part of a dual monarchy from 1867, but was on the losing side in World War I and its territory was reduced by 40 per cent. Communists seized control after World War II but were challenged by the pivotal 1956 Uprising. Hungary threw off the yoke of one-party rule in 1989; it's now an independent republic and member of the European Union.

PEOPLE

Ethnic Magyars, an Asiatic people of obscure origins who do not speak an Indo-European language, make up just over 92 per cent of the population. Non-Magyar minorities who make their home here include Germans, Serbs and other South Slavs, Roma, Slovaks and Romanians. About 52 per cent of Hungarians say they are Roman Catholic, while another 19 per cent are Protestant.

MARKETPLACE

Hungary is among the worst economic performers of the 10 Eastern European states that joined the European Union in 2004, with an annual growth rate of slightly more than two per cent. Unemployment has persisted to hover just above the six per cent level nationwide. Although the jobless rate is only about five per cent in Budapest, it reaches as high as 20 per cent in the northeast.

TRADEMARKS

- Roma music
- Paprika (with everything)
- Sweet Tokaj wine
- An obscure and difficult language
- Cowboys on the Puszta (Great Plain)

URBAN SCENE

About two-thirds of all Hungarians live in urban areas; the vast majority – roughly one-fifth of the country's total population, in fact – lives in Budapest, an Art Nouveau gem straddling the Danube. Many of Hungary's provincial towns and cities, however, offer a wealth of fabulous art and architecture – Sopron and Kőszeg have the strongest medieval flavour, and Pécs has the greatest monuments of the Turkish period. Eger, Győr and Veszprém were rebuilt in the baroque style during the 18th century. Outside the capital, the best examples of Art Nouveau architecture can be found at Kecskemét.

TRADITIONS

Hungarians reverse their names in all uses, and their 'last' name always comes first. Thus John Smith is never János Kovács to Hungarians, but Kovács János. Hungary also has one of the richest folk traditions in Europe, and this is where the country has often come to the fore in art. Look out for exquisite embroidery, the acme of Hungarian folk art, at Hollókő and Mezőkövesd, and stunning pottery at Hódmezővásárhely, Karcag and Tiszafüred.

CATCHING UP WITH A LOCAL ON THE STREETS OF PEST »

RANDOM FACTS

○ Budapest is the sixth-largest city in the European Union, after London, Berlin, Madrid, Rome and Paris.
○ Hungary has one of the world's highest rates of suicide, surpassed only by Russia and several other former Soviet republics.
○ There are three distinct Magyar dog breeds: the giant white komondor, a sheepdog with a corded coat; the short-haired vizsla pointing dog; and the unforgettable mop-like puli herding dog.
○ The word 'coach' comes from Kocs, a small village in western Hungary where lighter horse-drawn vehicles were first used for journeys between Budapest and Vienna.

ON DISC

Liszt, Bartók and Erkel form the holy trinity of classical music in Hungary, one of the most musical nations on earth. Add to that Hungarian folk music (think Márta Sebestyén in the film *The English Patient*), haunting Roma music sung a cappella (as opposed to the saccharine-sweet versions heard in Hungarian restaurants from Budapest to Boston), and a vibrant pop-music scene (Budapest's annual Sziget Music Festival is Europe's biggest) and you've got a helluva band.

CUISINE

Hungary has been producing wine since Roman times and much of it is excellent, especially the reds from Villány, the whites from around Lake Balaton and

sweet Tokaj wine. Hungarian cuisine may not be as seminal as French or Chinese, but it is interesting. It makes great use of paprika and has some unique cooking methods, such as twice-cooked vegetables in *rántás,* a heavy roux of pork lard and flour. But vegetarians beware: Hungarians are consummate carnivores.

IMPORT

↗ Christianity from Roman soldiers, and later missionaries from Rome
↗ Paprika from India via Turkey and the Balkans
↗ Grapevine root stocks resistant to phylloxera lice from California
↗ German and Slovak settlers after the Mongol invasions of the 13th century
↗ Lipizzaner horses (probably) from Lipica, now in Slovenia

EXPORT

↖ Ballpoint pen, patented by Laszlo Bíró in 1938
↖ Rubik's Cube, developed by Ernö Rubik in 1980
↖ Vitamin C, discovered by Dr Albert Szent-Györgyi in 1932
↖ Actress Zsa Zsa Gabor
↖ Magician Harry Houdini

⌃ A FOLK DANCER PROUDLY WEARS A TRADITIONAL EMBROIDERED VEST

ESSENTIAL EXPERIENCES

○ **Viewing Hungary's splendid capital, Budapest, from Fishermen's Bastion on Castle Hill**
○ **Touring the endless Great Plain by horse or bicycle**
○ **Stepping back in history at Boldogkőváralja Castle**
○ **Attending a classical-music concert at Esterházy Palace at Fertőd**
○ **Enjoying fine Hungarian cuisine from fiery paprika-spiced beef *gulyás* and chicken *paprikás* to strudel**
○ **Wine tasting in the evocatively named Valley of the Beautiful Women near Eger**
○ **Learning a folk craft at the traditional village of Hollókő**
○ **Sailing along the scenic northern shore of Lake Balaton**
○ **Taking the waters at Sárvár thermal spa**

MAP REF // M11

BEST TIME TO VISIT **APRIL TO JUNE, SEPTEMBER TO OCTOBER**

⌃ BUDAPEST SHOE SCULPTURE COMMEMORATES HUNGARIAN JEWS

≫ PASSING TIME IN BUDAPEST'S CENTRAL MARKET

HAND-PAINTED TRADITIONAL EASTER EGGS, BUDAPEST ≫

SLIDING THROUGH THE HEAT OF SUMMER AT SIOFOK RESORT ON THE EDGE OF LAKE BALATON ≫

TEXT BRETT ATKINSON

CZECH REPUBLIC

IN THE NEW CENTURY, THE CULTURAL HEART OF EUROPE PROVES IT'S AS MUCH ABOUT A DYNAMIC FUTURE AS A THRILLING PAST.

CAPITAL CITY PRAGUE   POPULATION 10.2 MILLION   AREA 78,870 SQ KM   OFFICIAL LANGUAGE CZECH

≈ TEST YOUR TASTEBUDS ON THE STAR OF CZECH BEERS, PILSNER URQUELL, IN PRAGUE'S STARÉ MĚSTO (OLD TOWN)

LANDSCAPE

The landlocked Czech Republic boasts some spectacular and diverse features. Incorporating two river basins, Bohemia, in the west, is drained by the Labe (Elbe) River, and Moravia, in the east, by the Morava. Each basin is circled by squat, forested hills. Between the low-slung ranges, the rolling plains are studded with farmland, and beech, fir and spruce forests. The climate is temperate, with cool, wet winters, warm summers and distinct spring and autumn seasons. Snow can linger well into March.

HISTORY IN A NUTSHELL

Czech history involves a long succession of upheaval. When the forthright Hussites rejected Catholicism in 1418, it ignited the Hussite Wars; when two Hapsburg councillors were thrown from a window in Prague Castle in 1618, it kicked off the Thirty Years' War that eventually engulfed all of Europe; when Hitler annexed the Sudetenland in 1938 it triggered World War II; and when the communists seized power in 1948, it led to the crushing of the optimistic Prague Spring with Soviet tanks in 1968. Finally, in 1989, the outcome was more positive, and the Velvet Revolution overthrew Czechoslovakia's communist regime in a bloodless uprising. The Czech Republic and Slovakia separated in 1993, the Czech Republic embracing democracy, and becoming a member of the European Union in 2004. In recent years, this long-desired democracy has produced government instability, as the country's fledgling political culture overcomes the legacy of four decades of totalitarian rule.

PEOPLE

The population of the Czech Republic is largely homogeneous, with 90 per cent of the country identifying as having Czech heritage. Around two per cent of the country is Slovakian, and there are substantial communities from other border countries, including Germany, Poland and Hungary, and immigrants from Vietnam. The significant Roma community is still subject to discrimination and economic deprivation. Since the Czech Republic joined the European Union, there is a growing number of expats living and working in the country, especially in Prague – lucky people!

MARKETPLACE

Since 1989's Velvet Revolution, the Czech Republic has been more successful than most former communist countries in making the transition to capitalism. Overseas investment has boosted manufacturing, and Czech products are now in greater demand following the country's accession to the European Union. Challenges remain, however, with incomes and living standards increasing faster in Prague than elsewhere, and unemployment remaining high within the Roma population and in the country's former industrial base in the north. The newest challenge is the scattering of young Czechs, who are seeking work in other European countries, seizing opportunities their parents didn't have during the Cold War. Fast-forward a few years, though, and most of them should return with skills and energy to move their country forward.

TRADEMARKS

○ Beer
○ Castles
○ Ice hockey
○ Super models
○ Affordable, live classical music
○ Socks, sandals and Speedos at the beach

URBAN SCENE

Prague and Český Krumlov are rightly celebrated as standout examples of architectural overachievement, but Olomouc and Telč are equally stunning. Olomouc

THE NICEST WAY TO TAKE A BREAK FROM A HARD DAY'S LABOUR »

combines a fascinating ecclesiastical history with the energy of a university town. Set amid a gorgeous Renaissance cityscape, cosy bars and restaurants punctuate its narrow laneways. In Telč a delicate town square is surrounded on three sides by ancient fish ponds. Topped by the 16th-century Water Chateau, the town's square is framed by Renaissance façades, heritage hotels and venerable cafés.

NATURAL BEAUTY

While the communists quarantined Czech society, the ideological standoff benefited isolated areas of the country. On the country's southern border, the Šumava National Park is laid out across 125 kilometres of largely unpopulated wilderness. The area was a sensitive border zone during the Cold War, and was spared the industrial damage inflicted on the country's north. Pristine forests host increasing populations of lynx, eagles and deer, and hiking and cycling paths allow outdoor buffs to experience nature's best. The northern border zones are peppered with idiosyncratic landscapes. The stunning Sandstone Rocks of Labe include the imposing Pravčická Brána, the biggest natural stone bridge in Europe. Further east, the Adršpach-Teplice Rocks showcase alien and otherworldly vistas of sandstone pinnacles fringed with forests, punctuated by hidden lakes, and crisscrossed with hiking trails.

RANDOM FACTS

○ At the Chodovar spa in West Bohemia, bathing in beer is part of the treatment.
○ The sugar cube was invented in the former Czechoslovakia.
○ Pop icon Madonna was threatened with legal action by plastic-explosive manufacturer Semtex for registering a business called Semtex Girls in 2006.
○ Museums sometimes request you wear felt slippers over your shoes to protect the floors and keep the noise levels down.

≪ THE MOVING MEMORIAL TO THE VICTIMS OF COMMUNISM, PRAGUE

ON FILM

○ *The Unbearable Lightness of Being* (1988)
○ *Kolya* (1996)
○ *Divided We Fall* (2000)
○ *Český sen* (Czech Dream, 2004)

ON PAPER

○ *Metamorphosis* by Franz Kafka
○ *The Good Soldier Šejk* by Jaroslav Hašek
○ *Closely Observed Trains* by Bohumil Hrabal
○ *The Book of Laughter and Forgetting* by Milan Kundera

IMPORTS

↗ Jazz clubs
↗ Tex-Mex restaurants (or should that be 'Czech-Mex'?)
↗ Funky 'Middle East-meets-Asia' teahouses
↗ An addiction to kitsch English-language 1980s music
↗ Nouveau-riche Russian tourists
↗ Democracy (brought back by popular demand in 1989)

EXPORTS

↖ Pilsner Urquell and the original Budweiser, two of the world's best beers
↖ New York socialite Ivana Trump
↖ NHL ice hockey star Jaromir Jágr
↖ Bata shoes
↖ Semtex plastic explosive
↖ The word 'robot'

ESSENTIAL EXPERIENCES

○ **Beating the tourist hordes on an early morning stroll across Charles Bridge in Prague**
○ **Conducting your own beer taste test in Plzeň and České Budějovice**
○ **Negotiating the bizarre landscapes of the Adršpach-Teplice Rocks and the Sandstone Rocks of Labe**
○ **Boosting your health and cultural credibility at a classical-music festival in the rejuvenating spa town of Mariánské Lázně**
○ **Cycling through the rolling landscapes around Mikulov to exuberant local wine festivals**
○ **Treating yourself to coffee and cake in Telč's gorgeous, old town square**

GERMANY
POLAND
Sandstone Rocks of Labe
Liberec
Ústí nad Labem
Adršpach-Teplice Rocks
Hradec Králové
✪ PRAGUE
Mariánské Lázně
Plzeň
Ostrava
Olomouc
Telč
Brno
České Budějovice
GERMANY
Český Krumlov
Mikulov
AUSTRIA
SLOVAKIA

MAP REF // L10

BEST TIME TO VISIT APRIL TO JUNE, SEPTEMBER

≪ IT'S NOT THE BEER: GEHRY'S DANCING HOUSE IS ASLANT, PRAGUE

⌃ UNESCO-PRESERVED 16TH-CENTURY ARCHITECTURE KEEPS THE RENAISSANCE ALIVE IN THE TOWN OF TELČ

COMMUNAL EARLY-MORNING POND FISHING, SOUTH BOHEMIA ⌃

WINTER'S THE TIME TO SLIP SOUNDLESSLY THROUGH THE TRANQUIL ŠUMAVA MOUNTAINS ⌃

SLOVAKIA

COMPACT AND RIDDLED WITH FORESTED HILLS AND FOOTPATHS, SLOVAKIA IS AN EXCELLENT PLACE TO TAKE A HIKE, BUT IT'S OFF THE WELL-MARKED TRAILS THAT AGE-OLD VILLAGES, STONY CASTLES AND A LIVING FOLK CULTURE ARE TO BE FOUND.

CAPITAL CITY **BRATISLAVA**   POPULATION **5.4 MILLION**   AREA **48,850 SQ KM**   OFFICIAL LANGUAGE **SLOVAK**

≪ EVERYONE'S HAVING FUN AT BEŠEŇOVÁ'S THERMAL BATHS ON THE VÁH RIVER – COULD IT BE THE LITHIUM IN THE WATER?

LANDSCAPE

Pine-clad hills, alpine peaks, rocky gorges – 80 per cent of Slovakia is more than 750 metres above sea level. Things flatten out near the capital, Bratislava, which sits on the Danube River plain. The moderate, temperate climate can get rainy, and river flooding in the spring months is not uncommon. Up in the mountains, ski areas are usually open from December into April at least, and higher passes and trails may still have snow into June.

HISTORY IN A NUTSHELL

Slavic tribes settled this area in approximately the 5th century AD, but it wasn't long before the Magyars (Hungarians) took over. Slovakia was then part of Hungary for more than a thousand years, until after World War I when it first became part of Czechoslovakia (which in turn became a Communist Bloc state post-World War II). The Czechs and Slovaks parted ways in the Velvet Divorce of 1993 and the independent nation of Slovakia joined the European Union in 2004. Prices of consumer goods and services are on the rise, and some voters are turning back towards the Communist Party, but adopting the euro is the targeted next step in development.

PEOPLE

Slovaks are for the most part Catholic (69 per cent), with smaller numbers identifying as Protestant (11 per cent), Greek Catholic (four per cent) and other faiths. While around 85 per cent of the population claim Slovak heritage, there are a few minority groups – Hungarians make up 11 per cent of the population, and Roma comprise between 1.7 per cent and four per cent, depending on what source you trust. Young people are usually fresh and open in their attitude and approach to life, and the stoicism of the older generation hides a boundless generosity.

MARKETPLACE

Market reforms and privatisation in the years leading up to European Union membership have spurred on international investment in Slovakia, especially by auto manufacturers. The GDP growth rate has risen to a strong eight per cent; however, the unemployment rate remains around eight per cent. An average monthly salary in Slovakia is equivalent to about €500. Standards in general are higher in Bratislava, where most families own at least one car, but lower within the remote villages of East Slovakia.

TRADEMARKS

○ Tall, gorgeous women with high cheek bones
○ Ice hockey obsession
○ Folk songs with the sounds *yee!* and *yip!*
○ Beer, red wine and *slivovice* (plum brandy)
○ Mountain hikes and amazing views

NATURAL BEAUTY

Take your choice of vistas: floating down the Dunajec River past 500-metre cliffs in a flat-bottom boat; surveying the High Tatra mountain range after taking a cable car ride to the top of Lomnický Peak; hiking through the woods in Malá Fatra National Park. Natural beauty is Slovakia's biggest drawcard. Nine national parks, and many more preserves, protect 23 per cent of the nation's land.

TRADITIONS

Folk ways and means still hold sway in this very traditional country. You can tell which holiday it is by what the street vendors are selling. Around Easter time, they hawk the braided willow-branch whips that boys in the village playfully chase the girls with, and the hand-painted eggs the girls are supposed to offer in return. Before 5 December, you'll see the chocolate santas that good little children get in their

GHOSTING THROUGH THE INTERIOR OF A RURAL CHURCH, ISTEBNÉ ≫

TRAVERSING ROCKY TERRAIN TO MOUNTAINTOP SPIŠ CASTLE ≫

shoes on St Nicholas' feast day. Later that month, portable fish tanks are set up on town squares so you can buy your carp for the traditional Christmas Eve meal.

IN STONE

The 12th and 13th centuries were the heyday of castle building in Slovakia, and today hundreds of ancient ruins dot the clifftops, all with public trails providing access. A few have been well preserved or restored and are open for formal tours, such as the seven-hectare-long Spiš Castle and the fairy-tale–worthy chateau Bojnice.

RANDOM FACTS

- There are 1160 government-registered sources of mineral or thermal spring water in Slovakia.
- You can tour two caves where ice formations are the major attraction – Dobšinská and Demänovská.
- More than 27 wooden churches in East Slovakia are on the national cultural register because they were made without nails.

⌃ EUROPEAN NATIVE SUCCULENT COMMONLY CALLED HENS AND CHICKS

⌃ AN OLDER WAY OF LIFE LINGERS IN HISTORIC KOŠICE

CUISINE

Filling, shepherd-inspired food is at the heart of traditional Slovakian home cooking. The national dish, *bryndzové halušky*, consists of small, gnocchi-like dumplings topped with soft, semi-sharp sheep's cheese and big bits of bacon fat. A light meal it isn't. *Bryndza* cheese is also spread on bread with onions, tucked into crescent moon-shape dumplings and melted into soup.

MYTHS & LEGENDS

Juraj Jánošík, Slovakia's 18th-century Robin Hood, rises tall over all other legends. While Jánošík is away at war, his mother dies and his father is beaten to death for taking time off to bury her. Vowing revenge, Jánošík goes on a thieving rampage against the ruling rich (though there seems to be some dispute as to whether he actually gave to the poor). He was eventually caught, tortured and killed, but his romanticised story lives on in movies, poetry and artwork – there's even an opera about him.

TOP FESTIVAL

Summer folk festivals bring traditional culture to life through dance, song, food and drink. The country's largest is at Východná in July – regional folk ensembles come from across the country to show off their colourful costumes and fancy footwork. All through the summer there are smaller events in villages, and at the numerous open-air village museums where local customs and architecture are preserved.

ESSENTIAL EXPERIENCES

- Stopping at one of the many pavement cafés on the winding Old Town streets of Bratislava
- Hiking through the High Tatra mountains by day and enjoying spit-roast chicken in a traditional *koliba* (rustic mountain restaurant) at night
- Soaking in healing hot spring waters at the nation's largest spa, Piešťany
- Scrambling up past waterfalls on a gorge hike in Slovenský Raj National Park
- Wandering though traditional log villages Čičmany and Vlkolínec
- Taking a night tour led by torch light of medieval Trenčín Castle

POLAND

CZECH REPUBLIC

Žilina
Martin
Vlkolínec
High Tatra Mountains
Čičmany
Malá Fatra National Park
Slovenský Raj National Park
Prešov
Trenčín
Banská Bystrica
Košice
Piešťany
Trnava
Nitra
Lučenec
BRATISLAVA
Komárno

AUSTRIA

UKRAINE

HUNGARY

MAP REF // M10

BEST TIME TO VISIT JUNE TO OCTOBER

⌃ LINEAR FOLK-DESIGN HOUSES PRESERVED IN ČIČMANY VILLAGE

Dior institut

≪ KIDS CLAMOUR TO CALL *ČAU* (HELLO) IN LEVOČA, SPIŠ REGION

DON'T CANCEL THAT TRAIN TICKET: RAIL CAR IN ČIERNY BALOG ≪

MICHAEL'S TOWER HAS BEEN MARKING TIME IN BRATISLAVA'S OLD TOWN SINCE THE MIDDLE AGES ≪

TEXT TIM RICHARDS

POLAND

HAVING SURVIVED ALL THAT FATE CAN THROW AT IT, POLAND IS A COMPLEX, FASCINATING COUNTRY WITH A WEALTH OF HISTORICAL REMNANTS AND A VIBRANT CULTURE.

CAPITAL CITY **WARSAW**   POPULATION **38.5 MILLION**   AREA **312,680 SQ KM**   OFFICIAL LANGUAGE **POLISH**

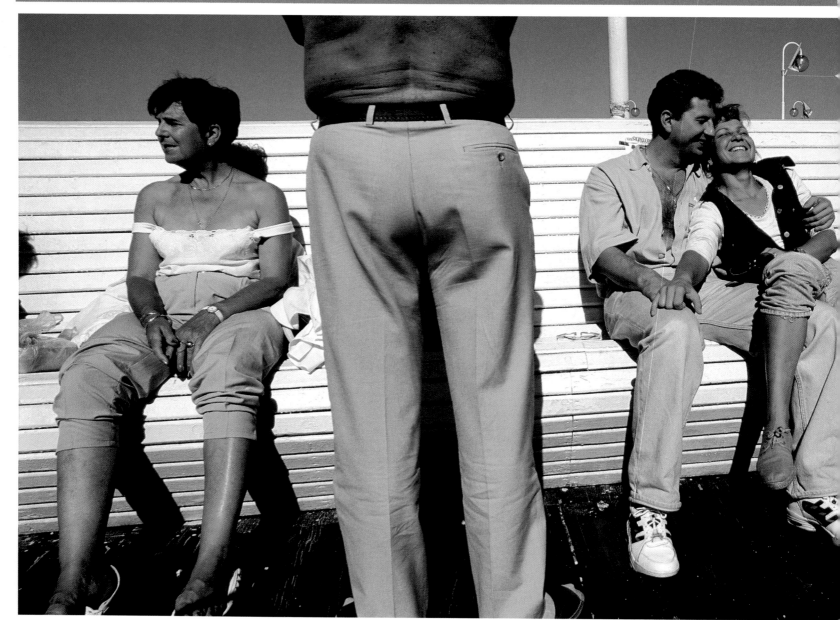

⌃ ROMANCE ALONG THE SOPOT BOARDWALK, DOWN BY THE BALTIC SEA

LANDSCAPE

Poland is largely a flat, fertile plain, stretching between the Baltic Sea to the north, and the Carpathian Mountains to the south. There's plenty of variety within those boundaries: the northeastern region of Masuria is dotted with a vast number of postglacial lakes, and various rivers divide up the countryside. On Poland's southern border, a series of mountain ranges – including the Sudetes, the Tatras and the Bieszczady (part of the Carpathians) – provide a dramatic contrast. Warm, wet summers contrast with chilly, often snowbound winters. Though Poland's environment has suffered from industrial pollution, it's also home to several Unesco Biosphere Reserves.

HISTORY IN A NUTSHELL

The history of Poland is not a light novel to be flipped through on the beach – it's a suspenseful thriller featuring dramatic setbacks and triumphs, with a hopeful epilogue at the end. From the moment their nation was founded in the 10th century AD, the Poles have vied with neighbouring peoples for territory; their greatest early rivals were the Teutonic Knights, warrior monks who spread their rule along the Baltic coast. Poland's golden age began in the 14th century, the nation blossoming into a vast empire that stretched to the Black Sea. By the end of the 18th century, however, Poland had been carved up by the German, Russian and Austrian empires, and disappeared off the map of Europe. Re-emerging after World War I, the reborn Poland was then subject to more than five years of Nazi occupation in World War II, followed by four decades of communism. After the fall of the regime, aided by the Polish trade union Solidarity and the influential Catholic Church, Poland rapidly re-established a market economy and joined the European Union in 2004.

PEOPLE

Poland was historically a multicultural and multilingual country, but the genocide and upheavals of World War II, and the forced resettlements that followed it, made the nation remarkably homogeneous in terms of ethnicity, religion and language. Some 97 per cent of the population is Polish, with small numbers from German, Belarusian and Ukrainian descent. Polish is spoken by 98 per cent of the population. Roman Catholicism is followed by 90 per cent of Poles, with tiny numbers of Protestant and Eastern Orthodox worshippers making up the balance.

MARKETPLACE

Poland's exports range from heavy machinery and chemical products to foodstuffs such as vodka and ham. Despite continued economic growth, unemployment remains high, and lingering corruption creates difficulties for business growth. Exports to other European Union nations, however, have steadily increased. The average Pole takes home the equivalent of €7500 per year. The nation's annual budget is €55 billion per year, in comparison with next-door neighbour Germany's annual budget of one trillion euro.

TRADEMARKS

- Vodka
- Dumplings
- The late Pope John Paul II
- Former Solidarity leader and former Polish president Lech Wałęsa
- Beautiful medieval city centres
- Communist-era concrete blocks

URBAN SCENE

Poland is blessed with numerous cities containing attractive historic centres. Kraków is the most significant – its Old Town district centres on a vast

PHOTOS FOR SALE IN WARSAW'S PICTURE-PERFECT OLD TOWN MARKETPLACE »

A RARE SIGHT: AN ENDANGERED EUROPEAN BISON TREADS SNOW-LADEN BIAŁOWIEŻA FOREST » cobblestone market square lined by attractive façades, with venerable historic buildings in the middle. The city is also blessed with the magnificent Wawel Castle and the atmospheric streets of Kazimierz, its former Jewish quarter.

ON FILM

- Schindler's List (1993)
- Trois Couleurs: Blanc (Three Colours: White, 1994)
- With Fire and Sword (1999)
- The Pianist (2002)
- Wesele (The Wedding, 2004)

RANDOM FACTS

- The most influential Pole in history was Nicolaus Copernicus, the 16th-century astronomer who asserted that the earth revolves around the sun.
- Adolf Hitler's former Russian Front HQ, the Wolfsschanze (Wolf's Lair), is now a tourist attraction situated in northeast Poland.
- One of Poland's most famous vodkas, żubrówka, is flavoured with bison grass, a favoured snack of wild bison.
- Warsaw's enormous Palace of Culture and Science, a gift from Joseph Stalin in 1952, is still one of Europe's 10 tallest buildings.

CUISINE

Polish food has a reputation for being heavy, and it's true that Poles do love their pork and potatoes. The signature dish is a plate of pierogi (dumplings) stuffed with fillings such as cottage cheese, minced meat, or cabbage and wild mushrooms. Excellent soups include żurek, a sour soup made with sausage and hard-boiled eggs, though barszcz (borscht) is more famous. Other distinctive dishes include bigos (a cabbage and meat stew) and gołąbki (cabbage leaves stuffed with mince and rice).

MYTHS & LEGENDS

A cobbler's apprentice once took up the king's offer of his daughter's hand in marriage to whomever could slay a dragon that was terrorising Kraków. Having noticed the king's knights make no impact with their weaponry, the wily worker left a sheep stuffed with sulphur outside the dragon's cave. The dragon ate the sheep, became enormously thirsty, drank the entire Vistula River, and then exploded. The apprentice lived happily ever after… with his princess.

IMPORT

↗ Jazz clubs
↗ Coffee chain stores
↗ Bulgarian wine
↗ Renaissance architecture
↗ Stag-party tourists

EXPORT

↖ Vodka
↖ Scientist Marie Curie
↖ Musician Frédéric Chopin
↖ Pope John Paul II
↖ Movie director Roman Polański
↖ Author Joseph Conrad
↖ Cool poster art

TOP FESTIVAL

On 21 March, some Poles celebrate the end of winter in a ceremony known as Topienie Marzanny (Drowning Marzanna). A straw effigy of the evil winter witch is immersed in water, sometimes after being set alight.

≫ SOUNDLESS FOOTSTEPS IN CHOCHOŁOWSKA VALLEY, TATRA MOUNTAINS

JON ARNOLD IMAGES // ALAMY

JONATHAN SMITH // LONELY PLANET IMAGES

ESSENTIAL EXPERIENCES

- **Drinking in the heady, historic atmosphere of Kraków's Wawel Castle**
- **Hiking or skiing in the lofty Tatra Mountains**
- **Meeting the rare European bison face-to-face in the forest near the village of Białowieża**
- **Taking a dip in the Baltic from the attractive seaside town of Hel**
- **Sampling traditional Polish cuisine in the cellar restaurants of Warsaw's Old Town**

MAP REF // M9

BEST TIME TO VISIT **MAY TO SEPTEMBER**

≫ SOVIET-ERA PALACE OF CULTURE AND SCIENCE, WARSAW

≫ 'PEARL OF THE BALTIC' MIĘDZYZDROJE ATTRACTS BEACH LOVERS WITH ITS WHITE SANDS AND TURQUOISE WATERS

MAN STANDS IN FOR A ROOK ON A GIANT CHESS BOARD ≫

POLAND'S BIRD POPULATION CONGREGATES IN THE 17TH-CENTURY OGRÓD SASKI (SAXON GARDEN), WARSAW ≫

TEXT STEVE FALLON

SLOVENIA

A TINY, YOUNG REPUBLIC IN SOUTHEASTERN EUROPE OF JAW-DROPPING NATURAL BEAUTY, SLOVENIA CAN LAY CLAIM TO BEING ONE OF THE GREENEST COUNTRIES IN THE WORLD.

CAPITAL CITY LJUBLJANA   POPULATION 2 MILLION   AREA 20,270 SQ KM   OFFICIAL LANGUAGE SLOVENE

≫ IT TAKES A GREEN THUMB AND SOME HARD WORK TO PRODUCE THIS HARVEST IN TEMENICA

LANDSCAPE

Slovenia is a Central European country about the size of Wales or Israel. It borders Italy, Austria, Hungary and Croatia, and counts 47 kilometres of coastline along the Adriatic. Most of the country is hilly or mountainous and 40 per cent is covered in forest. Alpine, Mediterranean and continental climates meet in Slovenia.

HISTORY IN A NUTSHELL

The Slovenian lands were settled in the 6th century by early Slavs, who formed the first Slavic state. These proto-Slovenes were subjugated in turn by the Franks, the Germans and by the Austrian Hapsburgs, who ruled them until the end of World War I. The Slovenes joined with the Serbs and Croats in 1918 to create a new multinational state, which went on to become Yugoslavia in 1929. At the end of World War II, Slovenia became a republic of the new socialist (though relatively open) Yugoslavia. In 1991, dissatisfied with the exercise of power by the majority Serbs, Slovenia declared itself an independent republic, successfully fighting a 10-day war against what was left of Yugoslavia. Slovenia has been a member of the European Union since 2004.

PEOPLE

About 82 per cent of the population identify as Slovene, descendants of the early Slavs. There are small indigenous communities of Hungarians and Italians, as well as ethnic Albanians, Bosnians, Croats and Serbs. About 58 per cent of Slovenians identify as Roman Catholic.

MARKETPLACE

Slovenia's accession to the European Union in 2004 opened up a vast export market for the country's goods, and it was the first of the 10 new European Union member-nations to adopt the euro as its national currency. Ljubljana is responsible for as much as 25 per cent of the country's GDP, which is a favourable €18,640 per capita. Unemployment remains a relatively high 7.8 per cent.

TRADEMARKS

- ○ Skiing
- ○ *Pršut* (air-dried ham from the Karst region)
- ○ *Potica* (nut roll cake)
- ○ The electric-blue Soća River
- ○ Three-headed Mount Triglav
- ○ *Zlatorog* (mythical chamois with the golden horns)
- ○ Lipizzaner horses

NATURAL BEAUTY

With so much splendour spread across the country, it's nigh on impossible to choose the 'best' spots. The hair-raising Vršič Pass, the Julian Alps in Triglav National Park, the Škocjan Caves, pristine Logarska Dolina (Logar Valley) in Štajerska and the unique (True) Karst region are all unforgettable.

TRADITIONS

Diners wish one another *Dober tek!* (Bon appetit!) before a meal. To do so is being *priden,* an important and much employed term in Slovene meaning 'diligent', 'industrious', 'hard-working' and, tellingly, 'well-behaved'. St Martin's Day (11 November), although not a public holiday, is important as the day on which the wine makers' *mošt* (must, or fermenting grape juice) officially becomes wine. In the evening, families traditionally dine on goose and drink new wine.

ON PAPER

- ○ *Deseti Brat* (The Tenth Brother) by Josip Jurčič
- ○ *Fužinski Bluz* (Fužine Blues) by Andrej E Skubic
- ○ *Hlapec Jernej in Njegova Pravica* (The Bailiff Yerney and His Rights) by Ivan Cankar
- ○ *Martin Krpan* by Fran Levstik
- ○ *Nekropola* (Pilgrim among the Shadows) by Boris Pahor

POET FRANCE PREŠEREN IS IMMORTALISED IN BOLD TONES BESIDE THE CHURCH OF THE ANNUNCIATION, PREŠEREN'S SQUARE, LJUBLJANA »

RANDOM FACTS

○ According to written references dating to the 17th century, skiing was born on the slopes of the Bloke Plateau in Notranjska province.

○ The average Slovenian man is called Franc, was born on a Friday in March, got married at age 30.3 and is now 38.7 years old. The average Slovenian woman is called Marija, got married at 27.3 years, has 1.2 children and is now 42 years old.

○ Slovenia is the third-smallest literature market in Europe; a fiction 'bestseller' in this country means sales of 500 to 800 copies.

○ The Karst region, a limestone plateau in Primorska province, was the first such area to be described and is therefore called the Classic, Real, True or Original Karst and always spelled with an upper-case 'K'.

MYTHS & LEGENDS

Slovenian folk tales are rife with fairies, witches and things that go bump in the night. Among the most common stories, however, are those describing the derring-do of 'superheroes', whose strong wills and unusual strength enable them to overcome evil and conquer their brutish enemies. Peter Klepec sweeps away his enemies with trees he's uprooted with his bare hands along the Kolpa River; Kumprej rules the Upper Savinja Valley in Štajerska with his mighty voice and fearsome blade; and Martin Krpan, of the Bloke Plateau in Notranjska, is a salt smuggler with superhuman strength and a big heart.

SURPRISES

○ Slovenes eat two things few other people do: dormouse, a tree-dwelling nocturnal rodent not unlike a squirrel, and horsemeat (especially colt).

○ Maribor is home to the oldest vine in the world, planted more than four centuries ago and still producing grapes and wine.

○ Slovenia is one of the few countries in Europe that is not football mad – basketball is the most popular team sport here.

TOP FESTIVAL

Slovenia's most colourful pre-Lenten festival is Laufarija, held at Cerkno in Primorska province. The festival takes place on the Sunday before Ash Wednesday and again on Shrove Tuesday. The symbol of winter and the old year, Pust, is put to death by some two dozen other characters representing various crafts and trades (the Baker, the Thatcher, the Woodsman, for example) or certain traits or afflictions, such as the Drunk and his Wife, the Bad Boy, Sneezy and the Sick Man. The costumes, made of leaves, pine branches, straw or moss stitched onto a burlap (hessian) backing, are quite elaborate and fashioned anew each year.

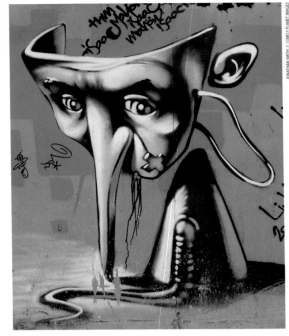
⌃ STREET ART GETS A LITTLE SURREAL IN LJUBLJANA

⌃ A SHRINE HAS BEEN LOVINGLY TENDED DESPITE SNOW, POSTOJNA

ESSENTIAL EXPERIENCES

○ **Viewing the Old Town from atop Ljubljana Castle**

○ **Canoeing or rafting down the unspoiled Soča River**

○ **Making your way up snowcapped Mount Triglav**

○ **Swimming or rowing out to the lovely little island with a church in Lake Bled**

○ **Crossing from Gorenjska into Primorska via the hair-raising Vršič Pass**

○ **Riding a white horse in Lipica**

○ **Dancing with death at the *Danse Macabre* fresco in the Church of the Holy Trinity in Hrastovlje**

○ **Descending into the wondrous underground world of the Škocjan Caves**

MAP REF // L11

BEST TIME TO VISIT **MAY TO OCTOBER, DECEMBER TO MARCH**

⌃ LJUBLJANA'S DRAGON'S BRIDGE IS A FEARSOME OVERSEER

GARY YEOWELL / GETTY

BOJAN BRECELJ / CORBIS

» A SLOVENIAN GARDEN OF EDEN SURROUNDS BLED ISLAND'S CHURCH OF ASSUMPTION, LAKE BLED

CULTIVATING HOPS IN THE SAVINJA VALLEY »

DANCERS CLAD IN SHEEPSKIN AND WEARING ELABORATE KURENT MASKS USHER IN SPRING DURING THE 10-DAY KURENTOVANJE FESTIVAL »

EASTERN MEDITERRANEAN & THE BALKANS

STRETCHED BETWEEN THE COOL CLIMES OF CENTRAL EUROPE AND THE HEAT OF THE MEDITERRANEAN, THIS COLLECTION OF COUNTRIES LURES WITH A PROMISING WHIFF OF ADVENTURE, THANKS TO THE BALKANS REVVING THE REGION'S POLITICAL ENGINE, AND THE EASTERN MEDITERRANEAN'S TOUCHES OF ASIA.

An area whose name comes from the old Turkish word for 'mountain range', the Balkans and the Eastern Mediterranean are surrounded by six seas – the Mediterranean, Adriatic, Ionian, Aegean and Marmara to the west and the Black Sea to the east – with two long mountain ranges running through its lands like backbones. A continuous chain stretches from the Carpathians through to Anatolian Turkey, and an offshoot of the Dinaric Alps to the west follows the coast of Croatia, Montenegro and Albania, crossing Greece and plunging into the sea, only to emerge again as a series of gorgeous islands.

Over the centuries different ethnic groups mingled, migrated and merged here, creating a part of Europe whose ethnic make-up is at times as mixed as a jumble sale. The history of the Balkans and the Eastern Mediterranean is as dynamic as the land itself, with a succession of empires fighting to control the strategic territories that connected the East and the West. Some of the world's greatest civilisations and empires originated from and shaped the region. The ancient Greeks set up the foundations of modern society, the Byzantines brought Eastern Orthodoxy, and the Ottomans introduced Islam, leaving behind a common cultural residue of gastronomy, a relaxed lifestyle laden with music, and social gatherings soaked in coffee and cigarettes.

The communist rule that dominated the former Yugoslavia, Bulgaria and Albania, among other countries, ended with the collapse of Yugoslavia, but the country's former republics are up and running again, and hoping for a better future. Roma minorities are dotted across the region, famed for their music, but often steeped in hardship. The region's prosperity varies widely, with Greece at the top of the heap as a European Union member since 1981. Bulgaria acceded in 2007, with Croatia looking to be next in line, but it is Turkey's European Union membership that is creating the most friction in Europe.

The Balkans and the Eastern Mediterranean hold some of Europe's aesthetic aces up their sleeves. Greece is truly a holidaymaker's magnet, with plenty to discover off the beaten track. Magnificent İstanbul, torn between modernity and tradition, is one of Europe's most spectacular cities. Cyprus has plenty of sunshine on tap and, despite tourist troupes, reveals charming traditional villages and deserted beaches. Croatia's gorgeous coastline has sprung to attention after years of war, and draws thousands of visitors, while Montenegro is waking up to the tourist boom and recent independence. Serbia kicks up a mighty dust with fabulous music festivals, and Bosnia and Hercegovina flaunts its diverse capital, Sarajevo, and medieval Mostar. Albania is perfect for the adventurous traveller, and Bulgaria's mountains and beaches pull visitors in. All this comes with a sprinkling of bombastic music, saucy food and traditional hospitality.

TEXT VESNA MARIC

CROATIA

JAM-PACKED WITH ANCIENT SITES, BEAUTIFUL BEACHES, PRISTINE NATIONAL PARKS AND HOSPITABLE, PASSIONATE PEOPLE , CROATIA IS A COUNTRY TO FALL IN LOVE WITH.

CAPITAL CITY ZAGREB   POPULATION 4.5 MILLION   AREA 56,540 SQ KM   OFFICIAL LANGUAGE CROATIAN

≫ LAND VERSUS SEA: THE INTENSE COLOUR OF DUBROVNIK'S TERRACOTTA ROOFS TRUMPS THE BLUE OF THE ADRIATIC

LANDSCAPE

Shaped like a wishbone, the thin southern fork is a chain of barren craggy mountains flanked by the clear waters of the Adriatic. While the mountain areas freeze in the winter and swelter in the summer, you can easily escape to the pleasant climate enjoyed by the coast and its 1200-odd islands. As the northern fork broadens out to reach into Central Europe, barren rocks are replaced by verdant fields in the valleys of the Sava, Drava and Danube Rivers.

HISTORY IN A NUTSHELL

Croatia has been occupied since Palaeolithic times. The Romans wrested control from the Illyrians (ancestors of the Albanians) in 168 BC, and 800 years later, as the Roman Empire was disintegrating, the Croatian tribes began to descend into the area. The Croats were united under King Tomislav in AD 925, who founded a nation that eventually collapsed under intrusions from Venice and Hungary. Narrowly avoiding an Ottoman invasion, Croatia instead was fought over, carved up, handed around and generally trodden down by Europe's 'Great Powers' until 1918. Hope then came with the formation of the combined Kingdom of Serbs, Croats and Slovenes, known as Yugoslavia after 1929. A Croatian fascist government was installed by the Nazis during World War II – although many Croats fought with Tito's communist partisans, who founded a federal Yugoslavia upon their victory in 1945. By 1990, tensions within the federation rose to the point where both Slovenia and Croatia voted for independence, sparking a complicated, ethnically divisive war. Peace has seen Croatia rebuilding its economy, enticing the tourists back and laying a path to European Union membership.

PEOPLE

A recent census shows a population that is overwhelmingly Croat (90 per cent) and Catholic (88 per cent). The biggest minority are the Serbs (five per cent), who live mainly in eastern Slavonia. The Eastern Orthodox faith is embraced by four per cent of the population, including most Serbs, and Muslims account for about four per cent. Among younger people English is widely spoken, although German still tends to be the second tongue in the north, and Italian takes its place in Istria and Dalmatia.

MARKETPLACE

The war in the 1990s hit Croatia's economy hard, with GDP dropping more than 40 per cent. Since then economic growth has been strong, but unemployment still remains at about 11.8 per cent. The average income sits at around €5000 per annum.

TRADEMARKS

○ Dubrovnik's mighty walls and terracotta roofs
○ Soccer obsessives
○ Catholicism
○ Sun-soaked beaches
○ Roman ruins

URBAN SCENE

Arriving in any Croatian town, you'll be struck by the vast number of people drinking in cafés and bars, and you'll be tempted to wonder: 'Does anybody work?'. Particularly in Dalmatia, the Croatian pace of life allows plenty of time for the serious business of socialising. As well as all the coffee drinking, this approach to life manifests in the evening promenade along the main street.

NATURAL BEAUTY

From above, the Adriatic seems unnaturally blue, as though someone's emptied dye into it. At close range, the warm waters (rising to 26 degrees Celsius in summer) are superbly clear, making for great diving or general splashing about.

TAKING TIME OUT IN A FRANCISCAN MONASTERY CLOISTER IN DUBROVNIK'S OLD TOWN »

RANDOM FACTS

- Despite its tiny scale, if you include all of Croatia's islands, the country's coastline stretches for 5835 kilometres.
- The Old Town of Split nestles within the walls of Caesar Diocletian's palace, built on the spot he considered the most beautiful in the entire Roman Empire.
- During the Homeland War of 1991 to 1995, Dubrovnik took 111 direct hits to its walls, 314 on its streets and squares and shells struck 68 per cent of its buildings.

TRADITIONS

The force feeding of guests is a national hobby. If you're lucky enough to be invited into a Croatian home, it's best to do so on an empty stomach. It's rude not to make an effort, but eating until you're sick is not officially required.

CUISINE

Predictably, seafood dominates along the coast, with risotto and pasta dishes, liberal splashes of olive oil and lots of garlic betraying the Italian influence. Inland, spit-roasted or barbecued meat is a favourite, while a Hungarian taste for paprika can be found in Slavonia. Wine is a part of everyday life and many villages have their own distinct grape varietals. In summer, red wine is often served chilled and it's common to water it down, but it's the mixing of red wine and Coca Cola that's most likely to horrify the purists.

SURPRISES

- Considered the most American of wine varietals, California's Zinfandel originated from Croatia.
- Notwithstanding Venice's better publicised claims, there is evidence that Marco Polo was a Dalmatian born in Korčula.
- Many Croatian teenagers are obsessed by rock-band Nirvana, rapper Tupac Shakur or death metal music.

TOP FESTIVAL

If the sheer marbled majesty of Dubrovnik is not enough to transport you back in time, during the July opening of the Summer Festival you'll find flaming torches lining the walls, soldiers in traditional garb manning the gates and the City Guard let loose with muskets. The programme is always packed with theatre and concert performances, which are held in many of the city's historic palaces, churches and squares.

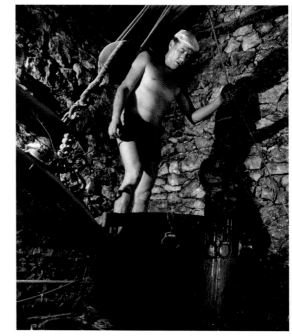

≈ CREATING LAVENDAR OIL AT A DISTILLERY ON HVAR ISLAND

≈ DUBROVNIK'S COLOURFUL GUNDULICEVA PORLJANA MARKET

ESSENTIAL EXPERIENCES

- Exploring the walled towns and crystalline waters of the Dalmatian islands
- Wondering if you're in an animated cartoon as you pass through flocks of butterflies in the spectacular Plitvice Lakes National Park
- Wandering the baroque streets of Varaždin
- Idling away an afternoon at a Zagreb street café
- Washing down squid-ink risotto with a glass of local wine at Diocletian's ancient palace in Split
- Marvelling at the perfection as you circumnavigate Dubrovnik's honey-coloured walls
- Avoiding kamikaze truck drivers as you travel the spectacular coastal highway
- Watching the sun set over Šibenik's stone Cathedral of St Jacob from the ancient St Ana Fortress

MAP REF // L11

BEST TIME TO VISIT **APRIL TO SEPTEMBER**

≈ PAG ISLAND WOMAN CONCENTRATES ON STITCHING INTRICATE LACE

≫ A MODERN IMAGE OF AN ANCIENT KING HERALDS A RUINED ROMAN AMPHITHEATRE, PULA

A RAIN-WASHED STRADUN, DUBROVNIK'S FAVOURITE PROMENADE ≫

LOCALS MAKE LIKE PARISIANS IN LUŽA SQUARE, DUBROVNIK ≫

BOSNIA & HERCEGOVINA

AN INTRICATE CULTURAL MOSAIC ONCE ASSOCIATED ONLY WITH ITS BITTER CONFLICT, BOSNIA AND HERCEGOVINA HAS TURNED INTO THE PERFECT EUROPEAN OFF-THE-BEATEN-TRACK DESTINATION, WITH ITS FUN-LOVING CAPITAL, SARAJEVO, AND THE CHARMING MEDIEVAL OTTOMAN TOWN OF MOSTAR ATTRACTING VISITORS CURIOUS TO DELVE BELOW THE SURFACE OF THINGS.

CAPITAL CITY SARAJEVO   POPULATION 4.5 MILLION   AREA 51,130 SQ KM   OFFICIAL LANGUAGES BOSNIAN, SERBIAN, CROATIAN

⌃ MOSTAR'S HAUNTING AND UNMISSABLE OLD BRIDGE ARCHES GRACEFULLY OVER THE NERETVA RIVER

LANDSCAPE

Bosnia and Hercegovina is a mountainous country in the central Balkans. Just a toe of land connects it to the Adriatic Sea through Croatia. There are two main national parks: Sutjeska, which is a Unesco-protected primeval forest that has a history reaching back 20,000 years, and the Hutovo Blato wetlands, a prime sanctuary for migratory birds. Bosnia and Hercegovina has a mix of Mediterranean and Central European climates.

HISTORY IN A NUTSHELL

The Slavs first arrived in the area during the 6th and 7th centuries AD. Over the years between 1190 and 1463, Bosnia and Hercegovina became one of the most powerful states in the region. The first Turkish raids came in 1383, and by 1463 the country was a Turkish province. The Austro-Hungarian Empire later took over in 1878. Continued foreign occupation caused grievances among the locals, culminating in the assassination of the Austrian archduke Franz Ferdinand and his wife in Sarajevo on 28 June 1914 by a young Bosnian Serb, Gavrilo Princip, which triggered the beginning of World War I. At the end of World War II, Bosnia and Hercegovina was absorbed into the Kingdom of Serbs, Croats and Slovenes, which was later to be named Yugoslavia, and then annexed by the newly created fascist Croatian state in 1941. Post-World War II, the country was given republic status within Tito's Yugoslavia. In 1991, Bosnia and Hercegovina followed the example of neighbouring Croatia and Slovenia and declared independence from Yugoslavia, much to the dismay of the Bosnian Serb population. Although the country was recognised internationally, internal talks between the parties broke down, launching a three-year war in April 1992. The conflict came to a close with the signing of the Dayton Agreement in 1995. The country now has a rotating presidency between Bosniak (Muslim), Croat and Serb candidates.

PEOPLE

Serbs, Croats and Bosniaks (Muslims) are all Southern Slavs descended from the same ethnic stock. In terms of religion, about 40 per cent of the population is Muslim, 31 per cent Orthodox, 15 per cent Roman Catholic, and 14 per cent follows other religions. The country has three languages: Bosnian, Croatian and Serbian, although these three are essentially one language divided across political lines.

MARKETPLACE

Bosnia and Hercegovina's main industries are metal mines, and tobacco and textile production. During the 1990s conflict, production fell by 80 per cent and unemployment soared. Growth has improved rapidly in postwar years, though a high unemployment rate (30 to 40 per cent) remains. Substantial amounts of reconstruction and humanitarian aid are still supplied by the international community but increasingly this assistance is on the decline.

TRADEMARKS

○ Emir Kusturica (film director)
○ Mostar's Old Bridge
○ Ivo Andrić, Nobel Prize–winning writer
○ 1984 Winter Olympics in Sarajevo

URBAN SCENE

Bosnia and Hercegovina's capital, Sarajevo sits in a valley surrounded by high mountains, its mosques, churches, houses and tower blocks sprouting across the cityscape. Sarajevo's heart, Baščaršija, pulses with artisan and souvenir shops, and smoky traditional cafés where the coffee is as dark and sweet as a particularly naughty sin. The more modern part of town is steeped in Austro-Hungarian heritage, with

CONTRASTS OF FUTURE AND PAST: A SOCCER GAME TAKES PLACE ON A 'FIELD' SCARRED BY WEAPONS' FIRE IN THE YUGOSLAVIAN CIVIL WAR »

grandiose buildings boasting their colours on the banks of the Miljacka River. Surrounding the city's mosques and churches are countless restaurants, bars, cafés, museums and galleries, all testament to the various cultural influences the city has known.

ON FILM
- *When Father was Away on Business* (1985)
- *No Man's Land* (2002)
- *Grbavica* (Esma's Secret, 2005)

ON PAPER
- *Bridge Over the Drina* by Ivo Andrić
- *Nowhere Man* by Aleksandar Hemon
- *Sarajevo Marlboro* by Miljenko Jergović

RANDOM FACTS
- Sarajevo's pavements are scattered with 'Sarajevo Roses', remains of mortar shells symbolically filled with red wax in places where the death count from bombing was high.

⌃ PEACE MONUMENT OUTREACHES ORTHODOX CHURCH, SARAJEVO

⌃ CROSSING MOSTAR, A CITY ONCE DIVIDED BY WAR

- It is said that the stones of the original Old Bridge in Mostar were assembled with an unappetising combination of horse hair, eggshells and wax paste.
- It is common to turn over your *fildžan* (coffee cup) after drinking Turkish coffee, and have your future read in the thick, dark residue.

TOP FESTIVAL
Film is Bosnia and Hercegovina's most successful and prolific art, and the Sarajevo Film Festival held annually in August has become the country's most celebrated festival. It promotes young filmmakers, commercial releases and art-house movies.

ECOTOURISM
While there is still a substantial way to go for Bosnia and Hercegovina's ecotourism scene to really take off, small but significant steps have been taken in the right direction. Some agencies are working to promote and preserve the country's pristine upland environment, organic food and medicinal plants; however, the country faces environmental problems, such as air pollution from metallurgical plants.

FUTURE DIRECTIONS
Bosnia and Hercegovina's future is hopefully on the up. Intercommunal relations have improved vastly, but national and political divisions hamper any real economic progress. Curious visitors are seeping in slowly, getting away from Croatia's tourist hordes and discovering the buzzing cultural and nightlife of Sarajevo. The presence of landmines, however, makes unimpeded movement through the wild countryside a lingering and serious risk.

ESSENTIAL EXPERIENCES

- **Looking up at Sarajevo's minarets, church spires and synagogue dome**
- **Watching young men dive off the Old Bridge in Mostar into the furious, foaming Neretva River below**
- **Taking in views of the sprinting waterfalls in Jajce's town centre**
- **Rafting on the speedy swirls of the Una River while surrounded by dark mountain gorges**
- **Wandering around Sarajevo's old bazaar, Baščaršija**

MAP REF // L12

BEST TIME TO VISIT MAY TO OCTOBER

⌃ IN MEMORIAM: MUSLIM WAR CEMETERY HEADSTONES, SARAJEVO

≫ SARAJEVAN WOMEN STEP OUT FOR A SPOT OF SHOPPING IN THE OLD TOWN

BASKING ON THE WALKWAY AT NEUM'S BUSY BEACH ≫

ORTHODOX PRIEST IN ELABORATE ROBES ADDRESSES WORSHIPPERS AT AN EASTER SERVICE IN SARAJEVO ≫

SERBIA

IRREPRESSIBLE, EXUBERANT AND EVER RESILIENT, SERBIA IS A REVELATORY LAND OF MUSIC FESTIVALS AND MOUNTAIN VILLAGES, ANCIENT SPIRITUALITY AND SPONTANEOUS BALKAN HOSPITALITY.

CAPITAL CITY BELGRADE   POPULATION 10.2 MILLION   AREA 88,360 SQ KM
OFFICIAL LANGUAGES SERBIAN, ROMANIAN, HUNGARIAN, SLOVAK, UKRAINIAN, CROATIAN

⌃ SHEEP DO WHAT SHEEP DO BEST OVER SNOWY HILLS IN A SERBIAN WINTER

LANDSCAPE

Serbia's varied terrain ranges from fertile plains in the northern province of Vojvodina to the ancient Stara Planina Mountain in the southeast. Forested hills and mountains such as Kapaonik, Zlatibor and Tara stretch across Serbia, as do three great European rivers, the Sava, Danube and Morava.

HISTORY IN A NUTSHELL

Along with other Slavic tribes, the Serbs migrated into the Balkans after the 6th century. They later accepted Orthodox Christianity. By the mid-14th century the Serbian Empire rivalled Byzantium. Ottoman Turks, however, would ruin the party. The 1389 Battle of Kosovo – then the heart of Serbia – presaged a long period of Muslim occupation, lasting until 1804. In 1815 a semi-independent Serbian principality was created. During the Balkan Wars (1912–13), Serbia allied with Montenegro, Bulgaria and Greece against the Ottomans, winning half of Macedonia thereafter. The assassination of Archduke Franz Ferdinand by a Serb nationalist in 1914 led to an Austrian declaration of war, setting off a chain reaction around Europe. After the Great War, the Kingdom of Serbs, Croats and Slovenes, later the Kingdom of Yugoslavia, was established. The defeat of the occupying Nazis in World War II by communists gave birth to the Yugoslav Federation, in which Serbia played the central role. During the 1990s, Serbia suffered economic sanctions, with the government of Slobodan Milosevic accused of stoking conflicts in Bosnia and Croatia. NATO's bombardment of Serbia in 1999 compelled the withdrawal from the Albanian-majority province of Kosovo. Milosevic was toppled in October 2000. In June 2006, Montenegro ended its formal association with Serbia; Kosovo declared independence in early 2008. Despite its turbulent recent past, Serbia is now a stable, democratic state.

PEOPLE

Serbia's extraordinary diversity is seen in the many ethnic groups interspersed with the majority Serbs, including Vlachs, Hungarians, Albanians, Germans, Roma, Croats, Bosniaks, Ukrainians, Slovaks, Romanians and Bulgarians. Religions include Orthodox Christianity, Islam, Roman Catholicism, Judaism and various Protestant and other Christian faiths.

MARKETPLACE

During Yugoslav times, Serbia was a major industrial power. The 1990s sanctions and war damage crippled the economy, however, and poverty remains endemic, especially in rural areas. Foreign support post-Milosevic has increased and Serbia is resuming its traditional role as the region's economic motor. It's increasingly appealing to foreign investors due to its strategic location, skilled workforce and large market, and is receiving major investments from American and European companies. Oil, mining and agriculture are major industries, and finance and ecotourism are looking promising.

TRADEMARKS

○ Magnificent mountains
○ Belgrade nightlife
○ Meat festivals
○ Brass bands
○ Sublime medieval monasteries

URBAN SCENE

Serbia's capital, Belgrade, hums with a unique and irrepressible energy, easily assimilating everything in its path and always hungry for more. Belgrade is a town of grand old buildings of the prewar Parisian style, where church bells ring out and old men covered in communist medals and fierce whiskers orate before bus drivers. At sunset, lovers look out over the city's two rivers, the Sava and Danube, from the Roman

COLOUR COORDINATION IS IMPORTANT WHEN PHONING HOME IN BELGRADE ≫

fortress of Kalemegdan high above. River boats rock under the weight of restaurants and bars at night, when the city as a whole reverberates with improvised revelry, the roar of taxis and the sizzle of grilled meat. Belgrade's women are faithfully fashionable, and the occasional flash of red hair alludes to vague Celtic ancestry. Bookstores are abundant, well visited and sedate, contrasting the bright graffiti, exuberance and basketball out on the street.

RANDOM FACTS
o One-third of all raspberries come from Serbia.
o Serbia has 270 species of birds – 80 percent of the total found in Europe.
o Ancient Sirmium, near Sremska Mitrovica, dates back to 5000 BC – one of Europe's oldest settlements.
o Serbs use two alphabets, Latin and Cyrillic, interchangeably.
o The Kacarevo Bacon Festival draws over 100,000 meat-lovers each February.

ON FILM
Emir Kusturica, Serbia's most famous film director, has been celebrating the contradictions, upheaval and comic uncertainties of modern Balkan life for three decades. Kusturica's critically acclaimed films include the Golden Palm–winning black comedy *Underground* (1995), and *Black Cat, White Cat* (1998), winner of the Venice Film Festival's Silver Lion. During the shooting of *Life is a Miracle* (2004), which won a Golden Globe, Kusturica envisioned creating a traditional mountain village for touristic and spiritual rejuvenation. This Drvengrad (Wooden Town) or Küstendorf project has also injected new economic life into westernmost Serbia. Of course, Drvengrad boasts a state-of-the-art cinema, where Kusturica holds occasional film classes.

FROM THE TRAVELLER

This composition reminds me of the complex history and culture of Serbian people. The Temple of St Sava in Belgrade is the largest Orthodox church currently in use in the world. After paying respect at the temple, a beautiful Byzantine structure with a massive central dome, I walked outside and saw an old man walking by the statue of Karađorđe Petrović, the leader of the First Serbian Uprising against the Ottoman Empire. Newly planted trees show hope for better days to come.

SINISA VLAISAVLJEVIC // USA

IMPORT
↗ Luxury cars
↗ Greek banks and medical students
↗ Hip-hop music
↗ NGOs
↗ Italian fashion brands

EXPORT
↖ Iron and steel
↖ Basketball stars
↖ Film directors
↖ Raspberries and plums
↖ Ethno music
↖ Mineral water

TOP FESTIVAL
For five days each summer, the 3000-strong village of Guča gets half a million extra inhabitants. They come to drink, dance and barbecue, serenaded throughout by the Guča Festival's roving brass bands. Drawing on Serbia's traditions of martial trumpeting and Roma orchestras, this cathartic and chaotic festival has become a pilgrimage for those in search of Serbian music and anarchic good fun.

SURPRISES
o Serbia is the most multicultural country in the Balkans.
o Four Serbian ethno songs feature on *Buddha Bar 8*.
o Serbia hosts southeastern Europe's biggest summer music extravaganza, the Exit Festival.
o The national apéritif is *šljivovica* (plum brandy).
o Serbia has a flourishing fashion-design scene.

ESSENTIAL EXPERIENCES

o **Experiencing Belgrade's pulsating nightlife**

o **Channelling the spirit of old Serbia in the Loznica-area villages and Banja Koviljača's mountain spa**

o **Gazing upon the ethereal frescoes at the 12th-century Studenica Monastery**

o **Stampeding with the herd at the Guča Festival, the world's biggest brass band gathering**

o **Sailing the blue Danube**

o **Visiting Drvengrad, Mount Zlatibor's eccentric traditional village dreamt up by Bosnian-Serb film director Emir Kusturica**

MAP REF // M12

BEST TIME TO VISIT **MAY TO AUGUST**

⌃ TRAFFIC IS BUMPER TO BUMPER IN BELGRADE

ED KASHI // CORBIS

≫ STUDENTS CATCH UP ON THE GOSSIP AT BELGRADE'S DKC CULTURAL CENTRE

LIGHTS UP SUN DOWN, CENTRAL BELGRADE ≫

THE BIG ONE GOT AWAY: BELGRADE FISHERMAN UNTANGLES A SMALL CATCH FROM HIS NET ≫

MONTENEGRO

MONTENEGRO IS A NATION THAT PACKS IN BOTH THRILLS AND TRANQUILLITY, FROM TOWERING MOUNTAINS SLASHED BY DEEP CANYONS TO A MASSIVE FJORD SURROUNDED BY BEACHES AND THE SPARKLING WATERS OF THE ADRIATIC.

CAPITAL CITY **PODGORICA**   POPULATION **684,740**   AREA **14,020 SQ KM**   OFFICIAL LANGUAGE **MONTENEGRIN**

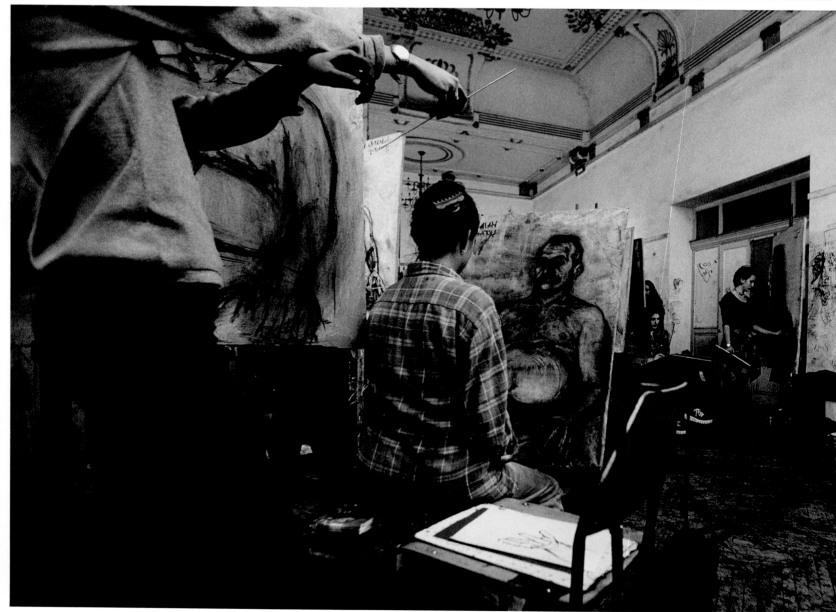

≪ STUDENTS PRACTICE THE ART OF LIFE DRAWING IN THE FORMER RUSSIAN EMBASSY, CETINJE

LANDSCAPE

Montenegro is a tiny, mountainous country, with a narrow coastal plain backed by rugged, high, limestone ranges. The coast stretches for 294 kilometres between the Croatian and Albanian borders. The Unesco-protected Durmitor National Park is a truly magnificent place for nature lovers, housing the 1.3-metre-deep Tara Canyon and Bobotov Kuk, the country's highest point. Montenegro has a Mediterranean climate, with hot dry summers and autumns, and relatively cold winters, with heavy snowfall in the mountains.

HISTORY IN A NUTSHELL

Only tiny Montenegro was able to keep its head above the Turkish tide that engulfed the Balkans for over four hundred years from the 14th century onwards. From 1482 Montenegro was ruled from Cetinje by *vladike* (prince-bishops). With the defeat of the Turks in 1878, Montenegro secured its territories, later recognised by the Congress of Berlin. Nikola I Petrovic, Montenegro's ruler, declared himself king in 1910 but was evicted by the Austrians in 1916. At the end of World War I, Montenegro was incorporated into Serbia. During World War II the region was given republic status within Yugoslavia; after the break up of Yugoslavia Montenegro remained in federation with Serbia. The two countries renamed themselves Serbia and Montenegro in 2003, and formed a looser federation, with a view to Montenegro's independence. Three years later, Montenegro held a referendum and, with votes exceeding the 55 per cent threshold, became an independent country on 3 June 2006.

PEOPLE

Montenegro's population comprises Montenegrins 43 per cent, Serbs 32 per cent, Bosniaks 8 per cent, Albanians 5 per cent and other groups (including Croats and Roma) 12 per cent. Orthodox Christianity is the majority religion, although Catholic churches and mosques are common in some areas – some churches even have Orthodox and Catholic altars next to each other.

MARKETPLACE

The dissolution of Serbia and Montenegro in 2006 means that Montenegro now has independent membership to international financial institutions, and the country is negotiating with the European Union in hope of eventual accession. High unemployment remains a major political and economic problem for this entire region. In recent years, Montenegro has attracted foreign investment in the tourism sector.

TRADEMARKS

- Dramatic coastline
- Soaring mountains
- Sveti Stefan, a fishing island-cum-exclusive holiday resort
- The *gusle*, a one-stringed musical instrument

NATURAL BEAUTY

Montenegro may be small, but it has an array of natural beauties: dramatic elevations with sharp, rugged peaks reaching into blue skies, cut through with canyons and scented with pine forests; the Adriatic Sea with its perfect Mediterranean towns; and Kotor Bay, hemmed in by majestic limestone mountains.

ECOTOURISM

Montenegro's government is keen to promote the country as an ecotourist's heaven, but in reality seems more in tune with foreign investors and developers. There are also environmental concerns, such as the pollution of coastal waters from sewage outlets, particularly in high tourism areas.

TAKING A QUIET MOMENT TO ROAM KOTOR'S COBBLED OLD TOWN »

ON PAPER

○ *The Mountain Wreath* by Petar Petrović Njegoš
○ *Black Lamb and Grey Falcon* by Rebecca West

WILD THINGS

Lake Skadar has 40 different kinds of fish, and counts as one of the largest bird reserves in Europe with rarities such as the Dalmatian pelican residing on its shores. Among the mammals that live in Montenegro's mountains are chamois, fox and hare. Bears and wolves are a very rare sight, though grey mountain eagles, white-headed vultures and falcons can be spotted in the skies above the snowy peaks.

MYTHS & LEGENDS

The Montenegrin town of Ulcinj was handed over from the Venetians to the Turks in 1571, and over the next 300 years gained in notoriety. It was well known as the centre of a thriving slave trade, which dealt in

some cases with small children only two or three years old, and those generally of North African descent. It was also used as a pirate base. Initially the pirates comprised mainly a few hundred North Africans and Maltese, but soon others – such as Serbs, Albanians and Turks – joined the ranks. The pirates are said to have made great fortunes from their innumerable robberies, swapping their small galley ships for large galleons almost overnight. The gangs changed their flags frequently while at sea, causing much confusion and chaos. At the end of their working day they would party on Ulcinj's Mala Plaža (Small Beach) and boil halva in massive cauldrons, stirring the piping-hot mass with an oar.

RANDOM FACTS

○ Montenegrins pride themselves on a 500-year-old reputation as valiant warriors.
○ Montenegro's people are among Europe's tallest, second only to the Dutch.
○ The country's most revered prince and poet, Petar Petrović Njegoš, is buried on top of Mount Lovćen, one of Montenegro's most spectacular landscapes.

FUTURE DIRECTIONS

Montenegro's future is growing brighter. After severing ties with Serbia (an alliance which, the government believes, was holding Montenegro back), the country is hoping to negotiate membership to the European Union. Tourism is increasing, and Montenegro is trying to combine its appeal as a small, undiscovered slice of the Mediterranean with its appeal as a luxury destination.

⌃ MONTENEGRIN ORTHODOX CHURCH CELEBRATES ST PETER OF CETINJE DAY

ESSENTIAL EXPERIENCES

○ **Climbing up to Kotor town's mountainside fortifications for breathtaking (and breathless) views of Kotor Bay**

○ **Rafting the Tara, the location of Europe's deepest canyon**

○ **Sunbathing on Montenegro's beaches in September, when the high season is over**

○ **Mountaineering, trekking, skiing and snowboarding in Durmitor National Park**

○ **Getting a dog-drawn sled to take you through the snow in the deep midwinter**

○ **Bird watching at Lake Skadar, one of Europe's biggest and most important bird sanctuaries and pelican habitats**

MAP REF // M12

BEST TIME TO VISIT **MAY TO OCTOBER**

⌃ TURQUOISE WATERS SURROUND SVETI STEFAN ISLAND RESORT

⌃ OSTROG MONASTERY NESTLES INTO ROCKY OSTROŠKA GREDA

≫ A MOMENT OF HOLY RITUAL AS A WOMAN IS CHRISTENED AT DAWN

TRANQUILLITY ON KOTOR BAY ≫

A SECOND OF SUSPENSE AS A DIVER HEADS INTO THE STILL WATERS AT BUDVA ≫

ALBANIA

A LITTLE LAND WITH A LOT OF HISTORY, ALBANIA'S CHEQUERED PAST HAS LEFT A FASCINATING LEGACY TO EXPLORE ALONG ONE OF THE LEAST-DEVELOPED STRETCHES OF EUROPE'S MEDITERRANEAN COAST.

CAPITAL CITY **TIRANA**   POPULATION **3.6 MILLION**   AREA **28,750 SQ KM**   OFFICIAL LANGUAGE **ALBANIAN**

≪ THE PARCHED AND CREVICED SHORE OF LAKE PRESPA CREATES HARD WORK FOR A WOMAN TURNING THE TOP SOIL

LANDSCAPE

A wild mountainous spine takes up three-quarters of the country, stretching its entire length. Bitterly cold in the winter, this area of Albania can be scorching under the summer sun. Running alongside the mountains and hugging the eastern edge of the Mediterranean is the coastal plain, no more than 50 kilometres at its widest and climatically mild.

HISTORY IN A NUTSHELL

Tracing an unbroken lineage to the ancient Illyrians, the Albanians have occupied these lands for 4000 years. For centuries from 167 BC, the country was passed between imperial powers – the Roman, Byzantine, Serbian and then 400 years of the Ottoman Empire – until an untimely stab at independence in 1912. The Albanian pass-the-parcel continued through World War I and World War II, during which time the country was occupied by the Greeks, Serbs, French, Italians, Austro-Hungarians and Germans, before independence was finally secured at the hands of the communist partisans. Faced with its own intransigent Stalinism, Albania's alliances with Yugoslavia, the USSR and China all ended in tears, the country bunkering down to a period of isolation from 1978 until the end of the regime in free elections in 1992. An uncontrolled free market saw peasants pushed off collective farms, state-owned industry grind to a halt and 70 per cent of the population lose their savings in private investment pyramid schemes, resulting in near anarchy by 1997. Things have been steadily improving in recent years, with the country losing its ranking as the poorest in Europe and working to rebuild its shattered infrastructure.

PEOPLE

The population is overwhelmingly Albanian (95 per cent), with Greeks making up the largest minority (two per cent). The traditional estimates of religious affiliation (70 per cent Muslim, 20 per cent Orthodox and 10 per cent Catholic) are largely conjecture. Many of the population remain fervently atheist, while Protestant fundamentalists have sought to make inroads into the country.

MARKETPLACE

With an average per capita income of around €2000 annually, 19 per cent of its population under the poverty line and high unemployment, Albania faces many difficulties in catching up with its European neighbours. Oil reserves are estimated at 185 million barrels, but output from its leaky pumps doesn't come close to meeting domestic demand. However, it's not all doom and gloom – GDP growth remains strong, inflation low, and annual remittances of €450 to €600 million from citizens living abroad helps to correct the trade deficit.

TRADEMARKS

- Gloomy mountains
- Beautiful beaches
- The flag's double-headed eagle
- Action-movie gangsters
- Communist-era bunkers
- Colourful headscarves

URBAN SCENE

Got a drab, grey city with no money for urban renewal and a population desperately looking for a brighter future? The solution, it seems, is a few coats of paint. Tirana is a bright, bustling city where once-stodgy concrete monoliths now wear yellow and orange stripes, concentric pink and purple circles or perception-bending cubes in primary colours. Fashionable teens wander the boutiques of Blloku, once the exclusive residential enclave for Party members, while the bars are abuzz with people drinking coffee, or something harder.

GRIT YOUR TEETH, IT'S TATTOO TIME IN THE CAPITAL, TIRANA »

TRADITIONS

For 500 years the people of the northern mountains were governed by a code of laws called the Kanun, which outlined all aspects of social responsibilities, such as work, marriage, family and hospitality. According to the Kanun, if a member of a family (or one of their guests) is murdered, it becomes the duty of the male members of that clan to claim their blood debt by murdering a male member of the perpetrator's clan. This sparks an endless cycle of killing that doesn't end until a reconciliation is brokered, or all the male members of either familiy are dead. A couple of high-profile cases, including a shoot-out on a bus in 2006, suggest that this bloodthirsty tradition has made a comeback.

RANDOM FACTS

○ Albanian is related to no other European language.
○ The countryside is dotted with 700,000 nearly indestructible concrete bunkers, a legacy of Stalinist isolation.
○ The world's most famous Albanian, Mother Theresa, was actually born and raised in Macedonia.

ON PAPER

There is no better introduction to Albanian culture and society than reading the works of the country's pre-eminent poet and novelist, Ismail Kadare. *Spring Flowers, Spring Frost* (2000) is a wistful look at the transition from communism, and was the winner of the Man Booker International prize in 2005; *Chronicle in Stone* (1971) gives a semiautobiographical account of wartime experiences seen through the eyes of a young boy; *Broken April* (1990) follows the doomed footsteps of a young man who is next in line in the desperate cycle of blood vendettas; *The Successor* (2005) is an entertaining take on political machinations under the old regime; and *The Concert* (1988) provides insight into communist daily life around the time of Albania's break with China.

SURPRISES

○ People shake their heads for 'yes' and 'nod' them for no.
○ Even the remotest of river valleys is blanketed in discarded plastic shopping bags.
○ Everybody seems to drive a Mercedes Benz.

CUISINE

Heavily Turkish-influenced, Albania's cuisine is dominated mainly by roast lamb in the mountains and fresh seafood dishes near the coast.

ON DISC

Polyphony, the blending of several independent vocal or instrumental parts, is a southern Albanian tradition dating from Illyrian times. Local pop music is incredibly catchy, using elements of polyphony and traditional instruments, such as clarinets over a disco beat. The accompanying video clips inevitably involve a hunky lad in traditional costume chasing after a coy village lass.

ESSENTIAL EXPERIENCES

○ **Stumbling around the ancient ruins hidden within the forest at Butrint**
○ **Lazing along the Ionian Coast, where the olive and citrus groves give way to unspoilt white sand beaches**
○ **Clambering up the rocky path to the living citadel of rugged Berat**
○ **Sipping a Turkish coffee in the colourful, chaotic streets of the capital, Tirana**
○ **Spotting square-jawed, stern-browed, socialist-realist sculpture**

MAP REF // M13

BEST TIME TO VISIT **APRIL TO JUNE, AUGUST TO OCTOBER**

≫ EGGS BY THE DOZEN AT TIRANA'S CENTRAL MARKET

DONALD NAUSBAUM // ALAMY

FROM THE TRAVELLER

The old part of Gjirokastra is a tangle of steep, narrow streets winding over and around hills and ridges. This, and the punishing heat of August, added to my sense of disorientation. Every time I thought I had become irretrievably lost in the labyrinth of stone-and-slate houses, I mysteriously found myself back in the same place: the Qafa e Pazarit crossroads, a star-shaped junction where five streets come together. The cobbled lanes of the Old Town were never designed with vehicle traffic in mind and navigating them by car must be a stressful experience. This mirror is intended to help drivers make their way through the crossroads, but it also provides an unusual view of the citadel that looms over the town.

ALAN GRANT // IRELAND

≫ ALBANIAN BOY STANDS STRONG IN FRONT OF THE NATION'S FLAG

GREEN OLIVES ARE PLENTIFUL DURING HARVEST IN LUSHNJË ≫

COOLING OFF BENEATH 500-YEAR-OLD OTTOMAN-BUILT MESI BRIDGE, SHKODRA ≫

MACEDONIA

HOME TO UNEXPLORED MOUNTAINS, ANCIENT MYSTERIES AND A MÉLANGE OF CULTURES, THE FORMER YUGOSLAV REPUBLIC OF MACEDONIA IS WITHOUT DOUBT ONE OF THE BALKANS' MOST CAPTIVATING COUNTRIES.

CAPITAL CITY **SKOPJE**   POPULATION **2.1 MILLION**   AREA **25,330 SQ KM**   OFFICIAL LANGUAGE **MACEDONIAN**

⌃ A YOUNG GIRL GASPS DURING HER BAPTISM IN THE TRESKA RIVER BY AN ORTHODOX PRIEST

LANDSCAPE

The Central European and Mediterranean climatic zones meet in Macedonia, as the many dramatic changes of landscape reveal. Green northern plains descend into arid vineyards, becoming cowboy scrublands in the south. Heavily forested mountains such as Korab, Šar Planina and Kozuf predominate; Macedonia has 16 mountain peaks over 2000 metres. Weird rock formations, such as Kuklica's giant stone dolls, Matka Canyon, and the 'iron gates' of Demir Kapija dot the land. The country's natural masterpiece, three-million-year-old Lake Ohrid, stretches for 30 kilometres across the southwest corner.

HISTORY IN A NUTSHELL

Few countries have a history as complex, contentious and ancient as Macedonia. Well known for Alexander the Great and his 4th-century BC empire, modern Macedonia nevertheless owes more to the migrating Slavic tribes who came during the 6th and 7th centuries AD, and the spiritual and cultural influences they took from Orthodox Byzantium. The subsequent 6th-century Ottoman Turkish occupation brought an Islamic influence. The Ottomans were expelled in 1912 by Serbia, Bulgaria and Greece, all of which had irredentist designs. Today's Republic of Macedonia is the chunk awarded to Serbia in 1913 and later incorporated into Tito's Yugoslavia, representing roughly half of the geographical Macedonia. In 1991 Macedonia declared independence, causing Greek embargoes and threats over the question of which country had rights to the Macedonian name and legacy. Ethnic Albanian extremists rebelled in 2001, but peace has long been restored. Macedonia is now a European Union candidate country praised for its tolerant, multiethnic society.

PEOPLE

Macedonia's ethnic blend includes Orthodox Christian Macedonians, ethnically and linguistically related to Bulgarians and Serbs, comprising around 64 per cent of the population. Muslim Albanians account for about 25 per cent, while Turks (four per cent) and Roma (three per cent) are also represented. Other minorities include Macedonian Muslims, Vlachs, Serbs, Bosniaks and Jews.

MARKETPLACE

Macedonia's economy, traditionally agriculture-based with an emphasis on tobacco, wine and vegetable farming, is being augmented by tourism and construction. Bigger cities such as Skopje and Tetovo are modernising rapidly. Nevertheless, annual economic growth averages only four per cent, and average monthly salaries are under €200. With around 35 per cent unemployment, many people rely on relatives working abroad or on the grey economy. Goods and services in Macedonia are inexpensive by Western standards.

TRADEMARKS

○ Red peppers in the doorframe of a country home
○ Whimsical, double-fisted hospitality
○ Lost cities and buried treasure
○ Serene lake views from clifftop monasteries

CUISINE

All-natural local ingredients and a time-honoured recipe book, combining Eastern and Central European tastes, distinguish Macedonian cuisine. From the Ottomans come burek (a golden-brown filo pie with crumbly white cheese or ground beef), baklava and Turkish coffee. Meat dishes include smoked ribs, uviač (chicken or pork logs rolled in bacon and filled with cheese) and roast lamb. Vegetable dishes revealing a Mediterranean flourish

A NEW CHURCH MIDCONSTRUCTION AT LAKE OHRID ADDS TO THE AREA'S ARCHITECTURAL HIGHLIGHTS »

include *ajvar* (sweet red-pepper sauce), *pinžur* (green-pepper sauce with tomatoes) and the national salad, *šopska salata* (tomatoes, cucumbers and onion with soft white cheese). Macedonian wines, meanwhile, are Europe's last undiscovered oenological treasure.

ON DISC
A Yugoslav joke once warned: 'Don't go to Bosnia; they'll sing better than you. And don't go to Serbia; they'll dance better than you. And definitely don't go to Macedonia; they'll sing *and* dance better than you!' That the Macedonians are fearsome entertainers is evidenced by gifted musicians such as opera singer Boris Trajanov and classical pianist Simeon Trpčevski, frequent headliners and award winners on the international stage. Ethno groups such as Synthesis and folk-dance ensemble Tanec have carried on traditional Macedonian music and dance. Annual sell-out events such as Ohrid's Summer Festival and the Skopje Jazz Festival have drawn world-renowned artists Ray Charles, José Carreras, Herbie Hancock and Ornette Coleman.

RANDOM FACTS
- The ruined prehistoric astronomical observatory of Kokino is, according to NASA, the world's fourth-most important site with ancient astronomical significance, after Stonehenge, Angkor Wat and Egypt's Abu Simbel.
- Macedonia has the longest continuous mountain ridge in Europe (89 kilometres), all of it above 2100 metres.
- Lake Dojran's fishermen use cormorants to catch fish – a method found only in Macedonia and China.
- The oldest university in the Slavic world was St Clement's 9th-century academy in Ohrid.

WILD THINGS
Macedonia's forests host one of Europe's last brown bear populations, along with wolves, pine martens, lynxes and other predators. Protecting shepherds' flocks from the latter is the hulking national mutt, the Šarplaninec. Macedonia is a migratory route and home for numerous bird species. Giant storks nest on phone poles, the enormous bearded eagle soars over canyons and the rare Dalmatian pelican trawls the waterways. Lake Ohrid boasts 10 endemic fish species; the most famous, the Ohrid trout, survived the Ice Age because the lake (in parts almost 300 metres deep) never froze. The trout is a delicacy, but also an endangered one; think twice before ordering it.

ECOTOURISM
Macedonian ecotourism's considerable promise has been stymied by low foreign investment and litter. It also conflicts with local businessmen's affection for marble-pillared five-star hotels. However, the limitless opportunities for bird watching, natural spa treatments, hiking and other outdoor sports indicate strong eco-potential.

FUTURE DIRECTIONS
Since its independence in 1991, Macedonia's survival has been almost miraculous. Postcommunist ills – high unemployment, shady privatisation and official corruption – were heightened by a Greek economic embargo, and an ethnic Albanian uprising in 2001. Structural reforms and strong support from the West, however, have consolidated Macedonia as a European Union candidate country. The government has pledged more foreign investment, better international marketing and infrastructural improvements. Despite Greece's threat to block Macedonia's NATO and European Union accession if it does not rename itself, Macedonia's outlook is bright.

≫ COBBLER TENDS TO NEEDY SOLES, SKOPJE

ESSENTIAL EXPERIENCES

- **Exploring centuries-old mosques, churches and repossessed *hamams* (Turkish baths) in Skopje's Ottoman Old Town**
- Swimming above the ruins of ancient settlements in Lake Ohrid's tranquil, translucent waters
- Savouring local favourites at the Tikveš wine country's private wineries
- Strolling Bitola's neoclassical Širok Sokak pedestrian street and drinking with the beautiful people in its cafés
- Feasting, drinking and merrymaking at the Vevčani and Strumica carnivals
- Disappearing into the ghost villages and haunted plain of Mariovo

MAP REF // N13

BEST TIME TO VISIT **MAY TO AUGUST**

≫ GABRIEL IN FRESCO, CHURCH OF ST GEORGE, KURBINOVO, PRESPA

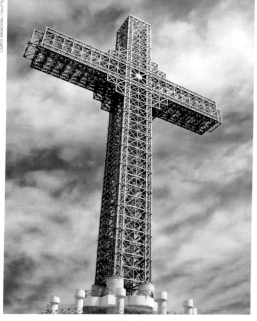

≪ THE OUTLOOK'S SUPERB FROM THE CHURCH OF ST JOHN AT KANEO, LAKE OHRID

MILLENNIUM CROSS PRESIDES ATOP MOUNT VODNO, NEAR SKOPJE ≫

A PICTURE OF PATRIOTISM AT A RALLY IN SKOPJE ≫

GREECE

STEEPED IN MYTHOLOGY AND HISTORY, BLESSED WITH ANCIENT AND NATURAL WONDERS, IDYLLIC ISLANDS AND GLORIOUS SUMMERS, GREECE POSSESSES AN ENDURING ROMANCE AND ALLURE.

CAPITAL CITY **ATHENS** | POPULATION **10.7 MILLION** | AREA **131,940 SQ KM** | OFFICIAL LANGUAGE **GREEK**

≈ BRILLIANTLY CLAD PARTICIPANTS GATHER ON PATRAS' GEROKOSTOPOLOU STEPS FOR THE SPECTACULAR PRE-LENTEN CARNIVAL CELEBRATIONS

LANDSCAPE

Spliced by dramatic mountain ranges and largely bordered by coastline, Greece has a remarkably diverse landscape for a country its size. Even its many islands differ radically from one another, from the strikingly barren islands of the Aegean to the lush Ionians. Central and southern Greece have a typically Mediterranean climate with hot, dry summers and mild winters, while the north has a more Balkan climate with freezing winters and humid summers.

HISTORY IN A NUTSHELL

Neanderthal tribes in Greece date back to 700,000 BC, but the Bronze Age triggered the rise of the remarkable Cycladic, Minoan and Mycenaean civilisations. Under Dorian rule, Greece split into independent city-states that competed in the first Olympic Games in 776 BC. The defeat of the Persians heralded Athens' golden age in 480 BC, but clashes with Sparta sparked the Peloponnesian Wars, marking the beginning of Athenian decline, the rise of Macedon, and Alexander the Great's expansion of the Hellenistic world. Greece later fell to the Roman and Byzantine Empires, then the Franks, Venetians and Ottomans, the latter ruling for 400 years. Greece gained independence – and a foreign monarch – in 1827. Suffering badly in World Wars I and II, and subsequent civil war, Greece was in turmoil again in 1967 when a military coup installed a dictatorship. Democracy was restored and the monarchy abolished in 1974. Greece has enjoyed relatively stable government since, joining the European Union in 1981 and hosting the Olympics in 2004.

PEOPLE

Greeks are notoriously proud, and renowned for their hospitality. Greece has a largely homogeneous population, with the majority identifying as Greek Orthodox. Once a nation of emigrants – more than five million people of Greek descent live abroad – Greece has seen a dramatic influx of migrants since the 1990s. Recent arrivals have boosted the Muslim population and demographics are changing: migrants now form nearly a tenth of the population.

MARKETPLACE

Greece has improved its economy and fast-tracked major infrastructure thanks to European Union funding, private and public sector spending and an Olympics-fuelled investment boom. Although it is a visibly wealthier society, economic disparities and a rural–city divide persist. Greece's significantly lower-than-average European Union incomes struggle against massive post-euro price hikes. Tourism is Greece's biggest industry.

TRADEMARKS

○ The Parthenon
○ Feta cheese
○ Ouzo
○ Pompom shoed Evzones (presidential guards)
○ Whitewashed island villages
○ The Olympic Games
○ Ancient Greek gods
○ *Zorba the Greek*

URBAN SCENE

Part ancient wonder, part concrete jungle, bustling Athens nonetheless oozes urban soul. Pedestrian promenades wind around ancient sites in the historic centre. Athenians enjoy a hedonistic lifestyle and vibrant street life, with lively outdoor cafés, quaint basement tavernas and terraces with superb Acropolis views. Moonlight cinema, funky late-night bars and music clubs, beach bars and all-night souvlaki joints fill with the throngs of Athenians out and about, determined to have a good time.

A TRICK OF LIGHT RENDERS THE STREETS OF MYKONOS AS A MOLTEN LANDSCAPE »

NATURAL BEAUTY

Beyond iconic islands jutting from dazzling azure waters, Greece is blessed with diverse natural wonders. Dramatic gorges in Crete and Epirus, rugged mountains and caves in the Peloponnese, and the volcanic landscapes of Santorini, Nisyros and Milos are a world away from hinterlands carpeted in wild flowers in the south, cascading waterfalls in Samothrace or the protected northern wetlands at Prespa and the Evros Delta.

ON STAGE

The ancient Greeks invented drama, and many plays from the 5th century BC are still performed today. Drama evolved from religious choral performances, during which Thespis is said to have broken ranks for what became the first solo performance. Thespian, the term for an actor, derives from this event. Theatre flourished in Athens between the 6th and 3rd centuries BC, when the tragedies of Aeschylus, Euripides and Sophocles and the comedies of Aristophanes were performed in annual drama contests.

RANDOM FACTS

○ About 170 of Greece's 1400-plus islands are inhabited.
○ Tourists to Greece annually outnumber its population.
○ Greek is Europe's oldest written language.

IN STONE

The celebrated classical period of Greek sculpture portrayed the body in a natural and idealised form rather than previous flat and stylised depictions. Statues of gods and men were represented nude or covered in masterful drapery. Few Greek masterpieces survive from this period, but those that did inspired famous Roman copies and the work of Renaissance artists such as Michelangelo.

CUISINE

Haute cuisine is a new trend in Greek dining. Greek food is best known for simple flavours, fresh ingredients and generous use of olive oil – the key to making vegetables, salads and legumes tasty. Regional specialities and local variations of traditional dishes abound. Eating out is a key part of the culture and sharing *mezedes* (appetisers) is popular.

MYTHS & LEGENDS

The ancient Greek gods continue to capture the popular imagination. Zeus, the supreme deity, had a wild time presiding over the ancient world from Mount Olympus with his fellow gods, who were mostly members of his unruly family. Hera, his wife, was also his sister; Athena, his daughter and the goddess of wisdom, was allegedly born from his head; Apollo, god of light, music and song, and Hermes, Zeus' messenger, were his sons by other lovers.

SURPRISES

○ Snow falls in many parts of Greece, including the islands, and you can ski in several mountain resorts.
○ Greeks drink more whisky than ouzo, the latter normally enjoyed with *meze*, not straight at a bar.
○ Cremation is forbidden in Greece.

ECOTOURISM

Greece is rather belatedly embracing ecotourism, which is now a miniscule but growing part of the tourism industry. Crete and the mainland promote alternative tourism, nature and adventure holidays, farmstays, and gourmet and wine trails. Overdevelopment and short-sighted opportunism unfortunately have spoilt many islands, leaving sad trails of cheap resorts.

ESSENTIAL EXPERIENCES

○ **Admiring the temples of the Acropolis**
○ **Island hopping around the Aegean**
○ **Enjoying spectacular vistas from Santorini's whitewashed clifftop villages**
○ **Visiting monasteries perched on rocky pinnacles at Meteora**
○ **Standing in the navel of the earth at ancient Delphi**
○ **Discovering the scenic mountain villages of the Zagorohoria**
○ **Exploring Crete's Minoan Palace of Knossos**
○ **Checking out the acoustics at the Epidavros theatre**
○ **Wandering through Rhodes' medieval Old Town**
○ **Envisaging the ancient Olympics at Olympia**

MAP REF // N13

BEST TIME TO VISIT **APRIL TO JUNE, SEPTEMBER TO NOVEMBER**

⌃ THE ANCIENT PARTHENON SURVIVES ON ATHENS' ACROPOLIS

⌃ A SANTORINI CHURCH WEARS THE NATIONAL COLOURS

≪ COUPLE READY THEIR FISHING NETS FOR A DAY'S TRAWLING OFF THE COAST OF SANTORINI

IT'S A DONKEY'S LIFE, SANTORINI ≫

A PERFORMER STRUMS MELANCHOLIC *REMBETIKA* MELODIES, BACKED BY IMAGES OF HIS FORERUNNERS, IN A PLÁKA RESTAURANT, ATHENS ≫

TURKEY

AS COLOURFUL AND COMPLEX AS THE CARPETS FOR WHICH IT IS FAMOUS, TURKEY INTERWEAVES A VENERABLE HISTORY WITH A SPONTANEOUS POPULACE, URBAN SOPHISTICATION WITH RURAL HOSPITALITY, IDYLLIC BEACHES WITH A RUGGED INTERIOR.

CAPITAL CITY ANKARA   POPULATION 71.2 MILLION   AREA 780,580 SQ KM   OFFICIAL LANGUAGE TURKISH

LANDSCAPE

Turkey is where the Balkans merge with the Mediterranean and tail away into the Middle East. İstanbul sits at the southeastern tip of Europe and spreads across into Asia and the landmass of Anatolia. The western and southern coasts boast quintessentially Mediterranean landscapes – rocky shores, translucent blue seas, pine trees, olive groves, poppies in spring and figs in summer. Eastward of the otherworldly geological formations of Cappadocia, in central Anatolia, the Turkish interior ripples away in a mountainous plateau all the way to Mount Ararat.

HISTORY IN A NUTSHELL

A meeting place, a marketplace, and often a battleground, Turkey boasts a history littered with fallen kingdoms, momentous events and noteworthy (sometimes infamous) characters. Around 1800 BC the Hittites were the first to emerge and dominate a miscellany of ancient cultures. Greek trading colonies – including the Troy made famous by Homer – then arose along the coast. Alexander the Great ricocheted through in 334 BC, to be followed by the Romans, who built their capital at Ephesus and later allowed Christianity to spread. When Rome was split in the 4th century, its

eastern half evolved into the Byzantine Empire, centred on Constantinople. The all-conquering Ottoman Turks then gradually swallowed up Byzantium and southeastern Europe, reaching their peak in 1566 under Süleyman the Magnificent. Thereafter the Ottoman Empire went into slow and enervating decline. In 1923, the Turkish republic was born under the stewardship of Kemal Atatürk, and since then gradual modernisation has brought Turkey ever closer to Europe.

PEOPLE

Seemingly a monoculture, Turkey actually consists of a patchwork of peoples and cultures. The Turks, from İstanbul sophisticates to hospitable Anatolian peasants, form the majority, while Kurds, found largely in the southeast, are the largest minority. There are also small communities of Greeks, Armenians and Jews. The Laz and Hemşin are native to the Black Sea region, and there are also smatterings of Balkan and Caucasian peoples: Circassians, Georgians, Kazakhs, Tatars and Albanians.

MARKETPLACE

After a long era of central control and underdevelopment, the Turkish economy is rapidly

modernising and private enterprise is being given free rein. Economists have long wrestled with rampant inflation and now have the upper hand; however, as urbanisation occurs apace, there are growing discrepancies between elites in İstanbul, Ankara and İzmir and those eking out a living in the provinces and villages.

TRADEMARKS

- Carpets (and persistent carpet spruikers)
- Mediterranean beaches
- İstanbul ferries
- Ablutions at the *hamam* (Turkish bath)
- Sizzling lamb kebabs
- Turkish delight
- Çay (tea) in tulip-shaped glasses

URBAN SCENE

İstanbul is the quintessential port city and marketplace. It was the capital of the Byzantine Empire for 1100 years, and then the Ottoman Empire for almost 500, but lost that honour to Ankara when the Turkish Republic was created. Still, it remains the financial, cultural and artistic heart of the Turkish nation; a bustling, burgeoning and vibrant entrepôt,

⌃ WHIRLING DERVISHES IN A SPIRITUAL SPIN, İSTANBUL

⌃ DILAPIDATED WINDMILLS LINE THE HILLTOP OUTSIDE THE TOWN OF BODRUM, MUĞLA PROVINCE

⌃ INSIDER'S VIEW OF İSTANBUL'S SUBLIME AYA SOFYA

PORTRAIT OF CONTEMPLATION: A TURKISH MAN HOLDS A STEADY GAZE WHILE INHALING »

» HERDERS TEND THEIR FLOCK ALONGSIDE HISTORICAL HARRAN'S UNIQUE BEEHIVE HOUSES

that is the only city to straddle two continents. Ankara, the administrative capital, little more than a backwater until 1923, is a thriving metropolis in the middle of the Anatolian steppe. İzmir, Turkey's third city, is a workaday industrial city, fronting the Aegean, with a large student population and pumping nightlife.

TRADITIONS
Hospitality runs deep in Turkey; it's second nature, not something that's thought about. Legion are the tales of travellers who have experienced spontaneous offers of sweets, refreshments and cups of tea, even invitations for meals or to stay in the family home. Indeed, life is lived with great spontaneity in Turkey, and it is always better savoured among friends – old or brand new.

RANDOM FACTS
○ The Virgin Mary is reputed to be buried near Selçuk.
○ Turkish people eat more bread per capita than any other nation.
○ İstanbul has a Jewish community that dates from 1492, when Jews were expelled from Spain by the Inquisition.
○ In 1768 Ahmet Çelebi was the first human to fly, with artificial wings, crossing the Bosphorus from the Galata Tower.

CUISINE
Many Europeans associate Turkish cuisine only with late-night kebabs. In fact, with the abundant fresh produce, bountiful seas and liberal borrowings from nearby Greece, the Middle East and the Balkans, the Turks boast a cuisine considerably more diverse and imaginative – in fact, it's downright mouthwatering. Turks are serious about their food, proud of their culinary traditions, and never miss an opportunity to share a meal with family, friends or passers-by. Many meals begin with – or may consist solely of – *meze*, a selection of dips and starter dishes that are mopped up with bread and washed down with *rakı* (aniseed spirit).

ON FILM
○ *Yol* (The Road, 1982)
○ *Hamam* (Steam: the Turkish Bath, 1997)
○ *Güneşe Yolculuk* (Journey to the Sun, 1999)
○ *Uzak* (Distant, 2002)
○ *Duvara Karsi* (Head On, 2004)
○ *İkilimler* (Climates, 2006)

ON PAPER
○ *İstanbul: Memories and the City* by Orhan Pamuk
○ *My Name is Red* by Orhan Pamuk
○ *Memed, My Hawk* by Yaşar Kemal
○ *Young Turk* by Moris Farhi
○ *İstanbul: the Imperial City* by John Freely
○ *The Caravan Moves On* by Irfan Orga
○ *Turkish Letters* by Ogier de Busbecq

IN STONE
○ Aya Sofya (İstanbul) Byzantine cathedral-cum-Ottoman mosque-cum-architectural treasure.
○ Süleymaniye Mosque (İstanbul) Masterpiece of Turkey's greatest architect.
○ Mevlana Müzesi (Konya) Opal-tiled spiritual home of the Whirling Dervishes.
○ Ishak Paşa Palace (Doğuubayazıt) Fortress with Mount Ararat as a backdrop.
○ Library of Celsus (Ephesus) Classic white-stone Roman ruin.
○ Sumela Monastery (Trabzon) Last redoubt of the Pontic Greeks.
○ Ruins of Ani (Ani) Melancholy, long-abandoned Armenian captial.
○ Beehive houses (Harran) Constructed entirely without wood.

MYTHS & LEGENDS
The 15th century saw Venetians opining that İstanbul, then known as Constantinople, was created by nature and ordained by history to be the centre of the world, and that a new emperor in the city would usher in the Second Coming. When the Turkish sultan, Mehmet, took the city from the Byzantines in 1453, much of Europe worried it was a harbinger of the end of Christendom.

SURPRISES
○ The Turks bequeathed coffee to Europe, while besieging Vienna.
○ Cherries originated near the Black Sea town of Giresun.
○ Harran is considered the longest continuously occupied city on earth.
○ Native Van cats have green-yellow eyes.

FUTURE DIRECTIONS
Turkey remains teetering on the edge of Europe; it's a candidate for inclusion in the European Union, but membership is still far from certain. Issues such as the status of Cyprus – the north of which is an unrecognised Turkish-run state – human rights and freedom of expression continue to be stumbling blocks, despite the fact that there was widespread jubilation when accession talks started in late 2005. The Turks' own ardour for the European Union appears to have cooled somewhat, and some in Europe baulk at the idea of a large, populous Islamic nation ever entering the union. Whatever the case, Turkey, vibrant and ambitious, remains the only Muslim state in the region with a thriving democracy.

ESSENTIAL EXPERIENCES

○ **Finding infinity in the soaring dome of İstanbul's Aya Sofya**
○ **Floating on your back in Ölüdeniz lagoon**
○ **Greeting the dawn in a hot-air balloon over Cappadocia**
○ **Pondering the futility of war on the battlefields of Gallipoli**
○ **Haggling for antiquarian books in İstanbul's Grand Bazaar**
○ **Watching the setting sun reflected in the snowy peaks of Mount Ararat**
○ **Tavern hopping and window shopping in Beyoğlu**
○ **Roaring across Anatolia on the night train to Lake Van**
○ **Daydreaming of Ottoman glories in the wooden houses of Safranbolu**

MAP REF // Q13

BEST TIME TO VISIT **MAY TO OCTOBER**

GAVRIEL JECAN // CORBIS

⌃ STRIKING REMAINS OF STATUES FROM THE 1ST CENTURY BC PRESIDE OVER MOUNT NEMRUT

VIEWS FROM A HOT-AIR BALLOON REVEAL THE FANTASTICAL VOLCANIC-CONED WONDERLAND OF NEVŞEHIR, CAPPADOCIA ≫

LOCAL BUS SPEEDS PAST PEDESTRIANS IN THE CITY OF DIYARBAKIR ≫

CYPRUS

CYPRUS IS A MIX OF EUROPE, ASIA AND AFRICA, WITH FASCINATING HISTORICAL REMAINS NEXT TO FABULOUS BEACHES, SHADY MOUNTAIN FORESTS OVERLOOKING KITSCH TOURIST RESORTS, AND A TRADITIONAL MEDITERRANEAN CULTURE WORTH DISCOVERING.

CAPITAL CITY NICOSIA (LEFKOSIA)   POPULATION 788,460   AREA 9250 SQ KM   OFFICIAL LANGUAGES GREEK, TURKISH, ENGLISH

⌃ CURIOUS WORSHIPPER POPS UP FROM A PEW DURING CHURCH SERVICE IN LAPITHOS, IN THE TURKISH NORTH

LANDSCAPE

The saucepan shape of Cyprus has a 100-kilometre-long mountain range, the Kyrenia (Girne), in the North. The large plain of Mesaoria (Mesarya) lies between the northern range and Troödos Massif, a vast mountain chain topped by Mount Olympus (1952 metres), which dominates the south of the island. Cyprus is a top spot for bird watchers, and there are some 1800 species and subspecies of plants. The island has an intense Mediterranean climate, with hot, dry summers and short, rainy winters.

HISTORY IN A NUTSHELL

Cyprus first saw human settlements between 10,000 and 3800 BC. The Chalcolithic period and Bronze Age lasted from 3800 to 1200 BC and the Phoenicians moved in between 850 and 750 BC. From 568 BC to AD 395, Cyprus was ruled by the Egyptians, Persians, Greeks and Romans, until the arrival of the Byzantines, who brought Orthodox Christianity to the island. Cyprus endured raids by the Arabs from 647 to 965, followed by the English in 1191; the Lusignans then ruled from 1192 until the Venetians helped themselves to the island in 1489. The Ottoman Empire swept through the land, ousting the Venetians in 1571, retaining control for three centuries. The British formally annexed Cyprus in 1914. Cypriot rebels, EOKA, waged guerrilla warfare against the British between 1955 and 1960, leading to an independent Cyprus with archbishop Makarios as its first president. Constitutional changes triggered intercommunal fighting, and in 1974 the Greek military junta organised a coup against Makarios and the Turkish army took over the northern third of Cyprus. The island was to live divided for the next 30 years, a division only intensified by the Turks unilaterally proclaiming the Turkish Republic of Northern Cyprus in 1983. The borders between the South and North opened for the first time in 2003, but when the UN called a referendum for reunification the following year, the Turks voted in favour while the Greeks voted against the plan. The Republic of Cyprus joined the European Union without the North in May 2004. A symbolic step towards the reunification of the island's capital took place in March 2007, when part of the division wall was knocked down.

PEOPLE

Cyprus is made up of Greek and Turkish Cypriots. The majority Greeks are Orthodox, and the Turks, who make up 18 per cent of Cyprus' population, are Muslim. Since the 1970s, which saw the partition of Cyprus, the North has had a large influx from mainland Turkey. Greek is spoken in the South, and Turkish in the North; English is also commonly spoken.

MARKETPLACE

The Republic of Cyprus' economy is dominated by the service sector, which accounts for almost 80 per cent of its GDP. The Turkish Cypriot economy has roughly one-third of the per capita GDP of the South, and is heavily dependent on financial transfers from the Turkish government.

TRADEMARKS
- Beautiful beaches
- An abundance of ancient remains
- Agia Napa nightlife
- Haloumi cheese

URBAN SCENE

Cyprus' most exciting city is its capital, Nicosia. Eased border-crossing restrictions have finally enabled the world to see the city – previously divided for more than 30 years – as a whole again. While Lefkosia (South Nicosia) developed into a city of restaurants, international chains and hip nightclubs, North Nicosia (Lefkoşa) remained stuck in time, with dilapidated

BACK-CRACKING MASSAGE KEEPS THIS NICOSIA MAN FLAT OUT IN A LOCAL BATHHOUSE

houses and charming traditional workshops. Both sides of the Cypriot capital offer a precious insight into the island's soul.

NATURAL BEAUTY

Cypriot beaches cater to all tastes: you can be surrounded by clubbers sleeping off their hangovers on Agia Napa beach, or spend hours strolling on deserted beaches of the North's Karpas Peninsula alongside sparkling waters. The Troödos mountain range offers brilliant hiking and mountain biking, and the Akamas Peninsula is perfect for springtime hikes among wild flowers.

ON FILM

- *Cyprus, Ordained to Me* (1963)
- *Camur* (Mud, 2003)
- *Living Together Separately* (2003)

RANDOM FACTS

- Fashion designer Hussein Chalayan, controversial British artist Tracey Emin and musicians George Michael and Yusuf Islam (Cat Stevens) all have Cypriot origins.
- Haloumi cheese is officially recognised by the European Union as a traditional Cypriot product, and therefore only made in Cyprus.
- The village of Geroskipou holds the world record for making the largest slab of Turkish delight in 2004.

MYTHS & LEGENDS

It is a common belief among Cypriots that theirs is the island on which the Greek goddess of love, Aphrodite, stepped out of the sea and went on to do what she did best. Legend has it that after emerging in a shower of foam and nakedness, Aphrodite spent most of her time receiving lovers at the Baths of Aphrodite, near Pafos. She became the island's patron, and has been embraced most fervently by the country's tourism board.

ECOTOURISM

Cyprus has a growing ecotourism scene, mainly represented by Agrotourism, an organisation dealing with small-scale hotels and village houses refurbished in the traditional style. Unfortunately, the mass development catering to package tourism still dominates the tourist industry here. The North has many small, family-run hotels, but no concerted effort towards ecotourism.

FUTURE DIRECTIONS

Cyprus' future is heading in a positive direction; however, division remains the dominant problem on the country's agenda, and solving this complex issue may take many generations.

⩓ A TERRACOTTA-DOMED CHURCH BECKONS TO DEVOTEES

⩓ ELDERLY LEFKARA MAN ENJOYS HIS MORNING BREW OUTDOORS

⩓ BLACK-CLAD ORTHODOX PRIEST IN THE WHITE HEAT OF SUMMER

ESSENTIAL EXPERIENCES

- Taking in the space and solitude of the Karpas Peninsula and its beautiful beaches
- Exploring the fairy-tale beauty of St Hilarion Castle, and the wind-beaten Gothic ruins of Kantara and Buffavento Castles
- Discovering the nooks of Nicosia's Old City, both South and North
- Wandering through ancient history at the stunning ruins of Ancient Salamis
- Hiking the Akamas Peninsula in spring, when wild flowers are in bloom

MAP REF // R15

BEST TIME TO VISIT **APRIL TO NOVEMBER**

≫ THE TRADITIONAL STREETSIDE STITCHING OF FINE LACE WOULD HAVE MOST OF US SEEING DOUBLE IN LEFKARA

PAPHOS CASTLE HOLDS STEADY AS FISHING BOATS SWAY IN PORT ≫

EXTRAORDINARY ANCIENT RUINS MAKE FOR PLENTY OF CLOSE ENCOUNTERS OF THE ARCHAEOLOGICAL KIND ≫

TEXT ROBERT REID

BULGARIA

COMPACT AND BEAUTIFUL, WITH ROCKY MOUNTAINS, GOLD-SAND BEACHES AND GINGERBREAD TAVERNS, BULGARIA IS HOPING TOURISM AND ITS NEWEST FLAG (THE EUROPEAN UNION ONE) CAN BOOST A SLOW-TO-START ECONOMY.

CAPITAL CITY **SOFIA**   POPULATION **7.3 MILLION**   AREA **110,910 SQ KM**   OFFICIAL LANGUAGE **BULGARIAN**

≈ SLIPPING OUTSTRETCHED THROUGH THE TRANSLUCENT BELLY OF A SNAKELIKE WATERSLIDE, VARNA

LANDSCAPE

Nesting in the eastern Balkans, Bulgaria is one-third mountainous terrain. The valleys to the south of the central Stara Planina range are home to enough roses to produce nearly 75 per cent of the world's rose oil. Bulgaria's eastern border meets the Black Sea, much of which is lined with gold-sand beaches (and a lot of Speedos). Bulgaria is called home by some 56,000 living creatures, including one of Europe's largest bear populations.

HISTORY IN A NUTSHELL

Thracians, Romans and Slavs settled in the area before Bulgaria's first incarnation eventually emerged in AD 681. During the next few (frequently violent) centuries, Bulgaria created its own language, religion and alphabet (Cyrillic – that's right, Russia imported it), forging an identity that fell into a 500-year hibernation during Ottoman rule. Next came the Nazis, then the Soviets, who pushed out Germany and set up a communist government. Bulgaria has waffled its way into the free-market world, but its entry to NATO in 2004 and the European Union in 2007 is making locals feel a bit more upbeat about their 21st-century prospects.

PEOPLE

Some 84 per cent of Bulgaria's population are Bulgarians and Slavs, who speak Bulgarian. About 10 per cent are Turks, many of whom speak only Turkish, and roughly five per cent are Roma. The sudden rise of late in 'New Bulgarians' – mostly middle-aged Brits and Western Europeans frantically buying beach property – has created an even more miniscule minority.

MARKETPLACE

Slow to restart after the collapse of communism, the Bulgarian economy has not been helped by in-house corruption that almost prevented the European Union from approving the country's membership. However, things are now improving. Oil and natural gas are among some of Bulgaria's better-known exports, but the average monthly salary remains less than €200.

TRADEMARKS

o 19th-century revival architecture
o Cyrillic alphabet
o Cheap ski slopes and beach resorts
o Female folk choruses
o *Mehanas* (traditional taverns)

URBAN SCENE

The bustling capital Sofia can feel ho-hum compared to some Eastern European capitals, but it's easy to enjoy the gold-brick streets around the centre and its pet mountain, Mount Vitosha (with its ski runs and berry picking), just outside the city limits. Many Bulgarians prefer Plovdiv, a lively town littered with Roman ruins, including a full Roman amphitheatre in a cobblestoned Old Town set on a hill. A former capital in the Stara Planina mountains, Veliko Târnovo is a lively student town, with an S-shaped river curling past the finest medieval citadel in the country.

TRADITIONS

Traditional music in Bulgaria is closely linked to national identity, and still very present in day-to-day life (particularly on TV). Hill towns Kotel and Shiroka Luka are home to famous schools that teach instruments such as the *gayda* (the Bulgarian goatskin 'bagpipe').

CUISINE

There are two kinds of Bulgarian food: Bulgarian food and pizza. The latter has taken off, in the form of ketchup-doused slices served on the street or finer

A PAINTED, DOMED CEILING HAS CHRIST LOOKING DOWN FROM THE HEAVENS ⤊

DECAYING 19TH-CENTURY HOMES CAN STILL BE SPOTTED AROUND INCREASINGLY MODERN SOFIA ⤊

servings at sit-down restaurants. Traditional Bulgarian food, on the other hand, is a Turkish- and Greek-influenced cuisine with many grilled meats, such as the *kebabche* (spicy meat sausage). Most days here begin with a cheese-filled *banitsa* pastry, sold from simple street stands marked 'zakuska' (breakfast). In the 1970s, the state-run Balkantourist created the ever-present *shopska* salad (tomato, onion, cucumber, goat cheese) for visitors wanting to try a 'Bulgarian staple'. Bulgarians took note, and now start most meals with this dish.

RANDOM FACTS

- Most towns have a street named after Bogomils, 10th-century vegetarian hermits who fought corruption by rejecting all things visual.
- Famous Bulgarian environmental artist Christo put up orange gates around New York's Central Park and covered Berlin's Reichstag in recycled materials.
- *Chalga,* or 'wedding music', is a synth-based disco music based on traditional Balkan melodies, and is both loved and hated (sample lyrics: 'We win, we lose, either way we drink, we're Bulgarians!').

⌃ WARMING UP AGAINST A RUINED STONE CHURCH, BURGAS

⌃ THE STRAW THAT BROKE THE DONKEY'S BACK

MYTHS & LEGENDS

Bulgaria's own Che Guevara is Vasil Levski, a charismatic revolutionary who put freedom before life – and lost his at age 35 in 1873 – after organising nationwide groups to stage attacks against the occupying Ottomans. His contribution to Bulgarian liberation has him hailed as a national hero. Vasil's legacy lives on, with stadiums, streets, schools and football teams named after him all over Bulgaria.

SURPRISES

- The Rila, Pirin and Rodopi mountain ranges in the south shoot up like the Alps, making for great hiking and skiing.
- Bulgarians shake their head for 'yes' and nod their head for 'no' – just ask '*da ili ne?*' (yes or no?) when confusion sets in.
- Red wine (which is dry and tasty) is produced throughout Bulgaria, such as in wee Melnik, where supposed 'hangover-free' wine is sold in tub-sized bottles.

TOP FESTIVAL

March is a great time to be in Bulgaria. At this time locals give each other red and white *martenitsa* dolls and bracelets, which are to help push out winter and welcome in the spring. The colours are chosen to appease the temperamental folklore figure Baba Marta (Grandma Marta). Bulgarian friends exchange the dolls and tie them to their wrists or clothes. As per the tradition, the *martenitsa* are worn until a stork is spotted – and there are some storks around, fortunately – after which the dolls get tied to a tree.

ESSENTIAL EXPERIENCES

- **Perusing Bulgaria's revival architecture in Koprivshtitsa and Plovdiv**
- **Elbowing a little space on Bulgaria's Black Sea beaches Sinemorets and Sunny Beach**
- **Cutting tracks through fresh snow at ski resorts Bansko, Borovets and Pamporovo**
- **Clambering around the remarkable Belogradchik Rocks with the medieval Kaleto Fortress built into them**
- **Trying the fiery *rakia* (home-brew brandy) in a cozy *mehana* (traditional tavern)**

⌃ SNOW-TIPPED TREES LINE THE WAY TO THE PIRIN MOUNTAINS

MAP REF // O12

BEST TIME TO VISIT **JANUARY TO MARCH, JUNE TO SEPTEMBER**

⊼ BLUE AND WHITE UMBRELLAS CREATE A BALKAN BEACHSIDE KALEIDOSCOPE

ALEKSANDER NEVSKI MEMORIAL CHURCH SHIMMERS IN SOFIA ⊼

THE CATCH IS HOOKED AND HUNG OUT TO DRY AT NESEBAR'S FISH MARKET ⊼

THE BLACK SEA & CAUCASUS

SEEN BY MANY AS EUROPE'S BACK DOOR, THE EXOTIC AND EASTERN REALM OF THE BLACK SEA AND CAUCASUS IS MADE UP OF THE LEAST-KNOWN OF EUROPE'S STATES, AND IT'S FOR THIS REASON THAT THE 'WILD EAST' PROVIDES SOME OF THE CONTINENT'S MOST OFFBEAT AND EXCITING EXPERIENCES.

Conventional understandings of Europe begin to blur as the continent slips away to Asia and the Middle East – it soon becomes clear that Eastern Europe is a lot more than just Slavs, snow and soldiers. Of course, Russia remains the local superpower, but today the sheer diversity of the region's one-time Moscow satellites is both surprising and impressive. Expect those long-held stereotypes to be blown out of the water and you won't be disappointed.

The Black Sea derives its name from the danger associated with crossing its waters in ancient times, when it was used as a place to exile troublemakers; however, its clear, warm waters and excellent beaches have been luring people here since Roman times. The coastlines of Romania, Ukraine, Russia and Georgia absolutely beg to be explored – check out Ukraine's most multicultural city, Odesa, and booming Batumi in Georgia, or experience the charms of the Russian Riviera at Sochi.

The Caucasus, where East and West grind up against each other, needs little introduction. Famed for dramatic mountain scenery and an equally dramatic history, here the Muslim and Christian worlds meet as Asia and Europe intricately interweave. It's a region that stands alone between the two continents, full of stunning variety, scenery and people for whom hospitality is a way of life. The Old City of Baku in Azerbaijan, Armenia's monasteries and the cave cities of Georgia will leave few unawed.

To the north is the colossus, Russia, a country so massive that no mere continent can contain it, and its vassal state, Belarus, a tiny appendage bearing the grand status of Russia's main 'ally' in the modern world. Both are fascinating countries – Russia for its mind-numbing complexity, throbbing paradoxes and beguiling peoples, Belarus for being a time capsule of that once ubiquitous Soviet way of life so feared the world over. Both countries stubbornly refuse to merge

into Europe's mainstream, preferring to stand apart as something not quite Europe, not quite Asia, in the long Slavophile tradition. The art collections and canals of St Petersburg, the stunning Kremlin in Moscow and the legacy of Stalinism in Minsk are all unmissable regional sights, rich in the dark and fascinating history of these countries.

As the European Union swells to ever more distant corners of this truly remarkable continent, Romania and Moldova will similarly disprove many stereotypes – why not party-down in Bucharest, a city that is relentlessly reinventing itself, and sample the wines of Moldova for a true taste of the new Europe?

TEXT TOM MASTERS

TEXT LEIF PETTERSEN

ROMANIA

DESPITE MTV'S INCREASING IMPACT, THE 'WILD WEST OF EASTERN EUROPE' IS STILL LARGELY ABOUT PEASANTS, STUPEFYING SCENERY AND THE COMFORTABLY UNDEAD.

CAPITAL CITY **BUCHAREST**   POPULATION **22.3 MILLION**   AREA **237,500 SQ KM**   OFFICIAL LANGUAGE **ROMANIAN**

⌃ A SHEPHERD CLOAKED IN FUR UNDERSTANDS THE IMPORTANCE OF KEEPING WARM IN THE FĂGĂRAŞ MOUNTAINS

LANDSCAPE

Romania's three distinct geographical regions encompass much of the country's outward appeal. The boomerang-shaped Carpathian Mountains are an outdoor enthusiast's contact-high. To the west are plateaus, where thriving peasant villages nestle amid undulating hills and valleys. The plains to the east hold the country's agricultural core as well as the Black Sea coast, which includes Europe's second-largest delta.

HISTORY IN A NUTSHELL

Adopting its present name in 1862 and current borders after World War I, Romania was previously one of Europe's hot potatoes: occupants, rulers and uninvited guests whirled through the territory like a university dorm room. Dacians, Greeks, Romans, Goths, Huns, Avars, Slavs, Bulgars, Magyars (Hungarians), Turks, Saxon Germans, Hapsburgs, Russians, Nazis and communists all made appearances, usually trading fierce blows along the way. Nicolae Ceauşescu's disastrous 25-year reign ended with his hasty execution on Christmas Day in 1989 and the country has been in slow recovery ever since. Romania narrowly won the thumbs up to enter the European Union on 1 January 2007.

PEOPLE

Romanians (about 90 per cent) comprise the vast majority of the country's population, with Hungarian (seven per cent) and Roma (three per cent) minorities, and a smattering of Ukrainians, Germans, Russians and Turks. Eastern Orthodox Christians, including subdenominations, are far and away the religious majority at about 87 per cent, with Protestants, Roman Catholics and Muslims making up the remainder. Hungarian, German and the Roma language are spoken in addition to official Romanian.

MARKETPLACE

The range of Romanian exports includes textiles, footwear, metals and metal products, machinery and equipment, minerals and fuels, chemicals and agricultural products. While persistent corruption and red tape continue to dog Romania's economy, macroeconomic gains have resulted in a palpable improvement in the country's widespread poverty, sparking the beginnings of a previously negligible middle class. Serious disinflation troubles have been curbed by revaluing the formerly dizzying currency: what was previously 10,000 lei is now equal to 1 leu.

TRADEMARKS

- ○ Dracula
- ○ Ceauşescu
- ○ Bucolic paradise
- ○ Castles and palaces
- ○ Painted churches

URBAN SCENE

Timişoara, Romania's fourth-largest city, is known by locals as Primul Oraş Liber (First Free Town). The first meaningful anti-Ceauşescu protests started here, directly leading to the dictator's downfall days later – by firing squad. Other noteworthy factoids: it was the first city in Europe to have electric street lamps (1884) and the second to introduce horse-drawn trams (1867). Named the 'city of flowers' because of the ring of parks that surrounds it, Timişoara is one of the country's most cosmopolitan and multicultural cities. Recently also dubbed 'Romania's economic showcase', there has been talk of applying the 'Timişoara Model' to other cities.

MYTHS & LEGENDS

There's just no ignoring it. Dracula is to Romania as bungee is to jumping. The fictional character of Dracula from Bram Stoker's Gothic horror story

BUCHAREST'S TRIUMPHAL ARCH CURVES STOICALLY AS HIGH-SPEED TRAFFIC WHISKS ALONG BENEATH »

Dracula (1897) is based on 15th-century Wallachian prince Vlad Țepeș, born in 1431 in Sighișoara. He was not a vampire (duh), but he was indisputably bloodthirsty. His punishment practices were cruel, even by medieval standards. He gained the name 'Țepeș', meaning 'impaler', due to his favourite form of execution – a wooden stake carefully driven through the victim's anus, to emerge from the body just below the shoulder in such a way as to not pierce any vital organs. This tactic is said to have prolonged death for an unimaginably painful 48 hours. Moreover, Țepeș enjoyed consuming a full meal while watching his Turkish and Greek prisoners writhe on stakes.

NATURAL BEAUTY

Romania has 12 national parks spread over more than 12,000 square kilometres, three biosphere reserves, and one natural World Heritage Site (the Danube Delta), of which only the latter has organised visitor facilities. Most of these areas are encased in the Carpathians and many are not accessible by public transport. Sadly, nearly all have suffered from some sort of environmental issue, ranging from piles of rubbish sullying otherwise stunning mountain vistas to a catastrophic cyanide-contaminated water spill into the Danube River. NGOs such as Pro Natura and the Transylvania Ecological Club are working to educate Romanians

We started out on a foggy, wet morning, arriving in Sucevița just as the weather broke. I couldn't help capturing a photo of one of the monastery's resident Orthodox nuns walking her straight and narrow line, considering the imposing scenes of judgement to be found on the walls just inside the gates ahead of her. Sucevița is the jewel of Romania's painted monasteries, the best preserved, with the most unusual of murals. These monasteries each hide a muraled church, in sapphire, emerald or garnet. Each a little faded now, but with years of character to share.

CLIFTON WILMSMEYER // USA

(and tourists) about how to diminish the impact of tourism on the environment.

ON FILM

- ○ *Glissando* (1985)
- ○ *Children Underground* (2001)
- ○ *The Rage* (2002)

ON PAPER

- ○ *The Phantom Church* translated by Georgiana Farnoaga
- ○ *Discover Romanian* by Rodica Botoman
- ○ *Call Yourself Alive?* and *Cheerleader for a Funeral* by Nina Cassian

RANDOM FACTS

- ○ Over half of Europe's bear population (some 5400) call Romania home.
- ○ Number of medals Romania has won in all Summer Olympics combined: 280.
- ○ Number of medals Romania has won in all Winter Olympics combined: one.
- ○ Between 1787, when the first marriage was registered, and 1980, there were no divorces in the village of Ieud in the Maramureș region.
- ○ It's estimated that it will cost €28.7 billion to repair Romania's notoriously treacherous roads.

FUTURE DIRECTIONS

Romania's 2007 whisker-thin acceptance into the European Union brings with it both much-needed funding as well as domestic economic growing pains. Meanwhile, Europe's last thriving peasant society fears unwelcome and unnecessary alterations to the lifestyle it's happily maintained for centuries.

- ○ **Indulging in Transylvania's 'big three': castles (Bran), palaces (Sinaia) and Draculas (Sighișoara)**
- ○ **Hiking (or skiing) some of Europe's most mind-bending peaks in the Carpathians**
- ○ **Soaking up the rich complexity of the painted monasteries situated in Southern Bucovina's bucolic ideal**
- ○ **Urbanising with culture and style in Timișoara and Cluj-Napoca**
- ○ **Submitting to the dominance of water, fish, birds (and mosquitoes) in the Danube Delta**

MAP REF // N11

≫ SERPENTINE ROAD STRETCHES TO BÂLEA LAKE, FĂGĂRAȘ MOUNTAINS

RICHARD I'ANSON // LONELY PLANET IMAGES

≪ CATCH OF THE DAY: FISHING FOR STURGEON IN THE DANUBE DELTA

TAXIS ARE NOSE TO NOSE WAITING FOR A FARE IN BUCHAREST ≫

CHILDREN TAKE A BUCHAREST BULL SCUPTURE BY THE HORNS ≫

TEXT LEIF PETTERSEN

MOLDOVA

MOLDOVA'S REPUTATION FOR EXCELLENT WINE AND STUNNING CELLARS IS FINALLY STARTING TO OUTSHINE ITS NOTORIOUS PAST AS A DEN OF ORGANISED CRIME, ARMS DEALING AND CIVIL WAR.

CAPITAL **CHIŞINĂU**   POPULATION **4.3 MILLION**   AREA **33,840 SQ KM**   OFFICIAL LANGUAGE **MOLDOVAN**

⌃ A COUPLE SEEKING REFUGE FROM TRANSDNIESTR PREPARE TO EAT A MEAL IN A HOSTEL

LANDSCAPE

Tiny and landlocked, Moldova is a country of gently rolling steppes, with one of the highest percentages of arable land in the world. Mineral and rock deposits are typically lignite, gypsum and limestone, the fervent mining of the latter producing staggering underground labyrinths utilised as wine cellars. Slow, politically hampered efforts are being made by environmental groups to protect Moldova's wetland regions along the lower Prut and Dniestr Rivers.

HISTORY IN A NUTSHELL

Straddling two historic regions – Romanian Bessarabia and tsarist Russia – Moldova has spent most of modern history being tugged like a wishbone back and forth between the two. The declaration of independence from the USSR in 1991 triggered continual domestic turmoil thereafter, ranging from human trafficking to simultaneous civil wars with the still-disputed Transdniestr area and the Gagauzia region. Historically, the country has been regarded as one of the poorest nations in Europe and one of the most corrupt in the world. Moldova is endeavouring to shake off these stigmas through commitments to combat corruption and human trafficking.

PEOPLE

Moldovans (who are mostly ethnic Romanians) account for the majority of the population at about 78 per cent, with the remainder comprising Ukrainian, Russian, Gagauz and Bulgarian minorities. In Transdniestr, however, Ukrainians and Russians make up 58 per cent of the region's population while Moldovans make up 34 per cent. Ninety-eight per cent of Moldovans are Eastern Orthodox Christians, and there is a recovering Jewish population of 1.5 per cent. Russian is widely spoken and Gagauz (a Turkish dialect) is mainly used in parts of the south.

MARKETPLACE

As a result of some ambitious economic reform, Moldova has returned to positive growth, with the service sector leading the way. Meanwhile, GDP per capita remains at a dismal €1500. The country's favourable climate and good farmland have resulted in heavy reliance on agriculture, including fruit, vegetables, wine and tobacco. Unfortunately, 40 per cent of Moldova's possible industrial output sits vexingly out of reach in Tiraspol, Transdniestr, running at only a fraction of potential productivity due to poor management and political disarray. The government's budget is meagre at less than €1 billion.

TRADEMARKS

o Wine
o The unrecognised 'country' of Transdniestr
o Organised crime
o Language debate (whether or not 'Moldovan' is actually a language or just a dialect of Romanian)
o Re-embracing communism

SURPRISES

o Moldova's government spends the largest percentage of its budget on education than any other country in the world.
o Moldova ranks among the highest in the world for the number of female professionals in its population.
o Monies sent home from emigrants working abroad comprise roughly one-third of Moldova's GDP.

TOP FESTIVAL

A hands-down winner, Chişinău's annual Wine Festival takes place on the second weekend in October. The country drops its visa regime for all nationalities for visits of up to 10 days at this time. Events include the parade of wine makers, professional and public wine tastings and performances by folkloric groups.

LANDMARK ALL SAINTS' CHURCH STANDS OUT ON A TOUR OF CHIŞINĂU

FARMER AND SONS KEEP WITHIN THE SPEED LIMIT ON THEIR WAY HOME

URBAN SCENE

Although Chişinău suggests a sea of concrete when viewed from a distance, in its heart the city boasts lush foliage, wide avenues and pleasant parks, circled by yet more parks and lakes. In the past 15 years, it has been transformed from dark and moribund into one of Europe's most party-bent capitals. Previously unlikely displays of wealth are abundant: fleets of BMWs and Mercedes dominate traffic, while fashionably dressed youth strut down boutique-lined avenues. The citizens are good-natured and the restaurant scene is particularly robust. Despite the current communist regime, the locals routinely submit to the Slavic-inherited impulse to enjoy life, day and night.

ON PAPER

- *Playing the Moldovans at Tennis* is Tony Hawks' hilarious account of his visit to a much bleaker Moldova in the mid-1990s to satisfy a drunken bet – his challenge was to defeat the entire Moldovan football team at tennis.
- *The Moldovans: Romania, Russia and the Politics of Culture* by Charles King is a more recent, textbook snapshot of this 'intriguing East Europe borderland'.

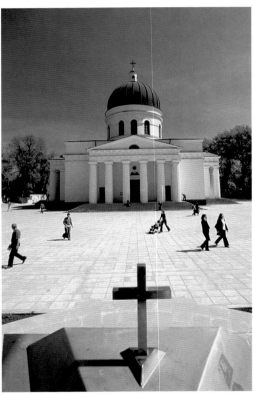

⌃ CHIŞINĂU'S IMPRESSIVE WHITEWASHED ORTHODOX CATHEDRAL

⌃ WINE-CELLAR WORKER MAY JUST HAVE THE BEST JOB IN TOWN

RANDOM FACTS

- Moldova has two of the largest wine cellars in the world – 120 kilometres and 200 kilometres of tunnels at Cricova and Mileştii Mici respectively.
- Dozens of Moldovans have famously 'escaped' the country by posing as the nonexistent national underwater hockey team and then applying for refugee status while attending world championship games – not once, but *twice* (Australia in 2000 and Canada two years later).
- Moldova has one of the highest percentages of people living below the official poverty line in the world.

ON DISC

Moldova has a surprisingly vibrant music scene, which is currently highlighted by two bands in particular: Zdob şi Zdub and Gândul Mâţei. Zdob şi Zdub (roughly translated as 'Bang and Boom') have been working Moldovan audiences into a lather since 1995 with their Romanian-folk-meets-Red-Hot-Chili-Peppers sound fusion. In 2005, with little preparation and virtually no financial support from their government, the group achieved a stunning sixth place finish in the legendary Eurovision Song Contest. Gândul Mâţei (Cat's Thought) nimbly run the gamut from lounge music to Coldplay-esque ballads to rocking *hard*.

MYTHS & LEGENDS

Just south of the city of Orhei, across from the parking lot of the Safari Café, Magnetic Hill is an ominous place where Nazis were reputed to have buried Jews alive. Strange happenings are alleged to occur in the area, including the phenomenon that gives the area its name. Reportedly, if one parks their car on the pavement right in front of the café, facing the main road, and slips it into neutral, the car will eerily advance despite the slight uphill incline.

ESSENTIAL EXPERIENCES

- Drinking in wine tours (and lots of them)
- Delving into the cave monastery at Orheiul Vechi
- Carousing in Chişinău
- Time travelling to Cold War USSR in Tiraspol, Transdniestr
- Appraising Soroca's fortress and opulent Roma homes

MAP REF // P11

BEST TIME TO VISIT **JANUARY TO FEBRUARY**

⌃ A WEAVER WORKS HER MAGIC BY SPINNING WOOL INTO YARN

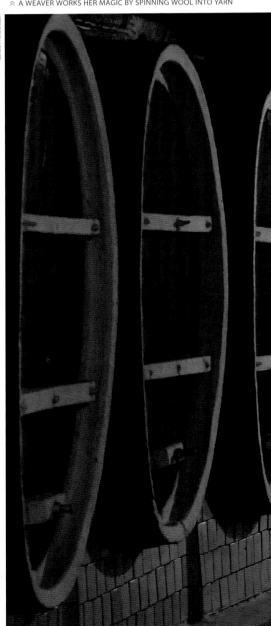

≪ A BUILDING IS BLINKERED BY A GIANT ADVERTISEMENT IN CHIŞINĂU

ACCORDIAN PLAYER LIVENS THINGS UP IN CHIŞINĂU ≪

YOU'LL BE SPOILT FOR CHOICE ON A DRIVE THROUGH MILEŞTII MICI, THE WORLD'S LARGEST WINE CELLAR, NEAR CHIŞINĂU ≪

UKRAINE

FROM THE CENTRAL EUROPEAN ELEGANCE OF ITS WESTERN REGIONS TO THE CHUGGING FACTORIES OF ITS INDUSTRIALISED EAST, THE EXPANSIVE LAND OF THE ORANGE REVOLUTION HAS A ROSY FUTURE, AND THE EXCITEMENT AND IMPATIENCE OF NEW-FOUND HOPE AND FREEDOM LINGER IN THE AIR.

CAPITAL CITY KYIV   POPULATION 46.3 MILLION   AREA 603,700 SQ KM   OFFICIAL LANGUAGE UKRAINIAN

≪ A YOUNG BOY DEMONSTRATES HIS DIVE TECHNIQUE TO PEERS AND ELDERS AT YALTA BEACH

LANDSCAPE

Ukraine is primarily vast, open steppe with humus-rich soil (chernozem) – an agricultural dream come true. Often referred to as 'the breadbasket of Europe', it is one of the world's most fertile regions. Two mountain ranges interrupt the plains – the Carpathians in the west and the Crimeans in the south. Of the four rivers crossing the country, the Dnipro is the biggest, most impressive and most beloved. In the north, the area still affected by the 1986 Chornobyl nuclear disaster is sealed off into an 'exclusion zone', although some Ukrainians have managed to move back to their homes there, and guided trips are possible for curious tourists.

HISTORY IN A NUTSHELL

Kyiv was once the capital of Kyivan Rus, the largest and mightiest state in Europe from the 9th to the 11th century. Weakened by internecine strife and Golden Horde invasions, the area was incorporated into the Polish kingdom in the 16th century. Meanwhile, the uncontrolled steppe in what is now southern Ukraine began to attract runaway serfs, criminals, Orthodox refugees and other outcasts. Along with a few Tatars, these people formed self-governing militaristic communities and became known as Cossacks,

deriving from the Turkic word for 'outlaw' or 'adventurer'. In the late 18th century, as a result of the Partitions of Poland, Russia took most of the land that is now Ukraine, and in 1783 Catherine the Great's army seized more land from Poland in the west, and from the Ottomans in the south. From 1932–33 a famine, allegedly engineered by Stalin, killed several million in Ukraine; six million more died as a result of World War II. After Ukraine declared independence from the USSR in 1991, it was plagued by overly authoritarian and corrupt government. Allegedly falsified presidential election results in October 2004 were the last straw, and the Ukrainian people took to the capital's main square for the Orange Revolution. This peaceful uprising led to new presidential elections and a Europe-focused direction for Ukrainian policy making.

PEOPLE

Ukrainians comprise some 78 per cent and Russians another 17 per cent of the country's population. Of those with religious beliefs, almost 97 per cent are Christian, most of whom follow some sort of orthodoxy. There are some very small Jewish minorities in all cities, while Muslim communities, primarily Tatars (of which there are only about

250,000), live for the most part in Crimea. Since independence, Ukraine's population has been steadily declining due to emigration, a low birth rate, alcoholism and poor health care.

MARKETPLACE

With its tremendous agricultural and industrial assets, Ukraine was by far the most economically vital republic of the Soviet Union. After independence, government squabbles over privatisation reforms, coupled with loose monetary policies, created hyperinflation in the early 1990s, and reliance on Russian energy continues to make the economy vulnerable. While official figures place unemployment at just three per cent, outside studies suggest it's more like seven per cent. Still, the economy is on the rise: the monthly wage is steadily growing and now averages around €140.

TRADEMARKS

- ○ Cossacks – the legendary, merciless and mercenary horseback warriors
- ○ Ruslana, Eurovision's wild-dancing winner in 2004
- ○ Chornobyl, the worst nuclear accident in history
- ○ The Orange Revolution
- ○ *Pysanky*, intricately hand-painted Easter eggs

A CHESS CHALLENGE BEGINS IN SHEVCHENKO PARK »

TOURING BY NIGHT ON A KYIV TROLLEYBUS »

URBAN SCENE

Kyiv surges with the whole spectrum of capitalist vitality: high-powered businesspeople zoom down cobblestone avenues in black SUVs, while gold-toothed babushkas hawk hot potato pies in underground pedestrian crossings. Everything's for sale in Ukraine's frenetic capital city, and enterprising marketeers have figured out some impressively creative ways to catch your eye with ads. This sort of anything-goes, free-for-all atmosphere is quite infectious, whether you're enjoying lovely cathedrals and monasteries by day or a raucous club scene at night.

NATURAL BEAUTY

The easternmost section of the Carpathian Mountains, in western Ukraine, is one of the least-developed areas in all of Europe. Among the undulating ridges lives a cluster of various ethnic groups, still living traditional lifestyles and using horse-drawn carts. Opportunities for camping, homestays, hiking and mountain biking abound, and skiing facilities are becoming more developed.

RANDOM FACTS

- Supermodel/actress/musician/designer Milla Jovovich was born in Kyiv.
- One of the world's only sculptures depicting a sitting Jesus Christ is on top of Boyim Chapel, in Lviv.
- Ukrainian Leonid Stadnik is believed to be the world's tallest man (2.54 metres).

≈ LOCAL BUS EN ROUTE TO THE CARPATHIAN MOUNTAINS

≈ STROLL DOWN TO THE THEMED RESTAURANT, YALTA BEACH

TRADITIONS

According to Hutsul (Carpathian) lore, the fate of our existence depends on the traditional art of *pysanky:* if the custom dies out, an evil serpent monster kept chained to a cliff will destroy the world. In making *pysanky*, wax-resist (batik) methods are used to ornately decorate hollow eggs with both pagan and Christian symbols for Easter.

CUISINE

The beetroot soup known as borscht is widespread throughout the former USSR, but Ukrainian *borshch* is widely recognised as the tastiest and most authentic. The popular *varenyky* (dumplings) are filled with virtually anything, sweet or savoury; *holubtsi* are cabbage rolls stuffed with rice and meat and topped with tomato-based sauce.

FUTURE DIRECTIONS

Although Ukraine has fervently enjoyed free speech as a result of the 2004 Orange Revolution, the new leadership has not sufficiently satisfied citizens' concerns over corruption and cronyism, and much of the population still faces financial hardship. Despite a Russia-leaning citizenry in the east, most political factions of Ukrainian government support the idea of future membership in the World Trade Organization and the European Union, although the European Union has responded rather apathetically to this, expressing concern over the already heavy enlargement agenda.

ESSENTIAL EXPERIENCES

- **Paying homage to the mummified monks of Kyiv's Caves Monastery**
- **Sipping the country's strongest coffee under Gothic eaves in Lviv, the hub of nationalist western Ukraine**
- **Feeling the burn on the way up Odesa's 192 Potemkin Steps**
- **Rambling through sweeping coastal panoramas on the world's longest trolleybus ride to palace-strewn Yalta**
- **Discovering the little-known treasures of Bakhchysaray, the heartland of the Crimean Tatars**
- **Exploring picturesque Kamyanets-Podilsky, a crumbling town towering high on an island of rock**

MAP REF // P9

BEST TIME TO VISIT **MAY TO SEPTEMBER**

≈ FEAST YOUR EYES ON SUMPTUOUS ST MICHAEL'S MONASTERY, KYIV

≈ NO NEED TO WORRY, YALTA BEACH HAS ROOM FOR ALL SHAPES AND SIZES

GETTING INTO HOT WATER UNDER POWER PLANT PIPES, SEVASTOPOL ≈

SMILING STEEL MILL SECURITY GUARD ALLOWS THE SIGN TO DO THE TALKING ≈

BELARUS

VOICES OF PROTEST ARE MUFFLED WITHIN THE SOVIET TIME CAPSULE THAT IS BELARUS – THE LAND THAT *PERESTROIKA* FORGOT AND *GLASNOST* GLOSSED OVER – MAKING IT PERHAPS THE MOST UNKNOWN, AND UNUSUAL, COUNTRY IN EUROPE.

CAPITAL CITY **MINSK**   POPULATION **9.7 MILLION**   AREA **207,600 SQ KM**   OFFICIAL LANGUAGES **BELARUSIAN, RUSSIAN**

⌃ FLOWER MERCHANT BOASTS HER RED GLADIOLUS ARE THE BEST OF THE BUNCH AT A MARKET STALL, MINSK

LANDSCAPE

Homogeneously flat and marshy, Belarusian vistas make up for a lack of variety with vast areas of pristine, undeveloped nature – including more than 11,000 small lakes. In the west of the country, the primeval forest Belavezhskaja Pushcha is home to some of the few remaining *zoobr* (European bison). Sadly, fallout from Ukraine's 1986 Chornobyl disaster contaminated a significant portion of southeastern Belarus, which is still considered to be uninhabitable.

HISTORY IN A NUTSHELL

Apart from a 10-month stint as the Belarusian Democratic Republic (declared under German occupation during World War I), Belarus did not exist as an autonomous entity until it declared independence from the USSR in August 1991. Before then the country switched hands between Lithuania, Poland and Russia, and became a founding member of the USSR in 1922. Nestled up against Poland, Belarus was particularly ravaged by the horrors of World War II, and the capital was virtually obliterated at that time. Since July 1994 Belarus has been governed by Alexander Lukashenko, whose presidential style is viewed as autocratic and authoritarian; US Secretary of State Condoleezza Rice has named Belarus one of six 'outposts of tyranny'.

PEOPLE

The population consists primarily of Belarusians (about 81 per cent), along with Russians (11 per cent), Poles (four per cent) and Ukrainians (2.5 per cent). Jews represent less than one per cent of the population, compared to 10 per cent before World War II. Atheism is widespread. Of believers, the ratio is 80 per cent Eastern Orthodox to 20 per cent Roman Catholic, and 15 per cent of Catholics are ethnic Poles. Hundreds of years of Russification and Sovietisation have diminished the distinguishing attributes of Belarusian culture, and today many Belarusians self-identify as Russian. Despite a spirited nationalist movement, the majority of the population (including President Lukashenko) speaks Belarusian poorly, if at all.

MARKETPLACE

With approximately 80 per cent of industry under state control, the present economy differs little from that of Soviet times. Government restrictions make private and foreign enterprises both undesirable and almost impossible. The current economic situation is largely seen as unsustainable. Officially 98 per cent of the population is employed, but many work in factories and warehouses that are overstocked with unsold, unwanted products, and underemployment is a serious problem. The average monthly salary is €170.

TRADEMARKS

- Home to some of the last remaining *zoobr*
- Europe's last dictatorship
- Staunch Stalinist architecture
- Shy but warm people
- Hit with nuclear fallout from Chornobyl

URBAN SCENE

Like the superhuman gymnasts the Soviet Union was once so famous for, Minsk has phenomenal flexibility, managing to keep one foot on hardline communism while dipping the other into the fast-moving white waters of cosmopolitan Europe. Inflated prices and poor selection make shopping a drag, but in addition to some funky bohemian cafés, there is a surprising variety of ethnic restaurants. Nightclubs – underground, elite and down-home alike – are becoming more impressive.

YOUNG MINSK SKATERS BUST SOME MOVES NEAR THE PALACE OF SPORTS »

NATURAL BEAUTY

When asked what it is they love about their country, most Belarusians will immediately start gushing about the natural environment – the thousands and thousands of lakes full of fish, the hectares and hectares of untouched flatlands where delicious berries and mushrooms grow wild and abundantly. During summer, the favourite local pastime is to enjoy these Belarusian bounties with an all-day picnic, ending with a campfire over which tasty meat shashlik are roasted.

CUISINE

Although very similar to Russian and Ukrainian cuisine, Belarus has a few unique dishes of its own. *Draniki* are the larger, thinner Belarusian version of Russian *olad'i* (potato pancakes); *kolduni* are the delicious, thick potato dumplings you'll find stuffed with meat; and *kletsky* are dumplings stuffed with a variety of fillings, such as mushrooms, cheese or potato. *Manchanka* are pancakes served with a thick meat gravy.

FUTURE DIRECTIONS

The future existence of Belarus could be in jeopardy if Russia makes a decision to raise the rock-bottom oil prices that almost single-handedly prop up the Belarusian economy. Lukashenko would be forced to stave off the price hike by handing Russia control of Belarus' gaslines, but he has vehemently opposed this idea and threatens (some would venture to say emptily) to sever ties with Russia if it raises the price. Talks of a monetary union – in which Belarus would take on the Russian rouble – are ongoing.

RANDOM FACTS

- Lukashenko has outlawed the use of foreign models in advertising and requires radio stations to play 75 per cent Belarusian music (a tall order for DJs, since most top Belarusian groups are banned for political reasons).
- Alleged John F Kennedy assassin Lee Harvey Oswald lived in Minsk for several years.
- Painter Marc Chagall was born in Vitsebsk.

TOP FESTIVAL

The night of 6 July is a celebration with pagan roots called Kupalye (meaning 'bathing'). During Kupalye, young girls gather flowers and throw them into a river as a method of fortune telling, while other festival-goers sit lakeside or riverside drinking beer in front of fires.

WILD THINGS

The *zoobr* is Europe's heaviest land mammal and Belarus' largest animal. The endangered species was hunted down to a few dozen by the early 20th century, but its numbers have risen to more than 3000 since protection was introduced. They can be spotted in Belavezhskaja Pushcha National Park, in western Belarus.

⌃ A SLIGHT CASE OF TAN-ENVY AT A LAKESIDE PARK, MINSK

MARTIN ROEMERS / PANOS PICTURES

Kurapaty is a forest outside Minsk where between 30 and 100 thousand people were massacred in 1941, probably by the Soviets who suspected large numbers of Belarusians of collaborating with the Nazis. Recently people have erected thousands of crosses in the forest to commemorate the dead. The forest is a haunting testament to those killed and to Europe's bloody past. But it also made me think of how quickly a region can recover from brutality.

DAVID BENDER // USA

- **Watching a dissident puppet show at a café across the street from the KGB building in Minsk**
- **Chasing a shot of fiery *samogon* moonshine with honey-dipped pickles at the interactive museum of Dudutki**
- **Succumbing to the sombre glory of Brest Fortress, the most epic of all Soviet World War II memorials**
- **Spotting an endangered *zoobr* (European bison) while wandering through the primeval landscape of Belavezhskaja Pushcha National Park**
- **Picnicking on wild berries, forest mushrooms, and fire-roasted shashlik alongside a pristine lake**

LATVIA

LITHUANIA

• Polatsk

• Vitsebsk

RUSSIA

Maladzechna • • Khatyn

• Orsha

☼ MINSK

• Hrodna

POLAND

Baranavichy • • Njasvizh

• Babrujsk

Belavezhskaja Pushcha National Park

• Salihorsk

Homel •

• Brest

UKRAINE

MAP REF // O8

≈ ONE OF THE LUCKY FEW TO OWN THEIR OWN LAND, THE MEDJEKO FAMILY WORKS HARD TO PITCH HAY DURING HARVEST

PAYING RESPECTS AT BREST FORTRESS, SOVIET WAR MEMORIAL ≈

BEACH BATHING AND GAMES CONTINUE DESPITE THE PRESENCE OF A DISUSED RIG AT HRODNA ≈

TEXT TOM MASTERS

RUSSIA

THE FLABBERGASTING DIVERSITY OF THE WORLD'S LARGEST COUNTRY ENCAPSULATES 11 TIME ZONES STRETCHING FROM THE BALTIC TO THE PACIFIC, VIA MOUNTAIN RANGES, VAST RIVERS, HUGE EMPTY STEPPE, PICTURESQUE TRADITIONAL TOWNS AND THE REMNANTS OF THE GREAT COMMUNIST EXPERIMENT.

CAPITAL CITY MOSCOW   POPULATION 141.4 MILLION   AREA 17,075,200 SQ KM   OFFICIAL LANGUAGE RUSSIAN

LANDSCAPE

When you're as large as Russia you can't help but take in almost every geographic phenomenon from permafrost, tundra and steppe to mountain ranges, volcanoes and semidesert. European Russia is surprisingly flat, becoming dramatic only in its southern stretches, where the vast peaks of the Caucasus form a natural border with Georgia and Azerbaijan. To the east, European Russia meets Siberia at the Ural Mountains.

HISTORY IN A NUTSHELL

Historically backward due to isolation from Europe and traditionally inward-looking rulers, Russia didn't begin its modern era until the early 18th century, when the visionary Peter the Great opened the country to Europe through the construction of St Petersburg on the Baltic. Flourishing under successive tsars to become a giant power by the late 19th century, Russia nevertheless suffered from a slow pace of reform. This in turn brought about a series of radical social upheavals, culminating in the Bolshevik coup of 1917, which created the world's first communist state. The 70-year USSR saw Stalin's purges and the building of a network of Gulag concentration camps, as well as mass industrialisation, education and health care. Communism finally gave way to democracy under Mikhail Gorbachev in the late 1980s. From 2000 to 2008 ex-KGB agent Vladimir Putin's authoritarian stance had many worried that Russia was turning back towards its repressive past. Putin's hand-picked successor, President Dmitry Medvedev, was elected in 2008 and looks set to continue on Putin's path with his influential predecessor by his side as prime minister.

PEOPLE

The vast majority of the population identify as ethnic Russians, although the number of nationalities that have been progressively absorbed into the mixed blood of modern Russia is hard to overstate. There are large numbers of 'national minorities', including Tatars, Bashkirs, Chechens, Dagestanis, Evens, Khanty, Chuvash, Karelians and Buryatians to name but a few.

MARKETPLACE

No longer a weapons superpower, Russia has successfully built itself up to be an energy superpower. Its massive reserves of oil and gas alone account for the country's impressive economic growth. Despite being riddled with corruption, Russia's marketplace has already become one of the world's most powerful.

TRADEMARKS

o Communism
o Fur hats
o Vodka
o Caviar
o Nesting dolls
o Bandits
o Snow, snow... and more snow

URBAN SCENE

There are two standout cities in Russia, whose almost polar differences sum up everything good about the country. Moscow, the national capital, Europe's largest city and Russia's economic motor, is one of the most exciting places to visit in the world. Neon, glitz and glamour are now the salient features of a city once known for communist austerity. Dubbed the 'northern capital', St Petersburg is one of the most beautiful cities in the world, with its wonderfully preserved late-18th- and 19th-century centre, its wide European avenues and networks of canals.

A RUSSIAN SOLDIER WITHSTANDS THE SNOW IN WINTER »

≫ LEAN YOUNG SOLDIERS TRAINING AT A RUSSIAN ARMY CAMP ARE A PICTURE OF DETERMINATION

JON ARNOLD // PHOTO LIBRARY

≫ COLOURFUL ONION DOMES OF ST BASIL'S CATHEDRAL ON RED SQUARE, MOSCOW

≫ THE WOOLLY HAIR ISN'T HIS OWN, BUT WHAT ABOUT THE BEARD?

PLENTY TO READ UP ON AT A KALININGRAD RAILWAY STATION NEWSPAPER STAND »

RELAXING BY THE NEVA RIVER IN ST PETERSBURG NEAR THE TSARIST PETER AND PAUL FORTRESS »

» AERIAL SURVEY OF KAMCHATKA PENINSULA'S STRIKING VOLCANIC LANDSCAPE

NATURAL BEAUTY

Where to begin? The lakes of Karelia, the impressive Volga Delta, the beaches of the Black Sea and the stunning amber-flecked coastline of Kaliningrad are just some of Russia's wonders. Despite being incredibly (some would say boringly) flat, European Russia looks stunning in the winter months when birch woods shimmer under thick snow, and lakes and rivers freeze to create a true winter wonderland.

TRADITIONS

Russians are deeply superstitious. Never try to shake hands over a threshold or doorstep – a Russian will recoil in horror as it's bad luck. Never place an empty bottle on a table or light a cigarette from a candle. Always give an odd number of flowers (even numbers are for a funeral), and if you step on a Russian friend's foot, present your own to be stepped on in return, otherwise the two of you will fight in the future.

ON FILM

Russia has a cinematic history to be proud of. Its most renowned visionary, Sergei Eisenstein, bequeathed a body of work that includes what is possibly the most famous film ever made – *Battleship Potemkin* (1925), sufficiently favoured by the communist authorities to allow the film a lavish budget. The other great genius of Russian cinema Andrei Tarkovsky offered complex and deeply personal visions of 20th-century history, the most singular of which is undoubtedly *The Mirror* (1975). Modern Russian cinema is booming too – *Night Watch* (2004) is Russia's most commercially successful film to date and is being given that signifier of greatness, the Hollywood remake.

RANDOM FACTS

○ There are more billionaires in Moscow than in any other city.
○ Vodka means 'little water', and is drunk as if that really were the case.
○ Dead for more than 80 years, Lenin's still looking pretty good; his body, displayed in a mausoleum on Red Square, is visited twice weekly by an embalmer.

ON PAPER

Russia is often experienced remotely by people who fall for its dark, enduring and deeply spiritual literature. While Russians consider Pushkin to be the father of its literary tradition, he's not well known in the West, where the great 19th-century novelists Tolstoy, Dostoevsky, Turgenev and Gogol have all fared far better in translation. Twentieth-century literature is just as rich – try Mikhail Bulgakov's wonderfully allegorical novel *The Master and Margarita* for a headlong plunge into both the tragi-comic reality and surrealism of life under the Soviets.

CUISINE

Despite a bad reputation worldwide, Russian food is often delicious and many people will be pleasantly surprised by its quality and taste. Don't miss borscht, blinis, *ukha* (fish soup), *stolichny salat* (chicken salad) or *zharkoye* (Russian hotpot).

SURPRISES

○ Almost any car in Russia is a taxi – stick out your hand, agree to a price and jump in; the system is extremely safe and reliable!
○ Russians are not as dour as they first seem – persevere and you'll have a friend for life.
○ It's not all snow, snow, snow: the summer months can be boiling, with temperatures more than 30 degrees Celsius.

FUTURE DIRECTIONS

President Dmitry Medvedev looks set to continue in Putin's footsteps. Many argue that Putin's legacy will be better than the reality of life under him – the oligarchs have been brought back under control, the economy is booming and life is slowly – achingly slowly – improving. Others argue that a country with a history as dark as Russia's can ill afford leaders who overlook human rights and fail to develop civil society and press freedom. Only time will tell, but the average Russian remains almost bafflingly optimistic.

≪ YOUNG ROYAL COSSACK CADET STANDS TO ATTENTION WHILE BEING FITTED FOR HIS UNIFORM, NOVOCHERKASSK

ESSENTIAL EXPERIENCES

○ **Taking a trip on the beautiful and extraordinary Moscow metro**

○ **Viewing the grand masters in St Petersburg's wonderful Hermitage collection**

○ **Experiencing true cleanliness with a traditional *banya* steam bath**

○ **Watching the world go by on the Trans-Siberian Express, the world's longest train journey**

○ **Hiking in the breathtaking Caucasus, which include Europe's highest peak, Mount Elbrus**

○ **Drinking and dancing your way through the formidable St Petersburg White Nights in June**

○ **Exploring the ancient city of Novgorod with its unique Kremlin and cathedrals**

FROM THE TRAVELLER

Summer in St Petersburg was delightful – a nice contrast to the manic bustle of Moscow. During the day, Dvortsovaya Ploshchad was the perfect people-watching place – roller-bladers manoeuvring their way across the square, snap-happy tourists, couples going for a stroll and the occasional Lada zipping by. In the late evening after the Hermitage had closed for the day, it was a resplendent place to be.

BELINDA ROY // AUSTRALIA

MAP REF // Q7

BEST TIME TO VISIT **MAY TO SEPTEMBER**

THE ICY SIBERIAN ENVIRONS ARE A DAILY AFFAIR FOR THIS FUR-WRAPPED DOLGAN REINDEER HERDER AND HIS CHILD »

MARK NEWMAN // LONELY PLANET IMAGES

» ELABORATE CHANDELIERS LIGHT THE PASSAGE OF A MOSCOW METRO TRAIN

STILL-ACTIVE KORYAKSKY VOLCANO ON THE KAMCHATKA PENINSULA »

TEXT **TOM MASTERS**

GEORGIA

LITTLE-KNOWN GEORGIA, TO MANY A NEBULOUS SOVIET REPUBLIC WITHOUT ITS OWN IDENTITY, IS IN REALITY ONE OF EUROPE'S BIGGEST SURPRISES – ITS STUNNING MOUNTAIN SETTING, RICH CULTURE AND FABULOUS CUISINE MAKE IT A REGIONAL HIGHLIGHT.

CAPITAL CITY TBILISI   POPULATION 4.6 MILLION   AREA 69,700 SQ KM   OFFICIAL LANGUAGE GEORGIAN

⌃ AN AGED BUILDING NEAR THE KURA RIVER IS IN NEED OF SOME TLC

LANDSCAPE

How can so small a country contain so much within its tiny borders? In the north, the massive peaks of the Caucasus take your breath away, while the verdant valleys of Tusheti and Kazbegi are no less impressive. The semidesert around Davit Gareja is a sight to behold, and the lush semitropical feel of Adjara with its gorgeous beaches will satisfy any sun worshipper.

HISTORY IN A NUTSHELL

Georgia's history is a familiar one of invasion. Surrounded by great powers on all sides – Russia to the north, Persia to the southeast and Turkey to the southwest – Georgia's unique language and culture are almost miraculous in the very fact of their existence. Having fared relatively well under communism – Georgians enjoyed some of the highest living standards in the USSR and few of the privations – things went downhill rapidly after independence and under the leadership of Eduard Shevardnadze. This decline in Georgia culminated in a popular uprising in 2003, often called the Rose Revolution, which saw Shevardnadze overthrown and the election of a pro-Western moderniser, Mikhail Saakashvili.

PEOPLE

Georgians are a fragmented bunch, their national identity cobbled together from multiple minor national groups, with varying success. The ongoing conflicts in Abkhazia and South Ossetia are a sad sign that the ethnic melting pot of Georgia is failing; on the other hand, places such as coastal Adjara and mountainous Svaneti have managed to assert their own strong regional identities without conflict with Tbilisi.

MARKETPLACE

The Georgian economy has vast potential and is growing, but still has a long way to go. Its major exports are wine, mineral water, fruit and vegetables. Traditionally Georgia's major export partner has been Russia; however, the Russian-Georgian relationship has so soured of late that Russia has for now banned the import of Georgian goods. This in turn is having a knock-on effect on the local economy, with Georgia being forced to find new markets in Europe.

TRADEMARKS

○ Mountain dancing
○ Stalin
○ Possible birthplace of wine
○ Polyphonic singing

URBAN SCENE

Without doubt the most beautiful city in the Caucasus, Tbilisi enchants with its gorgeous Old Town, dramatic cliffside setting and wealth of historic churches. Its central avenue, Rustaveli, has a modern, European feel, while the Old Town provides shady squares, beautiful 19th-century houses and a wealth of other quirky sights.

NATURAL BEAUTY

One Georgian legend states that when God was creating the earth he left the best bits till last, and gave them all to Georgia. It certainly is a country blessed by bounty: covered in lush vegetation, bisected by raging mountain torrents, covered in dramatic snowy peaks and sprinkled with national parks, beauty is one commodity that Georgia will never have to ration.

CUISINE

Georgia's great gift to the world is its fabulous cuisine – a good meal here will have you hooked for life. Staples include *khachapuri* (cheese bread), *satsivi* (cold chicken or turkey in a walnut sauce), *lobio* (spicy bean paste), and aubergines with walnut paste. The other great surprise is the variety and quality of Georgian wines available to accompany any meal.

TOUCHED BY THE PAST: WORLD WAR II VETERAN CONTINUES TO WEAR HIS SOVIET ARMY UNIFORM AROUND TBILISI ≫

BEER GUZZLING FROM A GOAT HORN DURING A MEN'S SUMMER FEAST, TUSHETI ≫

MYTHS & LEGENDS

Tbilisi, the charming national capital, means 'warm springs'. According to legend, King Gorgasali, the city's putative 5th-century founder, spied and chased a deer while out hunting one day. Pursuing it for some time, the king finally shot the deer and it fell into the hot springs, whereupon it was conveniently cooked for dinner. The city's sulphur baths are unmissable, but spare a thought for Bambi.

ECOTOURISM

While the word itself won't mean much to most people in Georgia, in fact ecotourism is developing fast on a local level. Fascinating homestays are found in almost every town. Those in the mountains can be particularly rewarding, where they really are community-enhancing projects, providing work for hosts and guides alike. The best are in Kazbegi, Tusheti and Svaneti.

FUTURE DIRECTIONS

The Georgians are aiming to join NATO and the European Union in the not-too-distant future, although Russia is less than content at the prospect, and the Saakashvili administration has been defined by clashes with its northern Goliath, with which several spats are ongoing. Some argue that without the support of Russia, Georgia will never be able to make a go of things economically, and sadly they may prove to be right. Despite Georgia's pro-European, pro-American government, few in the West care enough to make the necessary effort to help the country develop independently of Moscow. Georgians, however, are a tenacious and independent breed, so this challenge may well be one they'll rise to.

RANDOM FACTS

○ The name Georgia comes from the country's patron saint, George – he of dragon killing fame, and a Christian martyr who is also patron saint of England, Montenegro and Ethiopia.

○ *Chacha*, the local firewater, is distilled from grapes and is alarmingly alcoholic.

○ Uncle Joe (Stalin) is still much loved in his native Georgia, and you'll see pictures of the great dictator all over the country.

≫ ONLY THE DEVOTED: TSMINDA SAMEBA CHURCH HIGH IN THE CAUCASUS

STEPHANIE VICTOR // LONELY PLANET IMAGES

On my way up to Tsminda Sameba (Holy Trinity) church, Kazbegi, in northernmost Georgia, I noticed a lonely, ruined tower in the middle of the hike path. It was once used to overlook the valley, which was known from ancient times as the Georgian Army Road, as conquerers had to pass through the Caucasus here from the Middle East and Asia to Eastern Europe. I found out later that Georgians are very proud to be protectors of Europe. To me, this place was wonderful, with the serenity of the landscape and grace of the tower, and I'd never seen such gorgeous mountains. It represents Georgia as a nation at the crossroad of civilisations, struggling to keep its own identity.

MARKO PETROVIC // SERBIA

ESSENTIAL EXPERIENCES

○ **Getting a calorie injection with a hot plate of Adjaran *khachapuri* (cheese bread)**

○ **Communing with nature in the mountain villages of Racha and Tusheti**

○ **Relaxing in the cafés of cosmopolitan Tbilisi**

○ **Taking in the breathtaking monastery complexes of Davit Gareja and Vardzia**

○ **Dipping your toes into the warm waters of the Black Sea around Batumi**

○ **Hiking in the mountains around Kakheti, Kazbegi and Tusheti**

○ **Watching a performance of polyphonic singing and mountain dancing**

≫ CAR DELIVERS BREAD BY THE BAKER'S DOZEN IN TBILISI

STEPHANIE VICTOR // LONELY PLANET IMAGES

MAP REF // T11

BEST TIME TO VISIT **MAY TO SEPTEMBER**

≫ THERE'S A RELIGIOUS ICON TO SUIT EVERYONE IN THIS TBILISI SHOP

A BOY CRADLES HIS FAVOURITE PUP, CAUCASUS MOUNTAINS ≫

WAX TAPERS ARE LIT AND PRAYERS SUNG FOR ST MARY'S DAY, TBILISI ≫

ARMENIA

AN EARLY CHRISTIAN RELIC POSTED OUT NEAR IRAN ON A SPECTACULAR STRETCH OF MOUNTAINS, ANCIENT ARMENIA'S POSITION BETWEEN EUROPE AND THE MIDDLE EAST MAKES IT SOMETHING OF A CURIOSITY.

CAPITAL CITY YEREVAN   POPULATION 3 MILLION   AREA 29,800 SQ KM   OFFICIAL LANGUAGE ARMENIAN

≫ DOMESTIC DISPLACEMENT IN STEPANAVAN: MANY RESIDENTS STILL LIVE IN OIL CONTAINERS TWO DECADES AFTER AN EARTHQUAKE DEVASTATED THE REGION

LANDSCAPE

Landlocked Armenia occupies the mountainous eastern edge of the Anatolian Plateau, with rocky volcanoes in the west and twisting forested valleys in the east where the land slopes down towards the Caspian Sea. Most of the country is highland wilderness, with a small plain of vineyards and orchards around Yerevan. Lake Sevan is an enormous, stunningly blue alpine lake in the centre of the country.

HISTORY IN A NUTSHELL

Armenia dates back to an age when the Assyrians and Scythians were global powers, and it was later the first country to adopt Christianity. While earthquakes and invasions thinned out the heartland over the centuries, Armenians have protected their knowledge and culture in colonies across the known world. In the 19th century the Russian tsars conquered and protected a portion of Armenia, and the early 20th century brought massacres, genocide and then Stalin. While the present republic and its satellite territory, Karabakh, rest on just a fraction of the historic homeland, these are in fact the longest-lasting Armenian states since the 13th century.

PEOPLE

Disciplined and with a national love for knowledge (books are near sacred), Armenians also have a Mediterranean flair for the good life. A day spent in *keyif*, or 'companionable relaxation', balances all the hard work. Squeezed on two sides by much bigger rivals, Turkey and Azerbaijan, the first hint of prosperity in Armenia has been hard won. Something like 96 per cent of the population identify as Armenian, with smaller numbers of Kurds, Russians, Assyrians and Greeks in the mix. The biggest minority are the 50,000-odd Yezidi Kurds, highland herders with their own semipagan faith.

MARKETPLACE

The main exports are copper, gold and brandy. The economy shrank to peanut size during the Karabakh war of the 1990s, but with help from Armenia's wealthy diaspora, it is now growing madly. Unfortunately, not much new money spreads beyond Yerevan. Corruption is big business – the shadow economy is almost more important than the real one. The government has been quite effective in terms of reducing the number of people living in absolute poverty (those with less than a dollar a day) from a clear majority of the population a decade ago to less than 25 per cent today.

TRADEMARKS

- World-beating chess teams
- Good-looking noses (unfortunately cosmetic surgery is catching on)
- Vartivar Day (Water Day), when kids are allowed to drench everyone
- Openly stylish gangsters (black rayon, bling, stubble and sunglasses)
- Rousing folk music
- Genuine affection for steamy Brazilian soap operas
- Business acumen

NATURAL BEAUTY

In southern Armenia, the Vorotan Canyon slices through the high plateau like a jagged rip in the earth's fabric. The Tatev Monastery perches on a promontory on the lip of the abyss. Behind the monastery, the oak forests climb up to the raw Zangezur Mountains, a last refuge for the world's 20 or so Caucasian leopards.

TRADITIONS

Perhaps 95 per cent or more of Armenian names end with '–ian' or '–yan'. It means 'child of', as in Petrosyan (son of Petros), or refers to origins in a town, an occupation or even a personal characteristic. A few

CONTEMPLATING THE SIZE AND WEIGHT OF HISTORY INSIDE 10TH-CENTURY SANAHIN MONASTERY, NORTHERN LORI REGION »

names end with '–nts' (for instance, Vardanants), and some with '–uni' (Suni, Artsruni), which signifies an aristocratic connection.

ON CANVAS
Armenia practically invented the illustrated Bible – the best preserved are in Yerevan's Matenadaran institute. Red pigments used for illustration were made from the shell of a rare kind of scrub-dwelling beetle, which are today protected on a nature reserve near Echmiadzin.

IN STONE
Armenians have an obsessive streak – Levon Arakelyan of Arinj, a village on the edge of Yerevan, has been digging caverns under his house for 30 years. Around 40,000 people have visited the six halls, all hacked out and carved with a mere hammer and chisel.

RANDOM FACTS
○ Ancient observatories at Metsamor and Sisian hint at a common source for Indian and European astrology.
○ By tradition, the Armenian mother of the bride never attends the wedding service.
○ Unexpected income from Las Vegas flows in via Kirk Kerkorian, the American-Armenian casino king.
○ Winston Churchill fell in love with Armenian brandy, which Stalin supplied in large quantity.

CUISINE
Flatbreads, herbs and cured meats feature prominently in Armenian cooking. Accented with dishes typical of Lebanon (hummus), the Balkans (baklava) and Turkey (kofte, kebabs), Armenian cuisine emphasises subtle spices. The most feared dish is *khash*, a winter stew made of boiled-down cows' feet and served with vodka – it tastes like it sounds.

MYTHS & LEGENDS
Late in the 3rd century AD, Hripsime, a gorgeous nun, fled to Armenia with 70 other chaste women to avoid the lecherous Roman emperor Diocletian. Alas, King Tiridates of Armenia also took a fancy to them, and had them executed after they refused to break their vows. Driven mad with remorse, Tiridates was eventually cured by the Christian he had imprisoned in a well 15 years earlier. The healer, St Gregory the Illuminator, went on to convert the nation and build Armenia's first church. Hripsime is buried in Echmiadzin in a 6th-century church, said to be the most beautiful of the classical age.

SURPRISES
○ Apricots (*Prunus armeniaca*) are native to Armenia.
○ More cars run on liquefied petroleum gas here than any other country.
○ Cold War flashback – Russian troops still guard Armenia's borders with Turkey and Iran.

⌃ NORADUZ CEMETERY'S *KHATCHKAR* CRUCIFIX STONES DATE TO AD 996

ESSENTIAL EXPERIENCES

○ **Tracing the patterns on an intricately carved *khatchkar* (literally 'crucifix stone') at Echmiadzin, which is Armenia's 1700-year-old Vatican**

○ **Buying roses (in odd numbers only) from one of Yerevan's many florists**

○ **Toasting with fruit liqueurs (cherry, pear, mulberry) at a village banquet**

○ **Catching a glint off the icy dome of Noah's Mount Ararat, historic Armenia's holy mountain**

○ **Chattering along with the audience during an opera performance**

○ **Marvelling at the Vorotan Canyon**

○ **Puzzling over the age and purpose of Zorats Karer, Armenia's Stonehenge**

○ **Lighting a candle at Geghard Monastery (less messy than sacrificing a rooster at the monastery's *mataghatun*, or offering place)**

MAP REF // U12

BEST TIME TO VISIT **MAY TO JUNE, SEPTEMBER TO OCTOBER**

⌃ GIVE US THIS DAY OUR DAILY BREAD

≫ A LULL IN TRAFFIC: TWO MEN WAIT OUTSIDE A PETROL STATION NEAR SISIAN

≫ GOLD-HUED MINISTRY OF FOREIGN AFFAIRS, YEREVAN

WOMEN OFFER DEVOUT PRAYER IN VANADZOR ≫

TEXT MARK ELLIOTT

AZERBAIJAN

ENDLESSLY HOSPITABLE AZERBAIJAN IS A POTENTIALLY OIL-RICH PIVOT BETWEEN EUROPE, CENTRAL ASIA AND THE MIDDLE EAST, DIPPING ITS TOES IN THE CASPIAN SEA WHILE ITS SNOWY CAUCASIAN HEAD RISES AMID EUROPE'S HIGHEST MOUNTAINS.

CAPITAL CITY **BAKU**   POPULATION **8.1 MILLION**   AREA **86,600 SQ KM**   OFFICIAL LANGUAGE **AZERBAIJANI**

≈ A SHOT OF CAFFEINE MAY JUST MAKE THE DAY PASS FASTER

LANDSCAPE

Azerbaijan covers an astonishing range of climatic zones, from the rice and tea fields of the semitropical Talysh, to the dramatic High Caucasus, whose snowcapped peaks are taller than the Alps. In between there's plenty of dreary steppe, patches of desert and a Caspian coastline that sounds more magical than it looks. But on the mountain fore slopes, beautiful oak woods are photogenically patchworked with poppy-dappled cornfields – glorious.

HISTORY IN A NUTSHELL

Did Adam and Eve bite the world's first apple in an Azerbaijani Garden of Eden? If so, the site was probably in southern Azerbaijan. That's now within Iran, since Azerbaijan's ancient patchwork of khanates was divided in two through several 18th- and 19th-century Russo-Persian wars. As a modern nation, (northern) Azerbaijan first surfaced in 1918; however, just two years later it was submerged in the USSR, only re-emerging to full independence in 1991. The new nation then plunged straight into war with neighbouring Armenia over the status of Nagorno-Karabakh province. The result was the loss of over 15 per cent of Azerbaijan's territory. This area remains under Armenian occupation today, a bitter issue that's unresolved and by no means forgotten.

PEOPLE

Azerbaijanis form the vast majority of the population. Older statistical sources report significant minorities of Armenians, Russians and Kurds; however, most of these people left during the violent conflicts of the early 1990s, or live in occupied areas in or around Nagorno-Karabakh that are not accessible from Azerbaijan proper. Smaller, linguistically independent groups include the Persian-speaking Talysh plus various mountain peoples, including Lezghins, Xınalıqis and Avars. Some consider the Udis to be the last descendants of the mysterious Caucasian Albanians. Almost all Azerbaijanis follow Shia Islam but in a very characteristic, low-key local form that might surprise many other Muslims. Udis are nominally Christian and Mountain Jews populate Krasnaya Sloboda village near Quba.

MARKETPLACE

In Soviet days, Azerbaijan's economy was diversified from flowers and tea to plastics and petrochemicals. Today it's almost entirely dominated by oil. Booming crude prices have given Azerbaijan's economic growth figures a remarkably rosy glow. Baku has the air of a boom town, and speculative building adds daily to the dizzying new apartment high-rises being erected against all conventional wisdom in this earthquake-prone city. But Baku's fashionable façade disguises serious underemployment problems elsewhere in the country. Agriculture, the nation's main employer, has never fully recovered from the shock of the USSR's 1991 demise, which resulted in the dismemberment of *kolkhoz* collective farms. Heavy industries (except oil) were even worse affected, with Russian markets lost and most factories pillaged or left to rust.

TRADEMARKS

○ Caviar and carpets
○ Antiquated oil derricks stretching out on platforms into the greasy Caspian Sea
○ Burping mud volcanoes
○ Eddie Izzard jokes

RANDOM FACTS

○ In 1905 Baku was the world's biggest oil producer.
○ The Azerbaijani idea of a hangover cure is *xaş*, a garlic-supercharged stew-soup made from sheep feet and washed down with a vodka or two.
○ An estimated 700,000 refugees are still displaced from the 1988–92 war with Armenia.

TRADITIONAL FOLK DANCE GROUP RAISES THE ROOF AT A PERFORMANCE IN BAKU »

TRADITIONS

On paper, most Azerbaijanis are Shiite Muslims; however, 70 years of antireligious communism have left local Islam far removed from modern Islam. Local beliefs include many animist-like folk superstitions; holy rocks are kissed smooth; holy trees are considered *pirs* (shrines); and on the Abşeron Peninsula, pilgrims flock en masse to the vast Mir Mövsüm mausoleum to celebrate a 20th-century saint whose main claim to fame was being boneless. The main Muslim festival, Novruz Bayramı on 21 March, is in reality none other than Persian New Year and still features pre-Islamic fire jumping.

ON DISC

Azerbaijani pop combines whirling Turkish disco sounds with those Ace of Base–style '90s dance beats so popular in Russia. In contrast, Baku also hosts Eurasia's best jazz club and festival. But Azerbaijan's most iconic musical style is *muğam*, a wailing form of lyrical improvisation recognised by Unesco for its unique place in world culture. By far *muğam*'s best-known exponent is Alim Qasimov, who has been cited as one of the 20th century's greatest 'folk' singers.

SURPRISES

○ Mature forests backed by soaring mountains thrive just two hours' drive from barren deserts.
○ Opening scenes from the James Bond movie *The World is Not Enough* were filmed in the Baku oilfields.
○ Eric Clapton reputedly found the name for his song *Layla* in Azerbaijan's *Romeo and Juliet*–style classic *Layla and Majnun*.
○ 'We're about to land' announced on a plane in Azerbaijani sounds to a Turk like 'We're about to crash'.

⌃ QOBUSTAN'S FULL OF 'CHATTY' LITTLE MUD VOLCANOES

⌃ A ROMA CHILD LOOKS OUT FOR A FAMILIAR FACE

ON PAPER

Kurban Said's book, *Ali and Nino*, perfectly encapsulates Azerbaijan's curious balance between East and West, Russia and Persia, multiculturalism and fierce national pride. The tale relates a cross-cultural love affair between an Azeri Muslim and a Christian Georgian set against the backdrop of oil-rich, politically simmering Baku in the early 20th century. Perhaps predictably, the villain is an Armenian.

IMPORT

↗ British-style pubs for Scottish oil expats in Baku
↗ Islam
↗ Vodka
↗ Pro-US political posture
↗ Anthropologist Thor Heyadahl's curious ideas on ancient Scandinavian-Caucasus links

EXPORT

↖ Chess grandmaster Garry Kasparov
↖ Oil
↖ The 'world's greatest cello player', the late Mstislav Rostropovich
↖ Workers to northern Siberia's gas fields
↖ Jolfa artisans, 'kidnapped' in 1604 to build the fabulous city of Isfahan for Iran's Shah Abbas

ESSENTIAL EXPERIENCES

○ **Sleeping in an atmospheric arched cell of the 19th-century caravanserai in Şəki**

○ **Climbing the phallic Beşbarmaq Dağ pinnacle amid rock-kissing devotees wearing their Sunday-best skirts and high-heeled shoes**

○ **Sipping tea at Yanar Dağ in eerie silence except for the quiet hissing of natural gas flames licking away at the hillside in front of you**

○ **Renting a horse and guide to trek between the fabulous mountain village of Xınalıq and the waterfall-ringed hamlet of Laza**

○ **Chuckling at the flatulent impudence of Azerbaijan's lovable little mud volcanoes near Qobustan**

○ **Watching Lahıc coppersmiths operating their antiquated bellows as their wives gather spring water in traditional *jujum* pots**

MAP REF // V12

BEST TIME TO VISIT **MAY & OCTOBER**

⌃ KORANIC SCHOOL GIRL COMPLIMENTS A FRIEND'S CHOICE OF HEADSCARF

≪ ONSHORE OIL WORKERS GO TO GREAT LENGTHS TO DRAW OIL FROM THE GROUND

BAKU'S SHIKHOV BEACH HAS A BACKDROP OF ABANDONED OIL RIGS ≫

REUNION IS SWEET FOR TWO AZERBAIJANI FRIENDS ≫

SCANDINAVIAN & BALTIC EUROPE

THIS IS A LAND OF MIDNIGHT SUN, WHERE VIKING LEGENDS AND PAGAN-TINGED RITUALS ARE SHARED AROUND MIDSUMMER NIGHT BEACHSIDE BONFIRES, TOASTED WITH SHOTS OF VODKA; A LAND OF SAUNAS, WALRUSES AND REINDEER, NATURE WORSHIPPING IN THICK FORESTS AND TWILIGHT OVER FROSTY STRETCHES OF TUNDRA.

Scandinavian and Baltic Europe's landscape encompasses everything from the active volcanic belts of Iceland and magnificent edge-of-the-world granite cliffs along Norway's northern coast to the windswept sand dunes of western Lithuania, which once inspired Jean-Paul Sartre. It also pulls together the majestic fjords of Norway, Greenland's glacial valleys, the dizzying island archipelagos of Sweden and Finland, the mountains of northern Norway and the flatlands of Denmark and the Baltic countries.

This frigid corner of the planet also runs a wild economic and political gamut. At one end are some of Europe's most socialist countries, which have the highest standards of living on the planet; and on the other the Baltic countries, relatively recently freed of their repressive Soviet past and the newest euro members, with some of the lowest wages yet most-unfettered economies in the European Union.

'Scandinavia' in its strictest sense applies to Norway, Sweden and Denmark, but generally includes Finland and Iceland. The area has been populated by hunting

and agrarian tribes since the last ice age, but history buffs enthusiastically link Vikings with the region. The Vikings ruled the seas from the end of the 8th century until 1066, when an attempt to invade England fell flat.

The kingdoms of Denmark, Norway and Sweden were united between 1397 and 1536, after which Norway and Denmark remained together until 1814. Sweden moved politically closer to Finland; Iceland and Greenland stayed under the Danish crown. In the 19th century, Denmark and Sweden were the major regional powers, often at odds with each other. Norway was eventually ceded to Sweden and only became independent in 1905; Finland meanwhile became independent of the Russian empire in 1918, the year Iceland became independent of Denmark.

The Baltic Sea is the region's lifeline. An almost enclosed, shallow body of water, low in salinity and stretching more than 440,000 square kilometres, it harbours many secrets of Europe's stormy past. On its murky bottom lie the remnants of centuries-old battles, including two world wars.

The word 'baltic' comes from a proto-Indo-European root, balt-, meaning 'white', and points to the comparatively homogeneous nature of the area's population. While much has been made about recent waves of immigration to Sweden and Denmark, the region has a striking absence of visible minorities. Consequently, locals like to emphasise regional differences: how Latvians are unlike their Estonian neighbours, who in turn distance themselves from their Finnish cousins, to whom they are ethnically and linguistically related. The Finns are the Scandinavian odd one out, as it were, quite apart from Swedes, Norwegians and Danes who are linguistically and politically related. Further afield, Icelanders revel in their infamously remote natures, and Greenland's population is 85 per cent Inuit.

It's a heady mix that ensures everything is possible on a journey to the region – and that there will be a lot of fun along the way.

TEXT STEVE KOKKER

ARCTIC
OCEAN

Nordauslandet

Smith
Sound

Qaanaaq

Spitsbergen
Svalbard
(Norway)

Longyearbyen

Edgeøya

Baffin
Bay

Greenland
(Denmark)

Greenland
Sea

Barents
Sea

Disko
Island
Disko Bay

Ilulissat

Jan Mayen
(Norway)

Nordkapp

Tromsø

Kangerlussuaq

Narvik

Ivalo

Tasiilaq

Norwegian
Sea

Bodø

Kiruna

Rovaniemi

NUUK

Ísafjörður

Akureyri

ICELAND

Luleå

Oulu

Narsarsuaq

REYKJAVÍK

Seyðisfjörður

Trondheim

NORWAY

Umeå

SWEDEN

Vaasa

FINLAND

Tampere

Davis
Strait

Faroe Islands
(Denmark)

Shetland
Islands (UK)

Ålesund

Bergen

Gulf
of
Bothnia

Turku

HELSINKI

Lillehammer

Uppsala

Gulf of
Finland

Stavanger

OSLO

Örebro

STOCKHOLM

TALLINN

ESTONIA

ATLANTIC
OCEAN

Scotland

Göteborg

RUSSIA

Northern
Ireland

UNITED
KINGDOM

North
Sea

DENMARK

Århus

Baltic
Sea

Malmö

RĪGA

LATVIA

LITHUANIA

COPENHAGEN

Kaliningrad
(Russia)

VILNIUS

IRELAND

Wales

England

NETHERLANDS

POLAND

BELARUS

TEXT STEVE KOKKER

ESTONIA

THE LITTLE COUNTRY THAT COULD – AND DID – ESTONIA HAS A QUIET, SEDUCTIVE ALLURE THAT LULLS YOU INTO ITS EASY-PACED RHYTHMS AND NATURAL BEAUTY.

CAPITAL CITY **TALLINN**   POPULATION **1.3 MILLION**   AREA **45,230 SQ KM**   OFFICIAL LANGUAGE **ESTONIAN**

» TREAD CAREFULLY IN THE FABULOUS MÄNNIKJÄRVE PEAT BOG, ENDLA NATURE RESERVE

LANDSCAPE
Estonia's canvas is a strikingly flat one, with its highest peak, Suur Munamägi (318 metres), a mere tree-covered mound to most travellers. Southern Estonia (roughly the area south of Tartu to the Latvian border), however, is continuously and gently hilly, with lovely valleys in Viljandi and Rõuge. There are fine Devonian sandstone formations, such as in Taevaskoja, and impressive limestone cliffs along the country's northern shores, especially on the Pakri islands and at Ontika. Aside from thick forests and myriad small lakes, and even smaller rivers, Estonia's main feature is long stretches of rocky, forlorn but picturesque coastline, dotted with islands.

HISTORY IN A NUTSHELL
Loosely grouped tribes have been mucking about rather sternly on this windswept corner of the Baltic Sea's northeast for at least 5000 years (or, depending on the expert cited, perhaps almost double that). There was nothing akin to a feeling of nationhood until the 19th century – after centuries of domination by Denmark, the Livonian Order, Sweden, German land barons and the Russian Empire. Estonia became a republic of the USSR following World War II, after a brief inter-war stint as a free country. It became newly independent in 1991. The country immediately set its sights westward and officially became a European Union member in 2004.

PEOPLE
On the surface, Estonia appears an unusually homogeneous society, with but a smattering of visible minorities. Locals, however, tend to emphasise the differences between the two cultures that live side by side here: the native Estonians (68 per cent), and the Russians, Belarusians and Ukrainians (26 per cent and two per cent each respectively). Between the two world wars, Estonians comprised over 90 per cent of the population; most Russians have arrived as workers since the 1950s. Estonians are famously secular but nominally Lutheran, while the Russian speakers and the Seto peoples in southeastern Estonia are Eastern Orthodox.

MARKETPLACE
Much has been made of the Estonian 'economic miracle' since the restoration of independence. Of all the former Soviet Republics, Estonia was the most efficient at getting its house in order, privatising everything and instituting daring experiments, such as a flat tax system. Its GDP growth rivals China's; inflation and unemployment hover around four per cent. The average monthly wage, though, is still well below the European Union average at about €575. Estonia's economy ranks as one of the five freest in the world, well above the US.

TRADEMARKS
- The so-called Singing Revolution (which led to independence from the USSR)
- Highly wired and e-crazy society
- Young, creative, risk-taking entrepreneurs
- Little expression of emotion in public
- Conspicuous consumption (see the expensive, gas-guzzling cars in the capital)
- Enthusiastic overuse of the word 'suur' (big, great)

TRADITIONS
Estonians' deep connection with nature is reflected in the fact that most surnames denote an element in nature (Kirsipuu – 'cherry tree'; Meri – 'sea'). It's also reflected in traditions such as the bringing of flowers to dinner parties or gatherings. Saunas, once part of traditional feast-day preparations, are still de rigueur today at birthdays or important get-togethers, often in a country setting. Huge bonfires are still lit on Midsummer night festivities (24 June). Maausk (meaning 'land belief'), a pagan-tinged set of beliefs,

SOVIET-ERA MOSKVITCH CAR READY AND WAITING OUTSIDE ALEXANDER NEVSKY CATHEDRAL, TALLINN »

COBBLED ST CATHERINE'S PASSAGE STEPS BACK INTO TALLINN'S MEDIEVAL ORIGINS »

neoshamanistic in its nature-worshipping elements, has made a strong comeback recently. Singing is another tradition Estonians are associated with; foreigners comment that when spoken properly the Estonian language itself sounds like a song.

RANDOM FACTS

○ The government is constitutionally bound to balance its budget.
○ Estonians are the undisputed world champs in International Wife-Carrying Championships.
○ Estonia has the largest number of meteorite craters per land area in the world.
○ Estonia has the most Hummers per capita in the world after the US; but this small country of high consumers is consistently near the bottom of Happiest Nations lists.

MYTHS & LEGENDS

Birds play a central role in the earliest Estonian myths and legends – as the creators of the universe, as examples of how to live, and as the carriers of souls to the hereafter. The word for the Milky Way in Estonian is Linnutee, meaning 'bird's way'. Giants are also popular motifs: there's Suur Tõll, the hero of Saaremaa's folklore; Leiger, from the island of Hiiumaa; and Vanapagan, an antihero of southern Estonia. Most famous of all is the giant Kalevipoeg. His boulder-tossing adventures were written in the 19th century by Friedrich Kreutzwald, based on texts of old runic songs, but quickly became *the* iconic Estonian

myth. Kalevipoeg eventually dies after his sword cuts off his own feet, but is expected to rise again, along with a new era for Estonia.

IMPORT

↗ Foreign investment and ownership of nearly all enterprises
↗ Polish construction workers
↗ Plasma TV screens, high technology and luxury items
↗ British stag parties
↗ As little from Russia as possible, save for natural gas

EXPORT

↖ Software development (Skype, Kazaa and Playtech)
↖ Composer Arvo Pärt, model Karmen Kaas and artist Mark Kostabi
↖ Peat and textiles
↖ Vana Tallinn, a sweet liqueur with a wallop
↖ Cheap alcohol and cigarettes (mainly by Finnish bargain-hunting tourists)
↖ Revival of the flat tax system

↗ RUSSIAN-STYLE ORTHODOX ALEXANDER NEVSKY CATHEDRAL, TALLINN

ESSENTIAL EXPERIENCES

○ **Meandering through the narrow cobblestone streets of Tallinn's Old Town and peeking into its romantic, medieval courtyards**

○ **Getting the toxins beat out of your naked body by a Baltic buddy wielding birch branches inside a sauna, then jumping into a cool lake afterwards**

○ **Experiencing the thrill of being alone on one of the country's 1520 tiny islands**

○ **Sharing a local beer with fun-loving university students in a dive bar or out on the parklands of otherwise quiet, lyrical Tartu**

○ **Wondering how a swamp could be such a fascinating place while visiting Soomaa National Park**

○ **Finding the nerve to sample a blood sausage – and then downing it with a swig of the smooth-tasting but hard-hitting national liqueur, Vana Tallinn**

○ **Listening to Arvo Pärt on your MP3 player while driving along a remote rocky shoreline**

FROM THE TRAVELLER

The Witch's Well in northern Estonia is a karst spring that gushes when the underground Tuhala River floods. The well is 2.5 metres deep, but when under pressure from the river water, it can spurt up to half a metre. Pressure from the river makes the well 'boil' and over 100 litres of water flows out every second. Legend has it that the Witch's Well boils when the Tuhala witches are whisking.

TARMO SOODLA // ESTONIA

MAP REF // N6

BEST TIME TO VISIT **JUNE TO SEPTEMBER**

A STONY SILENCE ENSUES BETWEEN THE TWO WILDES, OSCAR AND EDUARD, ON A BENCH IN TARTU

NOT A SHIRT IN SIGHT: WOMAN HANGS OUT FISH TO DRY, HIIUMAA

RESIDENT FELINES NO DOUBT THINK TWICE BEFORE A STROLL OVER TALLINN'S PRECIPITOUS RED-TILE ROOFTOPS

TEXT BECCA BLOND

LATVIA

IF YOU'RE LOOKING TO WIN EUROPE'S TRAVEL JACKPOT, CASH YOUR CHIPS IN LATVIA; STILL UNDISCOVERED BY THE TOURISM MASSES, THIS BALTIC SEXPOT IS POISED TO BECOME THE CONTINENT'S NEXT DESTINATION *DU JOUR*.

CAPITAL CITY RĪGA   POPULATION: 2.3 MILLION   AREA: 64,590 SQ KM   OFFICIAL LANGUAGE LATVIAN

≪ AN ELDERLY MAN HAND-PUMPS WATER TO TEND HIS GARDEN AND HOUSEHOLD

LANDSCAPE

A good half of Latvia's sweeping 494-kilometre coast faces the Gulf of Rīga, a deep inlet on the Baltic, shielded from the open sea by the Estonian island of Saaremaa. Latvia has a few hills steep enough to ski down, but with the exception of the Vidzeme Upland in eastern Latvia, which is the largest expanse of land in the entire Baltic region to boast an elevation of more than 200 metres, the country is as flat as a pancake. Latvia's highest point is Gaiziņkalns (312 metres).

HISTORY IN A NUTSHELL

The history of Latvia is a whirlwind of fierce struggle and downright rebellion. In 1201 at the behest of the pope, German crusaders conquered Latvia, founded Rīga and ruled for the next 700 years. Soviet occupation began in 1939 with the Molotov-Ribbentrop Pact, nationalisation, mass killings and about 35,000 deportations. Latvia was then occupied by Nazi Germany from 1941 to 1945, during which time an estimated 75,000 Latvians were killed or deported, before the country was reclaimed by the Soviets at the end of World War II. Latvia didn't gain full independence until 21 August 1991. Although one-third of Latvians voted against the country's successful accession to the European Union in 2004, today the general mood surrounding membership is optimistic, and Latvia has moved quickly to embrace the free market.

PEOPLE

Latvians narrowly comprise the majority of the population, numbering 58 per cent of citizens. Russians account for 29 per cent of the total population, with Belarusians (four per cent), Ukrainians (three per cent), Poles (2.5 per cent) and a small Jewish community (0.4 per cent) rounding out the rest of the demographics. Christianity first came to Latvia in the 12th century, quickly superseding Latvia's ancient deity-centric religion. Today the Roman Catholic Church has the largest Christian following, with roughly 500,000 adherents.

MARKETPLACE

Latvia's exports include wood and wood products, machinery and equipment, metals, textiles and foodstuffs. High inflation has so far hindered Latvia from making the transition to the euro, but unemployment looks to be on the improve. The latter is due in part to 'active economical migration' – economist speak for Latvians leaving their country to seek out work in other parts of Europe, mainly in Britain and Ireland. The average Latvian industrial worker brings home about €3900 per year.

TRADEMARKS

○ Rīga's Black Balsams liquor
○ Castles
○ Saunas
○ Amber

TRADITIONS

Latvian culture is steeped in superstition and rich in folklore. Customs and rituals, many dating back to pagan times, play integral roles in traditional Latvian life to this day. Step into a Latvian cemetery and you'll notice the sandy paths around the gravestones are meticulously raked, void of any footprints. This practice stems from the ancient belief that the spirit of the dead could follow the mourner home unless all living footprints were erased.

ON PAPER

The national epic, *Lāčplēsis* (The Bear Slayer), written by Andrējs Pumpurs in the mid-19th century, is based on traditional Latvian folk stories. The eponymous hero struggles against his enemy, a German Black

THE ORNATE (YET UNFORTUNATELY NAMED) HOUSE OF THE BLACKHEADS HAS BEEN RESTORED TO ITS FORMER GLORY IN RĪGA »

Knight, only to drown in the Daugava River at the moment of final triumph. The anticipated rebirth of *Lāčplēsis,* however, leaves hope for a better ending next time.

RANDOM FACTS

○ In many rural households it's considered lucky to have a green snake (which are nonvenomous) living in the home.

○ The divorce rate in Latvia remains among the highest in Europe – more than 60 per cent of marriages end in divorce and almost 40 per cent of children are born into one-parent families.

○ According to Latvian legend, Catherine the Great was instantly cured of a mystery illness in Riga after taking two sips from a cup of local Black Balsams liquor.

CUISINE

Step into a Latvian eatery and your nose will be hit by a mélange of rich smells – roasting meats, salted fish, boiled peas in bacon grease and the aroma of onions are just a sample of the varied offerings. Cheese is a staple in many dishes, and special semisoft cheeses, usually containing caraway seeds, are produced during holidays. The infamous Black Balsams is a thick, jet-black, 45 per cent proof concoction that has been produced in Latvia – and nowhere else – since 1752. Its recipe remains a closely guarded secret, but wormwood is known to be one of at least 14 different ingredients, and the liquor is believed to have medicinal value.

SURPRISES

○ In summer, the sun doesn't set until nearly midnight and then rises again four hours later.

○ Despite being almost as flat as a pancake (there are a few small hills) Latvia still offers downhill skiing – rooftops and dirt mounds create vertical drop during winter.

○ At 9.4 births per 1000 people (compared to 13.6 deaths), Latvia is reckoned to have among the world's lowest crude birth rates.

TOP FESTIVAL

The country's most important festival, Jāņi (St John's Night), takes place at summer solstice on 23 June. Latvians celebrate the longest night of the year by staying awake until the sun has set and then risen again – it is considered bad luck to go to sleep on this night. Revellers head to the countryside to celebrate: giant bonfires are lit, special beer is brewed and cheese made with caraway seeds is created especially for the national celebration.

≈ BOYS HAVING A LAUGH IN EMBROIDERED TRADITIONAL OUTFITS

ESSENTIAL EXPERIENCES

○ **Wandering Rīga's medieval cobbled streets, sliding past Art Nouveau flourishes and watching the sun rise over a skyline of spires and turrets**

○ **Getting an adrenaline rush bungee jumping, bobsleighing or skiing amid Sigulda's exquisite landscape**

○ **Soaking up sun and icy-blue Baltic Sea vistas in Jūrmala, Latvia's most boisterous seaside resort**

○ **Discovering the heart and soul of Latvia's rock-and-roll scene in progressive Liepāja**

○ **Feasting on fresh fish, gulping mouthfuls of crisp air and savouring the solitude of wild and windswept Cape Kolka**

≈ SECURITY IS STAUNCH AND STARCHED AT RĪGA'S FREEDOM MONUMENT

≈ ELABORATE BUILDING FAÇADE IN RĪGA'S ALBERTA STREET

MAP REF // N7

BEST TIME TO VISIT **JUNE TO AUGUST**

» LIEPĀJA FARMER TAKES TIME TO APPRAISE HIS NEW RED TRACTOR DURING THE HARVEST

SNOW LIES AT THE FOOT OF GEOMETRIC NEW SIGULDA CASTLE »

YOUNG PUNKS IN THE OLD TOWN FIND THE RELATIVE MERITS OF WAX VERSUS GEL A HOT TOPIC OF CONVERSATION, RĪGA »

TEXT NICOLA WILLIAMS

LITHUANIA

THE NATION THAT VANISHED FROM THE MAPS OF EUROPE IS BACK WITH A VENGEANCE: THE EXTRAORDINARY MAGNETISM OF REBELLIOUS, QUIRKY AND VIBRANT LITHUANIA HAS SUDDENLY MADE THIS TINY COUNTRY THE HIP PLACE TO BE.

CAPITAL CITY **VILNIUS**   POPULATION **3.6 MILLION**   AREA **65,200 SQ KM**   OFFICIAL LANGUAGE **LITHUANIAN**

WITOLD SKRYPCZAK / LONELY PLANET IMAGES

⌃ CHANGE IS IN THE AIR: ŠEDUVA'S OLD STONE WINDMILL HAS A NEW LIFE AS A RESTAURANT

LANDSCAPE
Lush forests and 4000 lakes cover a big chunk of this small, flat country, neighbour to Latvia, Belarus, Poland and the Kaliningrad region of Russia. At 294 metres, Juozapinės is (don't laugh) the country's highest point. Half of Lithuania's short Baltic coast lies along the Curonian Spit. Behind it spans the Curonian Lagoon, into which flows Lithuania's longest river, the Nemunas. Winters are dark, snow clogged and freezing cold. Summers are short, sweet and hot.

HISTORY IN A NUTSHELL
A powerful state from the 14th to 16th centuries, Lithuania subsequently fell under the Polish yoke. It emerged from World War I and the Russian Revolution as an independent country and enjoyed two decades of statehood until World War II, at which time it fell under Soviet control. Occupation by Nazi Germany during the war was followed by Soviet reconquest, after which Lithuania was merged with the USSR. Lithuania led the Baltic push for independence in 1991 and joined the European Union and NATO in 2004.

PEOPLE
Almost half the population lives in Lithuania's five major cities – Vilnius, Kaunas, Šiauliai, Panevėžys and Klaipėda. Lithuanians account for about 83 per cent of the population, Poles seven per cent and Russians six per cent. The smallest ethnic community is the Karaites, a Turkic minority originating in Baghdad, which – unlike the rest of Lithuania's staunchly Roman Catholic population – adheres to the Law of Moses.

MARKETPLACE
Lithuania's postindependence transition from a centralised to a free-market economy was no mean feat, and is now counted among Europe's fastest-growing economies. GDP is on the increase, inflation hovers at 3.5 per cent and the budget deficit is less than three per cent of GDP. Its national currency, the Lithuanian litas, has been pegged to the euro since 2004, although Lithuania's bid to adopt the euro in 2007 was rejected by Brussels. Lithuania still ranks among the poorest of the 27 European Union countries, its GDP per capita notching up no more than 50 per cent of the European Union average, and the average worker's monthly net salary hovering around €270.

TRADEMARKS
○ Basketball
○ Cuisine made of piggy parts
○ Europe's largest baroque ensemble
○ Initiator of the USSR collapse
○ Soviet sculptures
○ European Capital of Culture 2009

URBAN SCENE
Bizarre, bewitching and beautiful, Vilnius is incredibly small (can this really be a capital city?) with astonishing old-town charm, a skyline littered with Orthodox and Catholic church spires, and an addictive drinking, dining and party scene. Port city Klaipėda – gateway to the natural splendour of the Curonian Spit – was once the German town of Memel (it wasn't part of Lithuania until 1923). Its minute Old Town and the flow of ferries forging across the Curonian Lagoon into the Baltic Sea exude an appealing grit.

NATURAL BEAUTY
The Curonian Spit is Lithuania's most breathtaking natural feature. Split between Lithuania and Russian Kaliningrad, the stunning sliver of spit stretches for 98 kilometres, is four kilometres wide and is graced with fragile dunes of fine golden sand.

ON DISC
Romantic, folk-influenced composer Mikalojus Konstantinas Čiurlionis is considered Lithuania's finest

STEP PAST INNUMERABLE TOKENS ON THE HILL OF CROSSES, A PLACE OF CATHOLIC PILGRIMAGE NEAR ŠIAULIAI »

musician. He wrote Lithuania's first symphonies, *Miske* (In the Forest) and *Jūra* (The Sea), at the start of the 20th century; created piano pieces; and conducted and composed for string quartets. Dogged by depression for much of his too-short life, Čiurlionis died aged 35 of pneumonia.

RANDOM FACTS

- Lithuania was the last pagan country in Europe; it adopted Roman Catholicism in 1387.
- The geographical centre of Europe lies 25 kilometres north of Vilnius at a latitude of 54°54'N and longitude of 25°19'E.
- The gorgeously golden stretch of coast between Lithuania and Kaliningrad (Russia) provides 90 per cent of the world's amber.

CUISINE

Long, miserable winters are to blame for Lithuania's waist-widening diet based on potatoes, meat and dairy products. The climax comes in the form of *cepelinai* – airship-shaped parcels of potato dough stuffed with cheese, meat or mushrooms and topped with an artery-clogging sauce containing onions, butter, sour cream and bacon bits. Mushrooms, berries and game dishes dominate eastern and southern Lithuanian cuisine; beer sneaks its way into northern cooking pots; and fish reigns on the coast and in lake districts such as Trakai. Bread tends to black, rye and dry.

SURPRISES

- Summers are hot and cloudless with daytime highs of 30 degrees Celsius.
- Vodka is no longer fashionable (although smoked tea with vodka is hip in city-slicker circles).
- Wherever you stand in Vilnius, you can always see a church spire.
- Lithuanians eat *liežuvis* (cow's tongue), *vėdarai* (fried pork innards) and *balionių skilandis* (meat-stuffed pig's bladder), and smoked pig's ears, trotters and tails are popular beer snacks.

TOP FESTIVAL

In a similar vein to neighbouring Latvia, the biggest party of the year is Joninės or Rasos (Midsummer or St John's Day), a night of magic and sorcery on 24 June when wild witches are said to have run naked, bewitching flowers and ferns, people and animals in pagan Lithuania. Celebrations start on 23 June when Lithuanians flock to the countryside to seek the mythical fern flower during this special night that scarcely gets dark. Bonfires are lit, folk songs sung and fortune seekers leap over flaming cartwheels as they roll down a hill. Men adorn themselves with crowns made from oak leaves, and women with crowns of flowers.

⌃ A FARMER LOOKS SATISFIED WITH THE CONTENTS OF HIS POCKET

⌃ CHURCH OF THE HOLY SPIRIT RISES ABOVE THE STREETS OF VILNIUS

ESSENTIAL EXPERIENCES

- **Revelling in Vilnius' cobbled courtyards and orgy of Gothic, Renaissance, classical and baroque architecture**
- **Sampling the capital's vibrant café and bar scene**
- **Mushrooming and berrying in the Aukštaitija National Park**
- **Frolicking around the Unesco-protected Curonian Spit, Lithuania's own Sahara**
- **Hunting for amber after storms on endless stretches of fine golden-sand beaches**
- **Touring an underground Soviet missile base in the Žemaitija National Park**
- **Eyeballing the 13 Lenins at Druskininkai's Soviet Sculpture Park**
- **Partying on the beach until the wee hours in Palanga**

⌃ DECORATIVE TEAPOTS STREETSIDE IN VILNIUS

MAP REF // N8

BEST TIME TO VISIT **APRIL TO SEPTEMBER**

≪ SNOW CREATES A NEAR MONOCHROMATIC WINTER SCENE ON THE BANKS OF THE NEMUNAS RIVER

WHEAT HARVEST FEATURES ON A TRADITIONAL WOOD CARVING ≪

THE GOTHIC FORTIFIED TOWER AND BASTION OF KAUNAS CASTLE HAVE BEEN ON THE DEFENSIVE SINCE THE 14TH CENTURY ≪

TEXT ANDY SYMINGTON

FINLAND

PROGRESSIVE FINLAND MAKES NOISE IN THE TECHNOLOGY AND MUSIC SCENES, BUT ITS EPIC WILDERNESS OF FORESTS, FELLS AND LAKES IS THE PERFECT PLACE FOR CONTEMPLATION AND NORDIC PEACE.

CAPITAL HELSINKI   POPULATION 5.2 MILLION   AREA 338,150 SQ KM   OFFICIAL LANGUAGES FINNISH, SWEDISH, SÁMI

≈ CLEARLY MORE FUN THAN IT SOUNDS, THE BIRCH-WHACKING BEGINS AT THE SAUNA AFTER SWIMMING IN AN ICE HOLE

LANDSCAPE

Forests and lakes are the stereotype, the truth and the glory of Finland. Some 10 per cent of the country's surface area is taken up by water, the remains of glaciers that retreated at the end of the last ice age. The vast expanses of pine, birch and spruce forest shelter much wildlife, including that mobile roadblock, the elk. Further north, beyond the Arctic Circle, the trees peter out, and reindeer graze on lichen.

HISTORY IN A NUTSHELL

Settlers gradually began moving into Finland as the ice age retreated, and one group, the Sámi, were likely pushed northwards by newer arrivals in the south. In the 12th century Sweden launched an aggressive campaign of colonisation and Christianisation against the pagan Finns. Over the years, as Swedish and Russian power waxed and waned, the region became a conflict zone, until Sweden finally ceded it to Russia in 1809. The Russian Revolution enabled Finland to declare independence in 1917, but in 1939 Soviet territorial ambitions pushed Finland into the Winter War, a heroic but ultimately fruitless defence of Karelia; the government then accepted German aid to repel the Russians, and later faced a bloody struggle to expel the retreating German forces. During the Cold War years, Finland walked a tightrope between Moscow and the West; however, the country has emerged as one of the world's most stable and admired democracies. Finland has been enjoying sustained prosperity and achievement since joining the European Union in 1994.

PEOPLE

Finland is rather sparsely populated, and the majority of its people live in the urban clusters of the south. Some 92 per cent of the nation are Finnish-speaking Finns, but the five per cent of Swedish-speaking Finns have had a disproportionate influence on the history and economy of the country, and remain an important minority. In the north, the Sámi are the indigenous inhabitants of Lapland and have traditionally made a living from reindeer herding. Finland has a low proportion of foreign residents, some two per cent, although this is rapidly increasing.

MARKETPLACE

Finland is the model of a successful northern European state; average income is high, there is little poverty, and the country scores well on economic and development indices. While the booming technology sector is increasingly important, it's still the country's forests that provide some 35 per cent of export income.

TRADEMARKS

- ○ Saunas
- ○ Nokia
- ○ Moody rock and metal
- ○ Wacky festivals
- ○ Reindeer
- ○ Santa Claus
- ○ Design and architecture
- ○ Rally and racing drivers

NATURAL BEAUTY

Some of Finland's prettiest scenery is to be found in the Lakeland areas around Savonlinna and Kuopio, and in nearby Karelia. These are classic landscapes of dark forests and glinting sylvan pools and lakes, divided by characteristic gravel dunes, called *eskers*. The southern coast is studded with thousands of small islands perfect for sea-bound exploration, while the north has an epic, empty feel – vast wilderness under a big sky and distant sun.

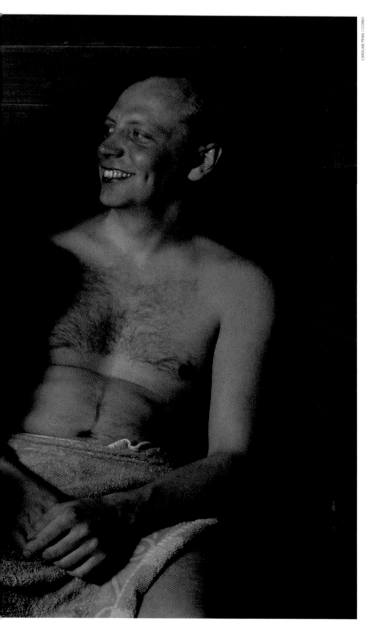

A CHILLING EXPERIENCE: ATTENDING MASS IN KEMI'S SNOW CASTLE CHAPEL »

REVERED CLASSICAL COMPOSER SIBELIUS IS HONOURED BY A TUNEFUL MONUMENT, HELSINKI »

ON DISC

Music is a large part of Finnish culture, particularly in summer, when music festivals are staged all over the country. Composer Jean Sibelius is well known, but melancholic Finnish tango and waltzlike *humppa* music get the dance halls pumping. In recent years, Finnish rock bands from the dark and heavy side of the spectrum have shot to international stardom: groups such as Nightwish, HIM and The Rasmus are household names worldwide, but there are numerous lesser-known bands that get aficionados' eyes sparkling. Up north, the traditional Sámi form is the *yoik*, a complex vocal solo that has been adapted into modern popular music with success.

MYTHS & LEGENDS

The *Kalevala* is a compilation of Finnish folk traditions collected and synthesised in the 19th century by Elias Lönnrot, an adventurous rural doctor. Regarded as the national epic, the *Kalevala* tells of creation, the struggle between good and evil, and more down-to-earth themes. Its central character is a heroic, grumpy, fallible bard-god named Väinämöinen, whose doings seem to involve echoes of both struggles between Finns and Sámi, and the coming of Christianity to Finland. JRR Tolkien based significant portions of his mythos on the *Kalevala*, and part of the language of the Elves in *The Lord of the Rings* on Finnish.

≫ FINLAND IS DOTTED WITH THOUSANDS OF LAKES AND ISLANDS

≫ A EUROPEAN BROWN BEAR SURVEYS THE SCENE, TAIGA FOREST

TOP FESTIVAL

The Savonlinna Opera Festival comes a close second, but for sheer Finnish nuttiness the Wife-Carrying World Championships in little Sonkajärvi takes the prize (with honourable mentions for weirdness to the Mobile Phone Throwing competition, and the Air Guitar World Championship). Participants race over an obstacle course with 'wife' (actually any consenting female) slung over their shoulder. The winning team gets the woman's weight in beer.

WILD THINGS

Finland's forests house a significant nation of mammals, including such 'respect' species as bears, wolves, lynx and wolverines. You've a better chance of spotting the iconic *hirvi* (elk), a mountain of muscle that writes off a couple of thousand vehicles a year on country roads. Finland is also home to some 240,000 reindeer. These are domesticated animals herded by the Sámi in the north. Finland's forests abound with birds, and its waterways with fish, but, for some, its most memorable creatures are the squadrons of biting insects that hatch with the first flush of summer's heat.

RANDOM FACTS

- Before telecommunications, Nokia's most successful product line was rubber boots.
- Despite painful temperatures, ice fishing is wildly popular – success is measured more in what is drunk than what is caught!
- It can get tedious driving around those lakes, so in winter people often take the short cut and drive across the ice; in some places, official roads are marked on the frozen surface.

ESSENTIAL EXPERIENCES

- Dashing through the snow in a reindeer sleigh in Lapland
- Sweating your issues away in a smoke sauna in Kuopio
- Flirting with the frontiers of sanity at one of the many truly bizarre festivals
- Trekking through the pine landscapes that underpin the Finnish soul in Karelia
- Upgrading your fashion sense with the latest design trends in bustling Helsinki
- Contemplating in a wooden cottage by a forest lake in the romantic Lakeland

MAP REF // N5

BEST TIME TO VISIT **JUNE TO SEPTEMBER**

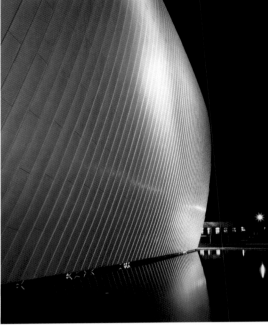

≫ ARCHITECTURALLY STUNNING MUSEUM OF CONTEMPORARY ART, HELSINKI

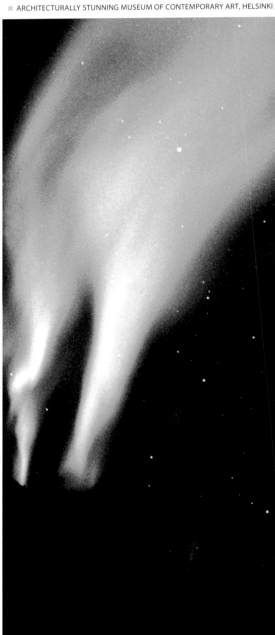

NIK WHEELER // CORBIS

KALERVO OJUTKANGAS // PHOTO LIBRARY

≪ JOCKEYS HOLD TIGHT AS REINDEER RACE FOR THE FINISH LINE NEAR INARI

DASHING THROUGH THE SNOW FROM ICE HOLE TO SAUNA ≪

MAGNIFICENT AURORA BOREALIS ILLUMINATES THE NORTHERN NIGHT SKY ≪

TEXT BECKY OHLSEN

SWEDEN

ONCE HOME TO VIKING BERSERKERS, SWEDEN IS NOW KNOWN FOR PACIFISM AND LIBERAL SOCIAL POLICIES, COMBINING UNTOUCHED LANDSCAPES WITH CUTTING-EDGE MODERNITY.

CAPITAL CITY **STOCKHOLM**   POPULATION **9 MILLION**   AREA **449,964 SQ KM**   OFFICIAL LANGUAGES **SWEDISH**

» A TUG OF WAR ENSUES AS A REINDEER RESISTS THE HERDERS' ROPE, LAPLAND

LANDSCAPE

Occupying the eastern strip of the Scandinavian Peninsula, Sweden shares borders with Norway, Finland and Denmark. This is a long, skinny country with a 7000-kilometre coastline and countless islands. The highest peak is Norrland's Kebnekaise (2111 metres). Parts of Skåne and the islands of Öland and Gotland consist of flat limestone and sandstone deposits. The Lake Siljan region was created by a three-kilometre-wide meteor some 360 million years ago.

HISTORY IN A NUTSHELL

Sweden came into its own during the Viking Age (800–1100), when pagan Norsemen raided and traded as far as İstanbul, Baghdad and America. Christianity took hold in the early 9th century, though pockets of paganism lingered. Stockholm was founded in 1252. In 1397 the Union of Kalmar allied Norway, Denmark and Sweden, but this pact steadily deteriorated until 1520, when a Swedish rebellion was led by nobleman Gustav Vasa. He was crowned king in 1523 and spent the next 37 years establishing the foundations of modern Sweden. More recent key events include the assassination of Prime Minister Olof Palme in 1986 and an economic recession in 1992 that sapped the country's confidence. Sweden joined the European Union in 1995, but voted against adopting the euro. Recent politics have shifted towards centre-right coalition Alliance for Sweden, but its hold is tentative at best.

PEOPLE

Sweden's population is concentrated in the cities of Stockholm, Göteborg, Malmö and Uppsala. Most people are considered to be of Nordic stock. The 17,000 indigenous Sámi people form a significant minority; likewise some 30,000 Finnish speakers. More than 20 per cent of the population are either foreign-born or have at least one non-Swedish parent. The majority of immigrants have come from other European countries, followed by lesser numbers from the Middle East. Lutheranism was the official religion until 2000, at which time Sweden established complete separation of church and state.

MARKETPLACE

After World War II and throughout the 1950s and '60s, Sweden set up and fine-tuned the welfare state, under which poverty was virtually eradicated. But during a world recession that peaked in 1992, the Swedish krona fell and interest rates shot up by 500 per cent. Unemployment rose to 14 per cent, and the government responded by hiking taxes, cutting welfare and tightening immigration. Since Sweden joined the European Union the economy has strengthened, with recent emphasis on biotechnology, IT and telecommunications in addition to the core areas of agriculture, fishing, forestry, mining and public-sector employment.

TRADEMARKS

- IKEA
- Swedish meatballs
- Tennis star Björn Borg
- Actress Greta Garbo
- Football coach Sven-Göran Eriksson
- Children's book character Pippi Longstocking
- Socialism

RANDOM FACTS

- Sweden hasn't gone to war since 1814.
- Sweden has a constitutional monarchy; Carl XVI Gustaf has been king since 1973, and Crown Princess Victoria is set to inherit the throne.
- Swedes are responsible for dynamite, taxonomy, the propeller, the zipper and the Celsius temperature scale.

A WOODEN HUT POPS ITS HEAD UP FROM THE DANDELION-COVERED GRASSY SLOPES »

NATURAL BEAUTY

Sweden's largely unspoiled landscape is one of the loveliest in Europe; forest covers more than half the country, and there are some 100,000 lakes scattered around, including the lovely Lake Siljan. National parks such as Norrland's Sarek and Abisko contain gorgeous, if challenging, hiking terrain. Islands off both coasts offer prime summer hang-outs. Beaches line the Böhuslan coast near Göteborg, and Gotland also has excellent beaches and flat woodlands. Even in Stockholm, beach access is plentiful, and sun worshippers line the water's edge all summer long.

ON FILM

- The Seventh Seal (1957)
- I Am Curious: Yellow (1967)
- The Emigrants (1971)
- Songs from the Second Floor (2000)
- Lilja 4-Ever (2002)

ON DISC

- ABBA
- Stakka Bo
- Dungen
- Sahara Hotnights
- The International Noise Conspiracy
- Peter Bjorn & John
- Cardigans

CUISINE

The staples of Swedish cuisine are fish, game, potatoes and milk. Open-face sandwiches and artful pastries fill the gaps. Coffee and *snaps* (spiced vodka) are equally key. The best way to get a thorough sampling is to visit a smorgasbord. *Husmanskost* (home-style food) includes such classics as meatballs with lingonberry (something like a wild cranberry) and *pytt i panna* (meat and potato hash). Sweden also embraces food from other cultures – pizza, sushi, tacos and Thai food are everywhere.

MYTHS & LEGENDS

Norse gods Odin, Thor, Loki and company are familiar figures throughout Scandinavia, and their names live on in the Swedish words for the days of the week. Odin, god of war, rides Sleipnir, an eight-legged horse with runes etched into its teeth. The god is said to have given one of his eyes in exchange for wisdom, only to learn of his own inescapable doom in the world-ending battle of good versus evil called Ragnarök. The dark myths recorded in the Icelandic *Eddas* are full of honour and sacrifice, tricksters and frost giants, and make perfect sense in a land that seasonally transforms from harsh to heavenly.

TOP FESTIVAL

Every Swede looks forward to Midsummer's Day, the first Saturday after 21 June. The longest day of the year in a country that's dark all winter, it's celebrated with rowdy sing-alongs, maypole dancing and copious consumption of seafood and schnapps. It's the country's biggest event: people take time off work and shops shut for the frenzied activities.

WILD THINGS

Sweden's geographical diversity entails a range of wildlife. Its large predators, mostly endangered, include the bear, wolf, wolverine, lynx and golden eagle. Elk (moose) are a Swedish icon, and around 260,000 reindeer roam the northern wilderness. Lemmings are a staple food for predators, whose population depends on their availability. There's also a vast array of bird life as well as fish and crustaceans.

≈ SINGING OUT LOUD AT GOTLAND'S MEDIEVAL WEEK

ESSENTIAL EXPERIENCES

- Gazing over the glittering beauty of Stockholm from the Söder Heights
- Marvelling at the complicated feat of dredging up and restoring the Vasa warship, now in Stockholm
- Singing your heart out to celebrate the daylight on Midsummer at Skansen
- Picking up handcrafted souvenirs at the Christmas market in Stockholm's Old Town
- Sailing or paddling among the 24,000 islands speckling the Stockholm archipelago
- Getting blown away on a tour of Sweden's prestigious glass-making factories
- Dodging reindeer on a Norrland highway
- Catching a view of the midnight sun at Abisko National Park

MAP REF // L5

BEST TIME TO VISIT **MAY TO SEPTEMBER**

≈ 'GOD'S HAND' SCULPTURE REACHES INTO A FIERY SKY, STOCKHOLM

» TAKE A RIDE THROUGH SCENIC SWEDEN'S FAIRY-TALE WINTER LANDSCAPE

SÁMI FAMILY IN TRADITIONAL GÁKTI GATHER OUTSIDE THEIR HUT »

ICE SPLITS AND THAWS IN A FROZEN COVE ON THE GULF OF BOTHNIA »

TEXT **KARI LUNDGREN**

NORWAY

BROWN CHEESE TO AQUAVIT, VIKINGS TO OIL TYCOONS, CODFISH TO MOOSE, FJORDS TO WATERFALLS, THE MIDNIGHT SUN TO THE AURORA BOREALIS: LIFE IN NORWAY IS VIBRANT, MYTHICAL AND EDGY.

CAPITAL CITY **OSLO** POPULATION **4.6 MILLION** AREA **323,800 SQ KM** OFFICIAL LANGUAGES **NORWEGIAN, SÁMI**

⊼ NORWAY'S OLDEST SLIPPERY SLOPE, THE 1892 HOLMENKOLLEN SKI JUMP, OSLO

LANDSCAPE

From the edge of the pack ice to the southern fjords, Norway is a rugged country characterised by the sea and mountains. Boasting more than 150,000 islands and numerous fjords that stretch for hundreds of kilometres inland, Norway's coast is one of the world's longest, and remains strikingly pristine and remote. More than two-thirds of the country is mountainous, with small farming communities tucked away within the fertile southern valleys.

HISTORY IN A NUTSHELL

Little remains of the vast Viking empire that once stretched across northern Europe and as far as the east coast of Canada, but there was a time when the sight of a Viking ship on the horizon inspired fear in many a Saxon heart. With the defeat of the Viking king Harald Hardråda in 1066 by Anglo-Saxons, and the raging destruction caused by the Black Death during the Middle Ages, Norway's power quickly declined. For over 500 years, until 1905, the country was ruled largely from afar, first by Denmark and then by Sweden. Since then, Norwegians have struggled fiercely to maintain their independence, actively resisting German occupation during World War II and, more recently, by choosing to remain outside the European Union. Today, Norwegians take pride in their role as a centre of global peace, typified by the celebrations associated with the Nobel Peace Prize, which is awarded annually in Oslo.

PEOPLE

Norway's population is predominantly of Nordic descent, with a small ethnic minority of Sámi (20,000) in the north. Norway's official language, Norwegian, has two recognised forms (Bokmål and Nynorsk), and Sámi is accepted as a second official language in six municipalities. More than 85 per cent of Norwegians are Lutherans.

MARKETPLACE

The UN consistently ranks Norway in the top four of the world's best places to live, and only Luxembourgers enjoy a higher average income. Much of this affluence is due to an abundance of natural resources: fisheries, forests, hydropower, minerals and, most importantly, petroleum. Norway is the third-largest exporter of oil worldwide, after Saudi Arabia and Russia, and oil and gas account for a third of all exports.

TRADEMARKS

o Brown cheese and pickled herring
o Vikings and trolls
o Midnight sun
o Majestic moose
o Fjords

RANDOM FACTS

o Henrik Ibsen, Norway's most famous and beloved author, lived self-exiled in Italy for 27 years.
o There are over 2600 kilometres of groomed cross-country ski trails in Oslo every winter.
o If Norway were rotated at its southernmost tip, it would stretch all the way to the boot of Italy.

URBAN SCENE

Often described as the 'Gateway to the Fjords', Bergen is one of Norway's most beautiful cities and the nation's cultural capital. Historically an important centre for maritime trade, during the 14th century the city attracted Hanseatic merchants, who built and preserved the wooden houses of the Bryggen (Old Wharf). Now a Unesco World Heritage Site, the Bryggen's yellow, red and white buildings are filled with galleries, shops and cafés, perfect for an afternoon stroll.

THE BRYGGEN'S RED AND YELLOW ROW HOUSES ARE PERFECT FOR AN AFTERNOON OUTING IN BERGEN »

NATURAL BEAUTY

The rugged islands and brightly painted fisherman's cabins of Lofoten, tucked as they are between the mountains, the sky and the sea, capture the isolated, harsh grandeur of the Norwegian coast. And the view across the Barents Sea from Nordkapp, brightly lit by the midnight sun, is hard to forget. But it is the soft, mossy greens of the inland forests and valleys of Telemark, the striking blues of the glaciers and lakes of Jotunheimen, and visions of golden summer meadows filled with mushrooms, berries and the occasional moose in Valdres, that fill Norwegian dreams during the dark winter months.

ON CANVAS

If the agonised, pale face of Edvard Munch's *The Scream* wasn't enough to turn the painting into an art icon, its absurd tendency to get stolen has done the rest. Twice, in a manner befitting the nimble fingers of Thomas Crown, *The Scream* has been plucked from the walls of Oslo art museums. Thefts and pop culture aside, *The Scream*, with its exaggerated colours and imagery, is considered to be a seminal work of the expressionist movement.

CUISINE

Leaving the ever-present boiled potato aside, Norwegian food is heavy on fish, game and cheese. Most Norwegians are fond of hunting and harvesting their own food, which results in delicious morsels such as moose meatballs, crayfish flavoured with fresh dill, and the highly prized *multe* (cloudberry) cream that only appears during holidays. Some of the more traditional items owe their origin to a basic lack of refrigeration: *lutefisk* (dried cod steeped in lye), pickled herring and smoked trout. And some products, such as Jarlsberg cheese, aquavit and smoked salmon, have become especially popular abroad. As for snacking, there is nothing more Norwegian than a *lumpe* (potato pancake) with *brun ost* (brown goat's cheese).

MYTHS & LEGENDS

In Norway, there is an *eventyr* (folk tale) for almost every landmark, tradition or experience. At Christmas, steaming bowls of porridge are left outside for the *Julenisse* (Christmas gnome) who guards the animals. In the summer, young men must beware of the impossibly beautiful *huldra*, a seductress who will try to tempt them into the woods. And the adventures of Askeladden, who invariably dupes his stupid older brothers, kills one or more trolls, gets the gold and marries the princess, is a bedtime staple.

SURPRISES

o Not all Norwegians are blonde and tall.
o Viking helmets did not actually have horns.
o The sun does shine during a Norwegian winter.

≫ THE FISHING'S ON HOLD FOR THIS STRANDED TRAWLER, LOFOTEN

ESSENTIAL EXPERIENCES

o **Communing with Norway's great explorers in Bygdøy's museums**

o **Breakfasting on *brun ost* (brown goat's cheese) and pickled herring**

o **Experiencing vertigo as you look down the dizzying drop of the Holmenkollen ski jump**

o **Yanking a fresh cod into your boat while fishing among the Lofoten Islands**

o **Plucking wild blueberries or cloudberries during a hike in Jotunheimen National Park**

o **Sailing down a Norwegian fjord**

o **Bathing in sunshine during a 1am visit to Nordkapp, the northernmost point in Europe**

o **Startling a moose while on a midnight summer saunter through the woods**

≫ LOOK THROUGH TO THE WEST NORWAY MUSEUM OF DECORATIVE ART

≫ A FISHERMAN'S PRIZE COD LEAPS FROM THE ICE, OSLO

MAP REF // K5

BEST TIME TO VISIT **JUNE TO OCTOBER**

≫ IDENTICAL TWINS DECKED OUT IN IDENTICAL TRADITIONAL COSTUMES

AN IMPRESSIVE SNOW DRIFT LINES THE ROAD TO GEIRANGER ≫

ACHIEVE THE ULTIMATE HIGH SCALING BLUE-TINGED NIGARDSBREEN GLACIER ≫

TEXT MICHAEL BOOTH

DENMARK

THE DANES MAY BE FEW IN NUMBER BUT THEY ARE AN EDUCATED, CULTURED, CONFIDENT TRIBE PROTECTIVE OF THEIR COUNTRY'S UNSPOILED NATURAL BEAUTY AND PROUD OF THE CREATIVE DYNAMISM OF THEIR CAPITAL CITY.

CAPITAL CITY **COPENHAGEN**   POPULATION **5.5 MILLION**   AREA **42,390 SQ KM**   OFFICIAL LANGUAGE **DANISH**

≫ FOLLOW THE YELLOW-BRICK ROAD OF RAPESEED FLOWERS

LANDSCAPE

Around half of all Danes live on the two main islands of Zealand to the east, home of Copenhagen, and Funen, in the centre of the country. To the west is the Jutland peninsula rising from northern Germany. The Danish landscape is almost uniformly made up of gently undulating hills; the climate is equally moderate – comparable to that of northern England, but perhaps a touch darker, colder and wetter.

HISTORY IN A NUTSHELL

The Vikings ensured that the Danes were known and feared throughout northern Europe from the 8th to 11th century. Unfortunately a series of overambitious kings saw them lose a large part of their empire during the 17th and 18th centuries. The British bombed Copenhagen twice in the early 19th century, but the country subsequently rebuilt itself culturally with the help of literary giants such as Søren Kierkegaard and Hans Christian Andersen and, in the 20th century, the Danes created an enviable social-welfare model and cutting-edge economy.

PEOPLE

The Danes consider themselves to be a close-knit nation, although regional variations are fiercely upheld. Thus rural Jutlanders are likely to distrust their cynical, cosmopolitan Copenhagen compatriots, and both of these groups in turn tend to look down on the countryside dwellers of Funen. Since the early 1960s, Denmark has welcomed immigrants from North Africa and the Middle East; however, in recent years the Danes' reluctance to allow their full integration has led to significant unrest among ethnic minorities and a right-wing backlash at the polls.

MARKETPLACE

The Germans used to think of Denmark as being a little like their private larder, so productive was the Danish agricultural sector; however, in the last 50 years the country's manufacturing and service sectors have grown so that today less than four per cent of the workforce is employed in farming. Denmark is a shining example of a modern, service-led economy – hi-tech and pharmaceutical industries are a speciality – but its wealth has been bolstered by oil revenues from the North Sea and its citizens pay some of the highest taxes in the world. Of impending long-term concern is the country's high level of public sector employment and welfare-state expenditure.

TRADEMARKS

- ○ Lego bricks
- ○ Bearded beer swillers
- ○ Windmills – for electricity as opposed to milling
- ○ Sleek interior design
- ○ Hans Christian Andersen's famously large nose

TRADITIONS

The Danes are compulsive candle-lighters – you'll find that even a summer breakfast table will be adorned with a flickering flame. Candles are a crucial ingredient of *hygge*, an ultimately untranslatable Danish word that is used to conjure a cosy, warm, convivial experience often involving an open fire, nonconfrontational conversation, freely flowing alcohol and perhaps a song or two. If a Dane ever thanks you for a *hyggelige* time, you can consider it the greatest of compliments.

RANDOM FACTS

- ○ The Danes give more overseas aid per capita than any other country.
- ○ The Danes have no word for 'please'.
- ○ The richest man in Denmark is oil and shipping tycoon and philanthropist Mærsk McKinney Møller.

LOOKING FOR LADY LUCK AT COPENHAGEN'S TIVOLI AMUSEMENT PARK »

VERNER PANTON'S RADICAL FURNITURE INSTALLATION IN THE DANSK DESIGN CENTRE REVEALS A MOLTEN LANDSCAPE »

URBAN SCENE

Founded a thousand years ago on the wealth of herring that shoaled in the Øresund Sea to the east, today Copenhagen blends picturesque, Dutch-influenced, 18th-century town houses and canals with radical, contemporary architecture – much of which houses leading cultural institutions. The spine of the city is Strøget, which claims to be the longest pedestrian street in Europe. You'll find it is lined with upscale, independent retailers, many of these having an interior-design bent. But there's another more intriguing, 'underground', anti-establishment aspect to the city, best represented by the alternative 'hippy' commune of Christiania, founded more than 30 years ago in a former military barracks.

ON DISC

- Kashmir
- Aqua
- The Raveonettes
- Junior Senior
- Whigfield
- Safri Duo
- Funkstardeluxe
- Niels and Chris Doky
- Michael Learns to Rock
- Metallica (well, their drummer Lars Ulrich at least)

TOP FESTIVAL

The Roskilde Festival is one of Europe's largest and most friendly open-air music events, attracting the world's biggest rock and pop acts – Radiohead, Bob Dylan, Morrissey and Scissor Sisters have attended, among others. Renowned for its carnival atmosphere, Roskilde Festival marks an important coming of age for young Danes. Each year, for four days in late June to early July, tens of thousands (up to 90,000 most years) migrate to the fields outside this former capital city to the east of Copenhagen.

CUISINE

The lure of Denmark's traditional cuisine has been stubbornly resisted by the world's gourmets. With the exception of the Danish open sandwich – or smørrebrød – Danish food is not generally known or appreciated beyond its borders. But the Danes themselves still love their frikadeller (sauceless meatballs), their pickled herring and a hundred ways with pork (including one dish that is made up entirely of fried pork fat). It might not be the most healthy or indeed appetising food, but it seems to keep the Danes well fuelled for the long, dark winters.

ON FILM

For such a small country, Denmark punches well above its weight in terms of its contribution to movie history. Denmark boasts pioneer movie makers such as Carl Theodor Dreyer and contemporary innovators such as the back-to-basics Dogma devotees.

- Travel with Greenlandic Dogs (1896)
- The Abyss (1910)
- La Passion de Jeanne d'Arc (1928)
- Babette's Feast (1987)
- Breaking the Waves (1996)
- Festen (The Celebration, 1998)
- Italian for Beginners (2001)

ESSENTIAL EXPERIENCES

- Catching some of the world's greatest pop and rock acts at the massive Roskilde Festival
- Paddling in the currents at the tip of Skagen
- Strolling along the vast – usually deserted – sandy beaches of western Jutland
- Chilling out in the alternative commune of Christiania
- Seeing Copenhagen from the sea on a canal and harbour tour
- Dosing up on caffeine in Copenhagen's cosy cafés
- Experiencing Denmark's Viking history at the Viking Ship Museum in Roskilde

↑ SANTA CLAUS IS COMING TO... COPENHAGEN'S WORLD CONVENTION

↑ BOATHOUSE RETREAT NEAR MARSTAL, ON THE ISLAND OF ÆRØ

MAP REF // K7

BEST TIME TO VISIT **MAY TO AUGUST**

MAKING A POINT: COPENHAGEN'S OPERA HOUSE ≫

COPENHAGEN STOCK EXCHANGE WITH ITS FAMOUS DRAGON SPIRE ≫

KIDS TAKE TO THE SKY ON AN INFLATABLE BOUNCER AT RINGKØBING FJORD ≫

TEXT FRAN PARNELL

ICELAND

A VAST VOLCANIC LABORATORY, ICELAND IS ALIVE WITH ERUPTIONS, GEYSERS AND HOT SPRINGS; AND THE INHABITANTS OF VIBRANT LITTLE REYKJAVÍK ARE FILLED WITH THE SAME ENERGETIC SPIRIT.

CAPITAL CITY **REYKJAVÍK**   POPULATION **301,930**   AREA **103,000 SQ KM**   OFFICIAL LANGUAGE **ICELANDIC**

⌃ RUGGED TRÖLLASKAGI PENINSULA OFFERS SOME CURIOUSLY CHALLENGING TERRAIN FOR WALKING

LANDSCAPE
Iceland's landscape is ridiculously varied. From high near-Arctic deserts, immense glaciers sweep southwards to a thin green belt of farmland. In the north, east and west, fjords wiggle their way around the coast. The country straddles two tectonic plates, meaning the country is riven, from northeast to southwest, by a highly volatile volcanic zone.

HISTORY IN A NUTSHELL
This icy, volcanic wilderness held little appeal for humans for much of its history. It was eventually settled by Norwegian Vikings in 874 – mainly exiles in trouble with the king and in urgent need of a bolt hole. They established a republic and lived peacefully until bloody power struggles began in the 13th century. Taking advantage of the chaos, Norway took control of the country in 1262, passing power to Denmark in 1397. For the next centuries, crippling trade embargoes and catastrophic volcanic eruptions reduced Icelanders to the poorest people in Europe. It was only during World War II, when British and American troops occupied the country, bringing money and infrastructure, that Iceland hauled itself from poverty and finally won its independence.

PEOPLE
Recent genetic research suggests that the original Viking settlers stopped off for a little R&R in Ireland and Scotland en route to Iceland – modern citizens have a mixture of Celtic and Norse genes. They speak Icelandic (a language that has changed very little since Viking times), fluent English and usually several other languages as well. The official religion is Lutheran Protestantism (about 86 per cent). A wave of immigration followed recent changes in policy that relaxed restrictions: six per cent of inhabitants are non-Icelanders, mainly from Poland and Denmark.

MARKETPLACE
Iceland relies heavily on fishing – around 70 per cent of the country's wealth comes from its fleet of trawlers. Declining fish stocks are a tremendous worry, however, and the government is actively trying to diversify the economy. Tourism is increasingly important; and highly controversial schemes have built factories and smelters, powered using the country's abundant geothermal or hydroelectric power. Unemployment is extremely low at 1 per cent, but the inflation rate is one of the highest in Europe.

TRADEMARKS
- Madcap singer Björk
- Hairy Vikings
- The 'Fire and Ice' cliché
- Frequent Miss World winners
- Passionate whale hunters

URBAN SCENE
Sparsely populated Iceland only has one city – cute, coffee-fuelled Reykjavík, where over one-third of Icelanders live. It has an international reputation for its thriving music scene and small-but-wild bars and clubs. More sober pleasures include a wealth of museums and art galleries – from the Saga Museum's entertaining model Vikings to Einar Jónsson's metaphysical sculptures. The multicoloured wood-and-tin houses of the Old Town contain quirky cafés and world-class restaurants. As for the setting, an unpolluted ocean rolls right to the foot of the city; whales and puffins can be seen just offshore.

NATURAL BEAUTY
Most visitors are drawn by the remarkable unspoiled wilderness, a vision of how life might look without motorways, urban sprawl and pollution. The biggest icecap outside the poles, Vatnajökull, dominates the

A FAMILY SHOW SOME MISPLACED FAITH IN THEIR UMBRELLAS BENEATH THUNDEROUS SKÓGARFOSS WATERFALL

southeast, sending rivers of frozen ice rolling stiffly to the sea. At the opposite end of the temperature scale, 22 active volcanoes plot their next outburst, and hundreds of geothermal areas litter the landscape – vents steam, and mudpots burp and gloop. The little-visited Westfjords and Eastfjords offer kilometres of winding coastline, scattered with colourful fishing villages. Almost every visitor takes a whirlwind tour around the Golden Circle, a microcosm of what Iceland has to offer: gushing geysers at Geysir; the rainbow-filled waterfall Gullfoss; and the ravishing national park Þingvellir, now a Unesco World Heritage Site.

ON PAPER

The terse, bloodthirsty medieval sagas – tales of feuding families, crossed lovers and doomed outlaws – are Iceland's greatest cultural achievement. For a taster, try *Egils saga*, *Grettis saga* or *Njáls saga*.

CUISINE

Traditional Icelandic food reads like a list of horror-film props – dishes include *svið* (singed sheep's head complete with eyeballs) and *súrsaðir hrútspungar* (pickled ram's testicles). Thankfully these gruesome items are only eaten during the February celebration of Þorri. Modern cuisine is a source of great pride: fine ingredients include tender Icelandic lamb (grazed wild in the mountains and hormone-free), and fresh fish and seafood, cooked following the most up-to-the-minute methods.

MYTHS & LEGENDS

In this land of twisted lava, boiling springs and deathly ice, it's no wonder that trolls and elves lurk in the wastelands, helping or hindering their human neighbours according to whim. Although nominally Christian, Icelanders hold a deep respect for the natural world and its manifestations – most people will not deny the existence of the Hidden People. There's even an extra Creation myth here: when Adam and Eve still lived in Eden, God paid a visit one day. Eve hadn't finished washing her children, so she hid the ones that were still muddy behind the ears. 'What man has hidden, let stay hidden,' declared God; and our elvish kin are invisible to us to this day.

RANDOM FACTS

○ Beer was illegal until 1989.
○ Students cannot graduate without passing a swimming test.
○ According to a recent survey, Icelanders are the happiest people in the world.

TOP FESTIVAL

Menningarnótt (Culture Night), held in August, is Reykjavík's biggest festival, attended by more than half the country. Musicians appear on every street corner, outdoor stages bloom in the city centre, fashion shows and films fill the museums and galleries, and the whole of Reykjavík takes on a carnival atmosphere. A mega-firework display rounds off the night.

ECOTOURISM

Talk about shooting yourself in the foot! Iceland's whale-watching industry was one of the fastest-growing in the country, and whale spotting the highlight of many a visitor's holiday. Then, in 2006, the government decided to resume commercial whaling, in spite of a nonexistent whale-meat market, international condemnation, and an instant drop in tourist bookings.

⌃ HAPPY HOUR IN THE SURREAL GEOTHERMAL BLUE LAGOON SPA

⌃ BRIGHT-BILLED ATLANTIC PUFFIN CLASPS A CATCH OF CARP

ESSENTIAL EXPERIENCES

○ **Wallowing in the Blue Lagoon**

○ **Gazing at nature's own sculpture park, the iceberg lagoon Jökulsárlón**

○ **Joining the merry, drunken crowds on Reykjavík's *runtur* (pub crawl)**

○ **Choking down a cube of *hákarl* (rotten shark meat)**

○ **Watching humpback whales dive**

○ **Wading through the ash of an active volcano**

MAP REF // F3

BEST TIME TO VISIT **MID-JUNE TO AUGUST**

≪ IT'S A BIRD, IT'S A PLANE… HALLGRÍMSKIRKJA CHURCH'S 75-METRE STEEPLE REARS UP IN REYKJAVÍK

PUREBRED STALLIONS PLAY-FIGHT IN SNOWY SKAGAFJÖRÐUR ≪

THE MAINSTAY OF THE ICELANDIC DIET, FISH ARE HUNG OUTDOORS TO DRY ≪

GREENLAND

NOT (QUITE) ALL ICE, THE WORLD'S BIGGEST ISLAND IS EDGED BY FAIRY-TALE FJORDS AND SPARSELY DOTTED WITH TINY, COLOURFUL HAMLETS LINKED ONLY BY AIR OR SEA.

CAPITAL CITY NUUK **POPULATION** 56,350 **AREA** 2.1 MILLION SQ KM **OFFICIAL LANGUAGES** GREENLANDIC, DANISH

LANDSCAPE

The majority of Greenland's surface is covered by an ice sheet up to three kilometres thick. Around its coastline, however, are some truly majestic fjords. These reach a spectacular climax in the far south, where some are lined with unbelievably dramatic sheer cliffs rising vertically up to 1500 metres and finishing in surreally jagged peaks. Other fjords have tamer, sheep-mown grassy foreshores that burst into colourful bloom in July. Landscapes are made memorable by wind- and sun-sculpted icebergs that crackle or even explode on warm summer afternoons as trapped air bubbles expand within them. Greenland's highest mountains rise to more than 3000 metres on the remote east coast.

HISTORY IN A NUTSHELL

Waves of Inuit tribes settled in Greenland as early as 2400 BC, but the current population started to arrive from northeastern Canada around the 9th century AD. Norse-Viking settlers from Iceland and Norway were colonising the southern fjords around the same time, only to mysteriously die out as the climate turned colder in the late 15th century. In 1605 Greenland was claimed as a Danish colony, and technically to this day it remains a part of Denmark; however, since 1979 the country has enjoyed extensive home rule.

PEOPLE

Most Greenlanders (88 per cent of the population) are of mixed Danish and Inuit blood; the remainder are Danes. No known descendents survive from the Viking colonists. Most Greenlanders are Lutheran Christians.

MARKETPLACE

The Greenlandic economy revolves around fishing, with seal hunting sustaining a few traditional villages. Half the GDP comes as top-up grants from Denmark. The high cost of extraction generally discourages extensive mineral-resource development; however, a new gold mine has opened near Nanortalik.

TRADEMARKS

- Polar bears (rarer than you think)
- Seal hunting (not seal clubbing)
- Mysterious, disappearing Vikings
- Father Christmas
- Turf huts and dogsleds

RANDOM FACTS

- The name 'Greenland' was one of the world's greatest marketing scams – it was coined by Iceland exile Erik the Red as a way to persuade fellow Vikings to follow him to an inhospitable, uninhabited land that was more icy-white than sheep-turf green.
- Greenland is the only country to ever withdraw from the EEC (now the European Union).
- The world's biggest island is also one of its least populated places: Australia has one hundred times more people per square kilometre.

URBAN SCENE

'Urban' and 'Greenland' aren't terms that fit neatly together. Most Greenlandic settlements house less than 2000 souls in colourful timber homes. These pretty settlements typically huddle fjordside around a central clapperboard church. But Nuuk, the capital, does feel strangely urban. Its vast 1950s apartment blocks create modern ghettoes of surprising ugliness in this otherwise pristine land. Much of the population was effectively forced here by the removal of supply routes to their widely scattered villages. Look carefully at people's washing lines: amid the laundry, Greenlanders still hang flanks of drying seal meat.

IMPORT

- Vikings, Inuits and Danes
- Alcohol and alcoholism
- Morose form of Evangelical Lutheranism
- Virtually all staple foods, including frozen New Zealand lamb (cheaper than the locally produced equivalents)
- Danish schoolteachers

EXPORT

- Snow crabs and shrimp
- The first known European explorers of North America
- Kayaks: the word comes from the Inuit *qajaq*
- Around 90 per cent of the cryolite needed to smelt the world's aluminium for much of the 20th century
- Icebergs

SURPRISES

- Coffee is a veritable national institution.
- There are no roads longer than 10 kilometres.
- The Ilulissat glacier produces 20 million tonnes of ice per day, equivalent to a whole year's domestic water consumption for New York City.

ESSENTIAL EXPERIENCES

- **Gawping at the mighty Ilulissat glacier as it calves enormous icebergs for your awestruck delectation**
- **Cruising the mind-blowingly dramatic fjords around Aappilattoq**
- **Dogsledding from beautiful Uummannaq**
- **Buzzing by helicopter across the magnificent peninsulas and island-dappled seascapes to superquaint Nanortalik**
- **Kayaking amid the ice floes from attractive Tasiilaq village**

MAP REF // F1

BEST TIME TO VISIT EARLY AUGUST

AN INUIT MAN IS TRIED BY ICE, SNOW AND WIND IN ONE OF EUROPE'S MOST CHALLENGING CLIMATES »

NO SEASONING REQUIRED: AN INUIT HUNTER READIES A MEAL FOR HIS DOGS »

BRILLIANT LICHENED ROCK AUGMENTS THIS PRETTY HILLTOP SCENE IN OQAATSUT, WEST GREENLAND »

THEMES OF EUROPE

TEXT ALISON BING

CAN THEY DO THAT IN PUBLIC?
EUROPE'S OUTRAGEOUS LANDMARKS

⌃ INSCRIBED STEEL BELLY OF THE WALES MILLENNIUM CENTRE, CARDIFF ⌃ THE LOUVRE'S GLASS PYRAMID CREATES DRAMA IN PARIS, FRANCE ⌃ ROME'S ANCIENT COLOSSEUM UNDER MODERN LIGHTS, ITALY

Right now some of the world's most brutal architecture critics are idling their Vespas at the foot of Capitoline Hill and grimacing. Not a traffic-jam scowl, mind you, but the same wince applied after tasting wine that has turned, or pasta that is not quite *al dente*. Such is the offence to Roman sensibilities of being stuck in traffic facing the Altare della Patria, known locally as the 'Splendido Orrore' (Splendid Horror).

The monument to honour Vittorio Emmanuele started in 1870, and Mussolini elaborated on it as a tribute to the Unknown Soldier and the motherland – but when American troops entered Rome in 1944, they irreverently dubbed the just-completed memorial the 'Typewriter'. The name stuck, especially as the white marble turned grey with pollution. Recently the memorial was scrubbed to its original glaring white, only to revive another nickname: 'Denti Finti' (False Teeth). The Unknown Soldier is now pitied not only for his anonymous demise, but for this monumental embarrassment in his name that's easily outclassed by any number of crumbling ruins in the immediate vicinity.

Zoom past this monument as Romans do and you'll soon arrive at the Colosseum, where ancient Romans passed many happy hours contemplating the deaths of others. Today this awe-inspiring ruin can induce Romans to slow to a point approximating the speed limit, in order to admire its artfully lit grandeur. But Rome's theatre of pain was controversial when it was inaugurated by Emperor Titus in AD 80, with the slaughter of some 11,000 exotic animals in its first 100 days. Eventually the novelty of gladiators fighting crocodiles wore off, and indifference and earthquakes conspired to make the Colosseum obsolete. But millennia-old controversy and rumours of Christians being fed to lions cling to the ancient stones like negatively charged ions, drawing crowds of visitors and keeping many a plastic-armoured gladiator gainfully employed.

Ever since the Colosseum, it's been an unwritten rule that all towering ambitions must be represented quite literally as such, expense and public protest be damned. But, as the Splendido Orrore shows, not all architectural attempts at grandeur succeed, or thrive on public controversy.

Given time and flattering lighting, can a colossal bone of contention such as the Splendido Orrore become a beloved landmark to rival the Colosseum? Consider the London Eye, the Eiffel Tower, or the Vienna Secession: each has been the object of public furore, yet has proved an essential backdrop for European vacation snapshots. Perhaps it's not the monuments themselves, but the public debate

swirling around them that makes them so eminently European – the spirited disagreements, as well as the hard-won points of commonality.

A SCANDAL IN THE MAKING

For many bureaucrats without Mussolini's autocratic powers to build splendid horrors, daring architecture is just not worth the risk to their careers. Zaha Hadid won a 1994 competition to build the Cardiff Bay Opera House, but local politicians scrapped the plans under pressure from local lobbyists wary of Hadid's reputation as a 'theoretical architect'. Hadid didn't exactly help matters by comparing her fragmented crystalline structures to the marshes of southern Iraq in their refraction of light and spatial division – an explanation unconvincing to many not privy to the charms of Mesopotamian swampland. The stigma effectively prevented Hadid from building in Britain for a decade and carried over to Berlin, where a Hadid structure was nixed. But in 2004 Hadid's radical designs won her the coveted Pritzker Prize, while the theme park–style replacement for her design was greeted with shrugs. With its glowing inscription, the round Wales Millennium Centre resembles a giant prop from *Lord of the Rings* inexplicably paired with a steel Thermos of a tower.

If the Wales Millennium Centre falls shy of its creative brief as 'unmistakably Welsh and internationally outstanding', it's not as far off the mark as London's Millennium Dome is to Tony Blair's promise of a monument that would represent 'a triumph of confidence over cynicism, boldness over blandness, excellence over mediocrity'. The hype for the £760 million National Lottery–funded public project would have been difficult to match even without New Labour's reputation riding on it. On a site admirably reclaimed from toxic power plant sludge in Greenwich, chief engineer Buro Happold tethered a cable-mounted white canopy 365 metres in diameter to 12 yellow, 100-metre-high poles arranged like numbers on a clock face – Greenwich Mean Time as interpreted by Cirque du Soleil.

But though the engineering solution was truly impressive, with the roof weighing less than the air contained within the dome, there remained the nagging problem of how to fill it. To ring in the year 2000, lavish dome displays were planned to capture life in modern Britain. The *Body Zone* exhibit that took visitors through arteries towards a loud, throbbing heart made adults queasy and frightened small children, and a home-town storytelling project sponsored by McDonald's seemed a distasteful display of cosiness between big business and government at public expense. After the millennium celebration, part of the dome

was set aside as a homeless shelter, and the project briefly saved face. But any remaining reference to the higher aims of British civilisation were stripped away when the venue was bought by American oil and telecom billionaire Philip Anschutz who renamed it The O2 after its major sponsor. This sports and music venue was inaugurated by Justin Timberlake in 2007.

The London Eye was also created for the millennium celebration with similar fanfare – and similar reservations. Locals expressed concern about how the proposed 'observation wheel' (not to be confused with the lowly French Ferris) would change the London skyline, as well as the wisdom of leasing public land to this privately owned attraction. Technical issues were another problem, delaying the public opening three months into the new millennium. Londoners with long memories feared a repeat of the 1906 disaster of the Great Wheel of London, when 74 people were trapped over London for 15 hours.

But once visitors drifted upward in 32 space-age capsules to a unique vantage point 135 metres over London, controversy seemed to shrink with the horizon. The all-seeing Eye took in postmodern London – the pastiche of industry and royalty, the beguiling theatres and stern clerical façades – and from the privileged perspective of a high-flying pigeon, suddenly it all seemed to make sense. Within its first couple of years, the London Eye had racked up eight million visitors to become London's most-visited attraction.

ANYWHERE BUT HERE

Not all monuments are built in the right place at the right time. Spain's Alfonso X would live to regret his 13th-century decision to build a chapel in what is conceivably the world's most inappropriate location: smack in the middle of the spectacular Great Mosque of Córdoba. Local legend has it that workers laid down their tools in protest when asked to tear down 63 of the 8th-century mosque's 1000 exquisite red-and-white-striped stone arches. Charles V of Spain initially approved construction of the Cathedral of the Assumption of the Virgin within the mosque in 1523, but when he saw the belaboured Gothic choir that had replaced the effortlessly soaring scalloped archways, he reportedly berated the architects: 'You've destroyed something unique in the world, and replaced it with something that could have been built anywhere.'

Architectural additions continued into the 18th century to correct the botched effort, but the *reconquista* remodelling would ultimately fail: the Great Mosque couldn't be eclipsed by an ordinary church. Still known locally as La Mezquita (the Mosque), the building has lately become the site of controversy, as Muslims have attempted to pray in the converted mosque that remains – despite its altar-ed appearance – an indelible triumph of Islamic architecture.

Another odd imposition dates from 1992, when a faux chateau opened its doors in a countryside full of real ones, about 32 kilometres outside of Paris. The encroachment of the Magic Kingdom on French *terroir* was galling to Gallic sensibilities – where the Romans failed to establish dominion, could Mickey Mouse succeed? The architecture of Le Chateau de la Belle au Bois Dormant (Sleeping Beauty's Castle) just made matters worse: at least it could have been a fake French chateau, rather than one modelled on Germany's Neuschwanstein Castle. Disney's ersatz European attractions may be ideal for a muggy Floridian climate that'll take any excuse for German beer halls and 'Matterhorn' log-rides, but it seemed ill-suited to a territory that had very narrowly escaped German annexation 50 years prior. Other attractions were based on European travel patterns to the US, emphasising wild-west mining towns, log-cabin lodges and adobe-style buildings.

Somewhere in the rush to complete the US$4.4 billion American fantasy, Disney overlooked the obvious: what Europeans occasionally enjoyed visiting across the Atlantic, they might not appreciate seeing permanently installed in their own backyard on real estate one-fifth the size of Paris. Objections were raised before one artificial brick was laid, and one critic called EuroDisney 'a cultural Chornobyl'. But the financially struggling attraction was recently saved by a prince from Saudi Arabia (naturally), who improved on the American model by serving wine and establishing better workplace conditions, and brought losses down €21 million in 2006.

So will the Royaume Magique have its corporate fairy-tale ending? Stranger things have happened in France – namely, the construction of an Egyptian funerary monument by a Chinese American architect in front of one of France's signature monuments. Historians, mystics and Mitterrand opponents were among the masses prepared to despise IM Pei's Glass Pyramid almost as soon as François Mitterrand announced the planned design for the Louvre's entryway in 1983. 'Pharaonic complex' was the popular diagnosis of Mitterrand's mindset.

But when the Glass Pyramid was unveiled, the overall response was an 'ooh la la' chorus. Pei's structure elegantly echoes the Egyptian obelisks that pinpoint many a Parisian place, neoclassical Parisian architecture and the museum's impressive antiquities collection. The transparent entryway afforded a view from the Louvre of the Tuileries and Arc de Triomphe, while providing access to an underground walkway system that abbreviated the trek from modern to ancient. If anything, the purpose-built pyramid made the rest of the Louvre seem a little haphazard, with its unwieldy wings and inconsistent application of 19th-century decorative flourishes. The main lingering criticism is downright bizarre: according to an urban legend revived in the bestselling novel *The Da Vinci Code,* the Pyramid is made of 666 panes of glass (the actual number is 673) and is part of some satanic scheme.

CRITICISM, GENTLE & OTHERWISE
Not all European monuments stand accused of satanic tendencies, but Europe has never been shy about critiquing the new additions to the local landscape. Twenty artists and writers published a letter in *Le Temps* newspaper on 14 February 1887: an un-Valentine to one Alexandre Gustave Eiffel and his design for a tower. Léon Bloy called the tower a 'truly tragic street lamp', and Guy de Maupassant dubbed it an 'ungainly skeleton upon a base that looks built to carry a colossal monument of Cyclops, but which just peters out into a ridiculous thin shape like a factory chimney'.

The drubbing Eiffel took for his tower was unsurpassed for almost a century, until young avant-garde architects Renzo Piano and Richard Rogers caused an uproar with their winning plan (out of 700 competition entries) for a new Centre Pompidou: a structure ingeniously turned inside out, with ducts painted in primary colours and open, multiuse interior spaces. The idea was equal parts Jules Verne and Notre Dame, a grounded spaceship with structural elements highlighted like a Gothic cathedral's flying buttresses. 'Too industrial' was the Eiffel-esque refrain, with one critic calling the 1978 building a 'Utopian oil refinery' and some residents disdaining it as 'the monstrosity'.

Six million people visit the Eiffel Tower each year and almost as many visit the Centre Pompidou – but before history could have the last word on their controversial projects, the architects spoke up. In the same newspaper that aired artists' protests, Eiffel retorted: 'Are we to believe that because one is an engineer, one is not preoccupied by beauty in one's constructions, or that one does not seek to create elegance as well as solidity and durability? ... Moreover there is an attraction in the colossal, and a singular delight to which ordinary theories of art are scarcely applicable.'

But while Eiffel came across a tad touchy, Renzo Piano seems to relish the controversy surrounding the Centre Pompidou. 'We were really bad boys,' he says. 'At that time Paris was full of institutions very, very severe, austere, made of stone. We wanted to break that sensation of intimidating building. And we wanted to create [a] totally different emotion... curiosity. Curiosity is a much better emotion than intimidation.'

Waiting out or laughing off criticism isn't always an option. Walter Gropius' Bauhaus School was lambasted almost from its 1919 inception, and accusations of Bolshevism followed the school's relocation from Weimar to Dessau. In the gilded, decadent Weimar Republic, Bauhaus' streamlined grey exterior and purpose-minded, pink interiors seemed suspiciously radical, and its directors and students alike were harassed by local authorities. Director Ludwig Mies van der Rohe issued campus memos requiring students to be quiet, well groomed and avoid political discussions. But the Gestapo remained unconvinced, and closed the school permanently on 11 April 1933.

The building itself miraculously survived. The pitched roof the Nazis added was later removed, and the rosy interior restored. One of the first modern buildings to be named a Unesco World Heritage Site, Bauhaus remains an ambivalent monument. Is it a tribute to the eventual triumph of quiet reason over extremism, or a reminder that no building should seek to rise above debate?

When controversy falls silent around them, even the most prominent buildings seem to fade into the background. Joseph Maria Olbrich built his 1898 domed Vienna Secession building as a deliberate provocation against Austro-Hungarian ossification. Secession president Gustav Klimt's provocatively sensual Beethoven Frieze was inaugurated here in 1902, inspiring a free-flowing aesthetic now known as Art Nouveau. But with time, skyrocketing auction prices for Klimts and over-familiarity of Art Nouveau through countless dorm-room posters, the Secession is today seen more as a jewel box than a radical manifesto in stone. Posters don't do the place justice: only by standing in front of the Secession amid the school-marmish formality of Vienna can its still-youthful exuberance really be appreciated.

UP FOR DEBATE
Rebellion is also alive and well at Vienna's 1986 Hundertwasserhaus. How Friedensreich Hundertwasser was ever entrusted with designing a €7 million public-housing project is no small wonder: the pioneering environmentalist and eccentric psychedelic painter had an avowed hatred of the straight line and a passion for bright colours and buckled floors, which he considered a 'symphony for the feet'. His design included a rippled building façade and floors to match, with room for 200 human tenants and 250 'tree tenants' planted on 16 terraces and inside many of the 50 apartments. Tenants who had to saw legs off their furniture and make way for trees have taken to the dissident spirit of the place, hanging banners protesting Austrian leadership under Jorg Haider outside their publicly funded housing.

Such ongoing debate is what keeps landmark buildings from blending into the scenery, and puts cities on the map. This is the secret to the 'Bilbao effect' – not a museum with a brand-name architect like Frank Gehry, a US$210 million price tag, a dramatic silhouette or dazzling details like titanium tiles. Gehry's Guggenheim museum in Spain's Basque country is no idle conversation piece, but provokes heated arguments about what it means to do justice to Basque culture, contemporary art and the modern European landscape. Say what you will about the Guggenheim Bilbao's free-form shape, but the free-form discussion it raises has been an unqualified success.

Europe's signature monuments have been steadily protested, mocked, honked at and quarrelled over, and perhaps that's as it should be. Europeans are well aware that they may live with their monuments for millennia, and have an appreciation of the collective grandeur a great monument can convey – and a distinct sense of outrage when landmarks fall short of that standard.

Public outrage seems to have been factored into many of Europe's most ambitious monuments over the last 2000 years and, more than any stylistic flourish in stone, that's what keeps them relevant today. After all, this is how the European Union came about: dissent was expected both within and among member nations, but they signed on anyway, imagining that all this active contention might give rise to something truly extraordinary.

PERIPHERAL VISION ON THE LONDON EYE, ENGLAND

PARIS' EVER-POPULAR EIFFEL TOWER, FRANCE

UNESCO-PROTECTED BAUHAUS BUILDING, DESSAU, GERMANY

TEXT RICHARD PLUNKETT

EUROPE'S UNRECOGNISED NATIONS

LOFTY VIEWS FROM CHÂTEAU DE BOURSCHEID, LUXEMBOURG ≪   BAGPIPERS PARADE ON THE BRITISH TERRITORY OF BERMUDA ≪   MONTENEGRO HAS COME TO EUROPE'S SHORE WITH INDEPENDENCE ≪

Scattered around the fringes of Europe are six unrecognised countries, with flags, capital cities and national anthems, vying to join the exclusive club of European nations. Even though the United Nations (UN) recognises the right of nations to self-determination, it is likely that only one of them will get the official stamp of approval in the near future. The rest will stay in the twilight, stubbornly holding out for the day, perhaps decades from now, when proper independence day celebrations can be held. They are all small, poor and lacking any important resources, and their recent histories sum up many of Europe's darkest themes. Independence isn't for everyone, though. Around the world there are atolls, cays and archipelagos which have chosen (well, most of them have chosen) to remain part of Europe, albeit with cheaper coconuts and nicer beaches.

MEMBERSHIP HAS ITS BENEFITS

The unrecognised countries are fragments of former European empires, trying to find their place in a successful and exclusive society of small and rich European countries and dependencies. In fact most of the world's richest places are European midgets. At the top of the list is the British territory of Bermuda, whose 66,000 inhabitants enjoy far higher living standards than other islands with colonial origins who chose to go it alone. As far as independent countries go, the Grand Duchy of Luxembourg is the wealthiest country in the world. The inhabitants of other independent midgets such as Monaco, San Marino, Liechtenstein and Andorra also do uncommonly well for themselves, usually because their homelands are tax havens for the extremely rich and great places for duty-free shopping splurges for the rest of us.

Joining the innermost European club, the European Union (EU), has helped a small country such as Ireland, with a population of four million (not including Northern Ireland), transform itself from a backwater exporting mostly beef and

migrants into one of the wealthiest places on earth. Since Estonia and Latvia broke free of Soviet mismanagement and joined the EU, they have turned themselves into little Baltic tigers, heading towards standards of living that new countries in Asia and Africa can't afford to even dream of. Europe's old colonial powers have a string of territories around the globe that get better schools, hospitals and welfare benefits than neighbouring places with their own seat at the UN. Membership of the Europe club means prestige, grants from cashed-up European development agencies, and an opportunity for the young people to live and work in Europe, then bring their ideas and money back home. These sorts of opportunities don't exist for new countries in poorer parts of the world, such as East Timor or Eritrea. If there are any guarantees of making a success of independence, Europe is the place to do it.

Over the past 20 years more new countries have emerged in Europe than anywhere on the planet. There are now 47 member states of the Council of Europe. The newest, Montenegro, won its political struggle for independence in 2006. Most of the unrecognised countries are also fragments of the communist empires that collapsed at the beginning of the 1990s. In many cases, these statelets remain unrecognised due to recent histories of violence and ethnic expulsions for which bigger, richer and older European countries have been forgiven. For the inhabitants of the six unrecognised statelets of Europe, the immediate future is more poverty and steadily shrinking populations, as the young and ambitious swap their unusable local passports for ones that actually allow you to pass through immigration.

EUROPE'S FOGGY FRONTIERS

There is a question about whether some of these shadowy countries can even be defined as European. What makes a country European or Asian has never been clear. Objectively, there is only one continent, Eurasia. Europe is more or less the western quarter of this continent, bordered on the west and north by the Atlantic and Arctic Oceans and by the Mediterranean Sea to the south. The boundary between Europe and Asia is usually drawn along the ridges of Russia's Ural Mountains, then along the reedy banks of the Ural River as it meanders through the steppes of Kazakhstan towards the Caspian Sea. This boundary leaves a portion of Kazakhstan bigger than Greece within Europe. Kazakhstan's president has argued that as his country has a greater proportion of its territory within Europe than Turkey has, Kazakhstan should be considered a part of Europe too.

Some influential figures, such as the late pope John Paul II, tried to define Europe as a kind of Christian heartland, an argument that has been picked up by European politicians who don't want Muslim Turkey to join the EU. Europe's leaders reject the idea and point to Muslim European states such as Albania, but the argument has some merit. Cyprus is an EU member tucked into a corner of the Mediterranean between Turkey and Syria. If it happened to have a mostly Arab Muslim population, it is unlikely it would be considered European. Being mostly Greek and Orthodox Christian must have helped its case. Armenia is placed even further to the east, between Turkey and Iran. If it too were Muslim and not Christian, it is less likely it would be a member of the Council of Europe. In that other council of Europe, the Eurovision Song Contest, Israel gets to submit terrible pop tunes while its neighbour, Lebanon, found it would have to change its legislation before it could conform with entry rules. The frontiers of Europe, and defining who is in and who is not, is ultimately not a question of geography or religion but of politics.

WAITING ON THE CONTINENTAL SHELF

Three of the unrecognised countries are in one of the most confusing Europe–Asia border regions, the Caucasus, a knot of languages and cultures between the Black Sea and the Caspian Sea. Two of these states, South Ossetia and Abkhazia, broke away from Georgia in the early 1990s. South Ossetia is the smallest and vaguest of the unrecognised countries – a pocket of 70,000 mountain villagers tucked up against the Russian border and under Russian protection. It is more or less a piece of the old Soviet empire that the Russians conspired to keep out of Georgian hands. As such it is unlikely to gain outside recognition.

The Abkhazians, who live on a scenic subtropical coast between the Black Sea and the Caucasus Mountains, made up less than 20 per cent of the population of their region in the 1980s. When Georgia fell into anarchy and civil war, straight after achieving independence in the early 1990s, Abkhazian nationalists picked up some impressive Soviet military hardware at bargain prices and became masters of ethnic cleansing. Abkhaz rebels (or freedom fighters – the difference depends on victory and official recognition) would abduct whole villages of ethnic Georgians and offer the Georgian military an ultimatum – withdraw from the local area or 1000 hostages would be killed. The ramshackle Georgian army would pull back, the hostages would be released and they'd follow the retreat from Abkhazia. By the end of the war nearly the entire Georgian population had been uprooted, and Abkhazians had created a majority for themselves in their new state.

The third unofficial nation of the Caucasus, Nagorno-Karabakh, is a product of an ugly brawl between Christian Armenia and Muslim Azerbaijan. Nagorno-Karabakh is a patch of stunningly pretty mountains in oil-rich Azerbaijan. In the early 1990s the 150,000-odd Armenians of Nagorno-Karabakh won a bitter war against Azerbaijan, and simultaneously expelled 500,000 Azeris to create a vacant zone between themselves and Armenia. In the terrible logic of ethnic war, Karabakh's Armenians torched every newly vacated house, reasoning that the Azerbaijanis wouldn't fight to return to homes that were blackened shells. Since then Nagorno-

Karabakh has held regular elections to bolster its credibility, but no country cares to recognise its status. In everything but official rhetoric, it functions as a province of Armenia. Although both Armenia and Azerbaijan sit on the Council of Europe, their dispute over Nagorno-Karabakh is far enough out on the fringe of Europe for the powers at the centre to largely ignore the problem.

Northern Cyprus is Europe's oldest unrecognised state. Since 1974 this ethnically Turkish territory occupying 40 per cent of the island of Cyprus has failed to win official recognition from anyone except its ally and sponsor, Turkey. The capital of Cyprus, Nicosia, is the last divided city in Europe. In the buffer zone that winds through the city there are oddities such as a Toyota showroom that still displays the finest 1974-model cars, untouched since the barriers went up. In 2004 a UN plan to reunite the two sides of Cyprus was approved by the Turkish side, and rejected by the mostly Greek side. The officially recognised Greek Republic of Cyprus has since joined the EU, while its counterpart across no man's-land is stuck with a moribund economy and a stalemate on the future of its little republic. The UN deal would have allowed Greek Cypriots to regain lost land and homes, but that wasn't enough to restore the damage done by the ethnic cleansing of 1974.

Closer to the heart of Europe is the oddest of the unrecognised states – Pridnestrovie, also called Transdniestr. It broke away from another newborn European obscurity, Moldova, in the early 1990s, with the help of a large Russian army base on its territory. It occupies a gnawed sliver of land between the Dniester River and Moldova's border with Ukraine, a fertile but generally unremarkable stretch of rolling farmland in the northwest corner of the Black Sea. It preserves all the hallmarks of the late, mostly unlamented USSR, including the hammer and sickle emblem on its coat of arms, statues of Lenin, an active secret police and a slightly sinister president named Igor Smirnov who wins stage-managed elections by hugely unlikely margins. It has a poor human rights record, especially against its Moldovan minority, but nothing like some of the other unrecognised states. Mostly it seems to be waiting in vain for recognition, because its political system is so wilfully out of fashion with the rest of Europe. Like Belarus, the only country to be kicked off the Council of Europe, it is shunned because of its dictatorial leadership. The hard questions may come if Pridnestrovie's people ever manage a successful transition to democracy like Ukraine's Orange Revolution, but still want to be separate from Moldova.

TOO SOON FOR FORGIVENESS

Ethnic cleansing is not particularly new to Europe. Croatians chased out Italians after World War II, while Czechs forced out Germans around the same time. Irish Catholics and Protestants were encouraged and sometimes forced to move across the new border when the Irish Free State was declared after World War I. Nazi Germany and the Ottoman Empire unleashed genocide against minorities. Slobodan Milosevic's Serbian forces tried to clear other ethnic groups out of their idea of a Greater Serbia, but ended up causing the removal of centuries-old Serbian communities when they were defeated. In the case of Poland, ethnic cleansing happened without much involvement by the Poles themselves. Before World War II, Poles made up about 70 per cent of the population of their country. After World War II, when the borders were redrawn and the German and Jewish populations had been killed or forced out, they found themselves comprising more than 95 per cent of the population. Essentially, the same process still goes on today. An old empire collapses, leaving a motley patchwork of peoples who don't conform to the new borders. Of the 20 million ethnic Russians who found themselves in someone

⌃ A FRIENDLY GAME OF BACKGAMMON IN NICOSIA, CYPRUS

⌃ SOKHUMI HARBOUR IN ABKHAZIA, GEORGIA

⌃ FAMILY STICKS TOGETHER IN DISPUTED NAGORNO-KARABAKH

else's country when the USSR split up, about half have moved back to Russia or left the region altogether.

But the message for most of the unrecognised statelets from the Great Powers is clear – the ethnic cleansing that went with their struggle for independence makes their states illegitimate. If they had enjoyed the clear ethnic majority of Kosovo, they might have had more luck. Kosovo, a province of Serbia, will be the next nation of Europe – the seventh to emerge from the old Yugoslavia. Although it has some of the Serbian Orthodox Church's greatest and most prestigious monasteries within its borders, the population is 90 per cent ethnic Albanian. Since 1999 it has been a UN protectorate. The formal path to independence was delayed by threats from Serbia and legal negotiations, but independence was declared – and recognised by some – in early 2008. One of the local causes of the delay has been mob violence against Kosovo's Serbian minority. The UN would like their future to be guaranteed in a new multiethnic state. This is probably overly optimistic – Kosovo's Serbs have been steadily leaving, and are likely to continue to do so. This is an example of another form of demographic shift in European history – the minorities tend to move out if they have their own national 'homeland'. West Germany had to wait 25 years for full recognition because of the Nazis. In the end it may be just a waiting game before ethnic changes, whether peaceful or violent, are deemed to be a historical fact.

COLONIAL RELICS

The end of the age of European empires left a bizarre variety of patches of dry land still under European control. France held onto the most. Thus the citizens of Europe officially include the Polynesians of the Wallis and Futuna Islands (north of Fiji if you want to find it on a map), the Muslim Africans of Mayotte, the Creoles of Guadeloupe in the Caribbean, and 7000 people of French descent who live on St Pierre and Miquelon, two bleak islands just off the east coast of Canada. France has also gone the furthest into integrating its outposts into the mother country. The jungles of French Guiana on the north coast of South America and the wind-blasted glaciers of Kerguelen deep in the southern Indian Ocean are just as much a part of France as Lyon or Bordeaux.

Many outposts are incredibly proud of their political links. The people of St Helena, an island in the South Atlantic, are unhappy that the UK, their mother country, keeps them at arm's length. They don't want to be simply an overseas territory, they want to be an English shire on a par with Kent or Devon. The people of Gibraltar, a British dependency on Spain's coast, solidly reject any notion of shared sovereignty or of independence and want to stay British. Across the Mediterranean on the coast of Morocco, the Spanish outposts of Ceuta and Melilla similarly want to remain Spanish. Other territories seem to lean towards independence when the future appears brighter without the European link. The Faroes, a collection of windy islands north of Scotland, are more in favour of separating from Denmark since oil prospectors started investigating the waters around their islands.

TRIBES & NATIONS

Even in the big nations of Europe, the process of tribal loyalties pushing for a separate identity rumbles away. Scotland's pro-independence movement seems to be slowly gaining ground. Celtic nationalist parties in Wales and Brittany dream of the same. France's Mediterranean island Corsica has a sporadically violent liberation movement. The independence movement among the Basques of northern Spain has spawned an active terrorist organisation called ETA, while other Spanish regions such as Galicia and Catalunya are also pushing for official separation. The western part of the Russian Federation has more than a dozen ethnic republics, including Europe's only Buddhist region, Kalmykia.

MICRO EUROPE

Even as the EU grows in size, stature and global importance, the continent gradually fractures into constituent pieces. The gap between independence from one multinational state and absorption into the bigger multinational entity of the EU can be quite a short one. Slovenia broke away from Yugoslavia in the early 1990s but felt unfairly dominated by the bigger republics of Yugoslavia. Yet less than 15 years later, Slovenia celebrated becoming one of the smallest and least influential members of the EU. What happens if Europe keeps splitting into smaller bits? Are Liechtenstein, Monaco, Andorra and San Marino the future? The ultimate example must be the world's only virtual state, the Sovereign Military Order of Malta. It issues passports, coins and stamps, and has diplomatic relations with 96 countries. This Catholic military order lost its last territory, Malta, in 1798. Yet its two main buildings in Rome, the Palazzo Malta and the Villa Malta, have extraterritorial status. In effect, they are embassies for a country that doesn't really exist – rather like the embassies of the EU itself.

TEXT **VICTORIA KYRIAKOPOULOS**

THE NEW EUROPE

SOLDIERS STARE THROUGH THE BERLIN WALL, GERMANY

TEXTILE WORKER HAND-STITCHES AN EU FLAG

CELEBRATIONS IN WARSAW AS POLAND ACCEDES TO THE EU CLUB

When arch enemies Germany and France agreed to form a common market for coal and steel in the aftermath of World War II, few would have believed it would be the building block for an unprecedented period of peace and prosperity in Europe. More than half a century later, that first cosy trading club of six rich nations has morphed into a motley union of 27 countries that make up the ever-growing European Union (EU).

The EU has become the world's leading trading power operating in a single market encompassing nearly half a billion people. Almost half the members have adopted a single currency, while its citizens can study, work and live freely throughout Europe and businesses and farmers have access to the world's biggest market. From a modest free trade zone established after the war it has grown into a complex and controversial broader economic and political union that is driving the fortunes of postwar Europe.

JOIN THE CLUB – THE ROAD TO INTEGRATION

With a history of war, division and conflict, visions of a united Europe have been broached since the collapse of the Roman Empire. In the mid-1800s, celebrated novelist Victor Hugo dreamed of a United Europe inspired by humanistic ideals where countries cooperated as equals.

As Europe reeled from the devastation of the two world wars, French statesman Jean Monnet – known as the EU's founding father – spread the idea that gradual European economic and political integration was the key to survival. British Prime Minister Winston Churchill weighed in with his 1946 speech touting a 'United States of Europe'. The wars had exposed the weakness of individual nations. Any illusions about European hegemony or any one nation's domination had been shattered by the rise of the new world superpowers – the US and the Soviet Union.

Obstacles to free trade contributed to mounting tensions leading to World War II and the Americans made free trade policies a condition for postwar economic aid under the Marshall Plan (which had its own anticommunist political agenda). It became clear France and Germany would have to work together to establish the new order in postwar Western Europe. In 1950, French foreign minister Robert Schuman proposed a common market for steel and coal. It was both a pragmatic economic initiative and a symbolic political move to secure peace in the region. By pooling coal and steel resources – the raw materials of war – the nations would work towards common goals rather than revert to old enmities. Two years later, France, Germany, Italy, Belgium, the Netherlands and Luxembourg signed the Treaty of

Paris, forming the supranational European Coal and Steel Community (ECSC).

The benefits of economic cooperation quickly became apparent. In 1957, a broader common market for trade and agriculture – the European Economic Community (EEC) – was established by the landmark Treaty of Rome. Ten years later the EEC, the ECSC and the European Atomic Energy Community merged into the European Community (EC), a key pillar of today's EU.

By 1973, the first new members – Denmark, Ireland and the UK – joined the common market and the EC began cooperating on social, regional and environmental policies. Greece joined in 1981, followed by Spain and Portugal in 1986, then the scene for further enlargement was set in 1992 by the Treaty of Maastricht, which created the EU, a political and monetary union with a broader role in security and foreign policy and police and judicial cooperation. When Austria, Finland and Sweden joined in 1995, the EU's ranks had grown to 15.

Europe's geopolitical map changed dramatically after the fall of the Berlin Wall in 1989. Germany's reunification and the collapse of communism and the Soviet Union posed new challenges and set in motion inevitable EU expansion to the north and east. The carrot of EU accession sped up economic and political reforms in the backward former communist regimes of Central and Eastern Europe. After the disintegration of Yugoslavia, the Balkan nations also looked to a future in Europe.

The dividing line between the capitalist West and former communist Europe was erased when a posse of ex-communist Eastern bloc states came on board in the EU's biggest enlargement in 2004. Overnight, the EU grew by 75 million people and 10 countries – Cyprus, the Czech Republic, Estonia, Hungary, Latvia, Lithuania, Malta, Poland, Slovakia and Slovenia. Bulgaria and Romania followed in 2007. It is a remarkable achievement given that in 1942, war-ravaged Europe was in economic ruins and had only four real democracies.

BRUSSELS & THE EU MACHINE

The EU is a largely supranational union of sovereign states, with a democratically elected Parliament, Central Bank, Court of Justice, a 22,000-strong bureaucracy and a range of institutions dealing with the complex machinations of the EU's policies, programmes and annual budget of more than €100 billion (about one per cent of its members' gross national income).

The EU has its own flag, anthem, National Day (9 May) and motto (United in Diversity). The European Commission and its legislative arms, the European

Parliament and the Council of Europe, are the three most important institutions. EU law consists of reportedly 80,000 pages of treaties, regulations, directives and legal opinions.

Since 1981, Brussels – originally chosen as the temporary EU base because of its central location and neutral position – has been the effective capital. But key institutions are also located in Luxembourg and Strasbourg, a costly split wasting taxpayers funds.

The first European Parliamentary elections in 1979 elected 410 Euro-MPs from nine member states. After the last enlargement, the number of MPs sitting on the benches was to be capped at 750. Seats are allocated roughly proportional to population and elections are held every five years. MPs are elected to Europe-wide political parties rather than national blocks. The presidency of the Council of Europe is rotated between member states every six months. With more than 343 million people eligible to vote, the EU is the second-largest democratic electorate in the world after India.

WELCOME TO THE EURO ZONE

Europe's single currency made its grand debut on 1 January 2002, when new euro coins and notes entered the wallets of 300 million consumers. In a huge leap of faith, a raft of national currencies such as Deutsch marks, francs, liras and drachmas were relegated to history as the euro became the official currency of 12 member states. It is one of the EU's most outstanding achievements, lowering the cost of business, eliminating currency fluctuations, allowing more integrated financial markets, making travel easier and prices across Europe more transparent and competitive. Europe's economic might was combined with a single currency capable of rivalling the US dollar.

Contrary to predictions of chaos, the switch to the euro went remarkably smoothly, though it led to massive price hikes in some countries. EU-critics took glee in the disappointingly slow economic growth in the first years, but by 2006, the European economy had bounced back and the euro was performing strongly. About 25 states and territories in and outside the EU have already pegged their currencies to the euro, including EU territories such as the Canary Islands and some African countries.

All EU members will eventually have to adopt the euro once they have satisfied the entry criteria, which includes sustainable low inflation and budget deficits below three per cent of GDP. But eurosceptic Britain has from the outset been reluctant to relinquish monetary control to Brussels, while Denmark and Sweden have rejected joining the euro zone. Of the new EU members, only Malta, Cyprus and Slovenia had any chance of joining in the near future.

Critics of the EU's one-size-fits-all monetary policy had a field day after it was revealed dodgy bookkeeping had led to Greece joining on false pretences, while violent unrest erupted in Hungary in 2006 after revelations the government had lied about its economic health as it pushed austerity measures in preparation for EU entry. Most Eastern European members have pushed back their target dates, conceding they were not ready to join the euro club.

RICH MAN, POOR MAN – EUROPE'S NEW DIVIDE

While the EU was set up as a coalition of equals, it could never be a level playing field with economic powerhouses such as Germany (population 82 million) sitting around the same table as tiny Portugal and the gap between rich and poor widening with the entry of even poorer nations in 2004.

The price of access to a bigger European market is that wealthier countries pay out hefty subsidies in structural, agricultural and administrative aid to help bring poorer members up to speed. Spain, Greece, Portugal and Ireland have long received more from the EU coffers than they pay in. About 35 per cent of the EU budget goes towards boosting the economies of poorer regions and billions in development funds are handed out to candidates in pre-accession aid. For many nations it has been a welcome cash cow.

Members' contributions are calculated according to their population and economic might. The biggest payments, proportionally, are made by the Netherlands, Sweden and Germany (followed by the UK, Italy and France). Luxembourg enjoys the highest standard of living, while the newest kids on the block, Bulgaria and Romania, are the EU's poorest.

GROWING PAINS

The EU treads a veritable minefield accommodating members with vastly different economies, taxation and social welfare systems, as well as issues peculiar to each nation and conflicts between member states. Progress has often been slowed down or paralysed by labyrinthine decision-making processes, bickering and constant stoushes over budgets and policies. Enlargement has made things even more complicated, not least because of the extra burden of translating into 20 official EU languages.

Fundamental disagreements have meant the level of integration has not been uniform. Britain and Ireland rejected the 1985 Schengen Agreement that eliminated border controls. The EU's newer states don't fully participate in Schengen, but Iceland and Norway (which are not EU members) do under special deals done with the EU. Exemptions and opt-out clauses from various agreements further complicate matters. Fearing a flood of cheap labour after the 2004 enlargement, some countries went against the EU's basic free movement principles and restricted access to foreign workers from poorer ex-communist states.

Member states can and often do veto major and minor decisions: the Czech Republic blocked plans to raise taxes on beer. Poland vetoed Russia–EU talks. The draft constitution unceremoniously scuttled by French and Dutch voters in 2005 would have made it difficult for single countries or minority groups to block decisions, but it, too, could only come into force if it was ratified by all member states. Founding members France and Germany remain the driving force and most powerful players in an increasingly unequal alliance but enlargement also potentially changes the balance of power. Eastern European members combined have more delegates in the European Parliament than Germany, while France and Germany can be outvoted by other coalitions.

During the Iraq conflict, the US inflamed these tensions by differentiating between 'Old Europe' (the relatively homogeneous Western Europe) and the 'New Europe' to the east. The EU is seen to be riddled with fraud and corruption, and has had to curb misuse and lack of accountability for distribution of EU funds. It is hardly one big happy family.

EUROSCEPTICS & EUROSNOBS

While a raft of nations have been clambering to join the privileged EU club, not all European countries are members and many don't particularly want to be. The EU comprises just over half the 47 nations and territories in continental Europe and excludes Russia – Europe's largest state in area and population. The Swiss voted against EU membership to protect their direct democracy and neutrality (not to mention favourable tax regimes and bank secrecy), but nevertheless enjoy privileged access to the EU.

The only country to ever defect from the EU was Greenland, which joined in 1973 with Denmark but withdrew 12 years later over a spat about fishing rights. It, too, enjoys quasi-member privileges. Denmark, Austria, Sweden and the UK remain the biggest eurosceptics, but anti-EU members of the European Parliament come from all over Europe.

While the British have reaped the benefits of EU membership, they fiercely guard their currency, borders and sovereignty, with UK polls revealing not just widespread indifference but calls for outright withdrawal. Euro-concerns range from worries about organised crime gangs infiltrating from the east to fears of eroding national identity in an increasingly homogenised Europe. Wealthier smaller countries resent carrying the increased burden of subsidies to poorer members, while others fear an influx of migrants from poorer states taking local jobs or industries relocating to nations with cheaper labour costs. Some would prefer the EU's powers were curbed and it stuck to being a free trade zone.

Europe-wide standards for industry and agriculture have given critics, and the UK press, a field day over often absurd interpretations of EU laws and directives, ranging from the definition of sausages, to the size or shape of fruit, passports for horses and donkeys, hair nets for fishermen and a universal length for condoms. The EU's website has a dedicated section dispelling an amusing list of 'Euromyths', but outrage over threats to national culinary treasures such as England's black pudding and Scotland's haggis or Greece's offal treat, *kokoretsi,* have been a constant feature of EU life.

At the core of perennial debate about the EU's various decision-making processes lie the fears about the creation of a European super-state at the expense of national sovereignty. Its harshest critics suggest the EU is becoming a Soviet-like totalitarian, undemocratic, bureaucratic juggernaut and warn citizens against complacency towards the increasing loss of influence over their lives.

THE WANNABES

Despite its shortcomings, EU membership remains an alluring goal. Theoretically, any European nation can join the EU, as long as it satisfies the accession criteria – sustaining a stable democracy, a competitive economy, respect for human and minority rights, and the administrative framework to implement EU law. However, as the EU's capacity to absorb new members is tested, the pace of enlargement is expected to slow.

Turkey has been knocking on Europe's door for more than 40 years, despite only a fraction of the massive country technically falling within Europe's borders. But after finally achieving candidate status, it stumbled in 2006 over its failure to open its ports and airport to EU member Cyprus. Resolution of the Cyprus issue is not the main sticking point for what could be an unattainable goal. Turkey is the hot potato of the EU: too big, too poor and the only Muslim country in what some have called – and want to maintain as – a Christian club. Many fear the relative poverty of its 72 million people could drain resources and lead to a flood of Turkish immigrants. Turkey's bid is sure to challenge both the boundaries and divisions in the EU. The former Yugoslav Republic of Macedonia's eventual entry is far less problematic, though it could be vetoed by Greece unless it resolves its name dispute with Greece. Corruption remains a major impediment for Croatia.

Potential candidate countries, including Albania, Bosnia and Hercegovina, Montenegro, Serbia and Kosovo are receiving development funds, but the Western Balkans face a major hurdle meeting the EU's criteria.

FUTURE EUROPE

European enlargement and integration have made the EU a powerful global trading power, the biggest world donor of development aid and in many ways reasserted Europe's cultural and political influence. In some shape or form, the EU touches on most areas of public policy in Europe, from trade and renewable energy to the environment, bioethics and protection of endangered species.

Along with prosperity and peace, the rocky EU road has brought citizens unprecedented opportunities and freedom to study, work, travel and trade within Europe's borders and compete in the globalised new world. The prospect of EU membership helped fast-track modernisation and strengthen democracy, human rights and legal reforms in many member states and aspiring candidate countries, continuing its original role as a mechanism for peace.

But the EU's rules and institutions were designed for a far smaller union and it risks suffocating under the weight of red tape and becoming one large dysfunctional family. Reviving or replacing the scuttled constitutional reforms or creating a new treaty to deal with the complex 27-member union will be an imperative. Future enlargement will remain a contentious issue as the EU absorbs its newest members and the next wave of aspirants fuels the ongoing debate about who can join and where the ultimate boundaries of Europe lie.

≈ KEEPING AN EYE ON TURKEY'S BID FOR EUROPEAN MEMBERSHIP

≈ SLOVENIAN KIDS ARE ECSTATIC TO BE PART OF THE UNION

≈ BERLIN IS INTRODUCED TO THE NEW EURO CURRENCY

TEXT REGIS ST LOUIS

REVOLUTIONARY IDEAS:
SIX THAT CHANGED HISTORY

ANCIENT ROME'S COLOSSAL *HEAD OF CONSTANTINE* ⩘

THE HOLY ST PETER'S BASILICA, VATICAN CITY ⩘

GREECE'S GOLDEN AGE PARTHENON ON THE ATHENIAN ACROPOLIS ⩘

Throughout more than 2700 years of recorded history, Europe has left a legacy of both the horrific and the sublime. Europeans have suffered through malicious rulers, persecution and cataclysmic wars. Yet Europe has also nourished some of the world's groundbreaking ideas – concepts so profound that they would create what philosopher Thomas Kuhn called a 'paradigm shift', when one reigning worldview is dramatically overthrown by another. The ranks of great European visionaries include kings, poets, scientists, philosophers and even working-class citizens, some of whom suffered great persecution in the advance of human progress. A brief journey through time highlights a few Europeans whose ideas have helped shape the modern world.

A GATHERING OF ATHENIANS

Few periods in human history spark as many superlatives as 'The Golden Age of Greece'. Indeed, the Greeks gave much to Western civilisation, including the oldest examples of European literature, the first playwrights and theatre, and the foundations for science, mathematics and philosophy.

One of their most important legacies is the gift of democracy, that now humdrum – but so poorly executed – exercise of government by the people. How and why it flourished in ancient Athens for a handful of generations then disappeared for over a thousand years is the subject of much scholarly debate.

Often the groundwork for radical change begins under perverse rule. Such was the case when the tyrant Draco (whose name means serpent) first codified the harsh laws of Athenian society: no matter the crime, from petty theft to murder, the punishment was death. Instead of bringing peace and prosperity to Athens, his laws only added to the instability, with egregious injustices unaddressed. During poor harvests, for instance, farmers could lose their land, or even their freedom (a citizen could use his own life as collateral for a loan).

In 594 BC, the crisis reached a breaking point and Solon (from a wealthy oligarch family) was chosen to revise the draconian laws. He created the template for all future Athenian governments, experimenting with a mix of oligarchy and democracy. Among his democratic ventures he established the *Ecclesia*, the assembly of citizens that met alongside the Acropolis; he created citizen-run juries; and he gave every Athenian the right to appeal to a jury. He also attempted to alleviate the debts of the poor.

The rule by citizen continued to evolve, and when Cleisthenes came to power (circa 525 BC), he expanded Solon's initiatives, ushering in the era of classical Athenian democracy. His goal was to sever the power of the oligarchs and prevent the rise of another tyrant. And so he placed sovereign power in the hands of the *Ecclesia*, replaced the four old tribal organisations (to whom his predecessors had answered) with 10 new ones, and the citizens indeed governed. They elected 10 top officials and drew lots to determine administrative posts. They enjoyed equality before the law and held all public servants accountable for their actions.

Winston Churchill once said 'democracy is the worst form of government, except all those other forms'. Athenian democracy had its human limitations. In ancient Athens, for instance, women were excluded from government. And yet it was a remarkable epoch that would last more than 180 years. It was also the spiritual ancestor to post-revolutionary France and the USA's 'government of the people, by the people, for the people', as Abraham Lincoln later described it – a concept that continues to entrance, mystify and even frighten rulers and citizens across the globe.

EDICT FROM ROME

Sometime between AD 98 and 117, a Syrian-born man, Ignatius of Antioch, was led into Rome's Flavian theatre (aka the Colosseum) and before a cheering crowd was torn to pieces by hungry lions. His death was one of the many gruesome ends met by early Christian believers, who over the course of three centuries would be periodically crucified, roasted alive or devoured by wild animals in the gory spectacles popular during Rome's imperial days.

What Ignatius never could have imagined is that a Roman emperor, Constantine (272–337), would embrace his obscure religion, and that Christianity would spread across the empire and beyond.

Although his mother was probably a Christian, there is little to suggest that Constantine practised her religion. Like other emperors, he was interested in gaining power, consolidating his empire and being worshipped himself. Besides, he committed some heinous crimes, even killing his eldest son Crispus when he feared a plot to overthrow him.

Yet Constantine is revered in the Eastern Orthodox faith (where he's considered a saint) and often credited as Rome's first Christian emperor. His connection to this western Asian religion began, according to one account, before a battle in 312. Constantine saw a cross in the sky together with the words, 'By this you will conquer'. Inspired, he had his army place the Christian monogram on their shields and marched his greatly outnumbered army into battle. Following his victory, he thanked the Christian God by issuing the Edict of Milan, which granted his subjects the freedom to practise whatever religion they chose.

Although Constantine didn't make Christianity the faith of the empire, he laid its foundations. He moved his capital to the shores of the Bosphorus (founding Constantinople, the seat of Christian power for over a thousand years) and built churches there and elsewhere, including St Peter's Basilica in Rome and the Church of the Nativity in Bethlehem. He also presided over the Council of Nicaea (which codified early Christian doctrine) and enforced Sunday as a day of rest. On his deathbed, Constantine was baptised.

While scholars debate the life of Constantine his legacy is clear: Christianity gained a firm foothold in Europe, where it would play a major role in political, social and cultural life for many centuries to come.

UPHEAVAL IN THE HEAVENS

At the end of the 15th century, human knowledge was still largely rooted in the thinking of the ancient Greeks. Aristotle's ideas about nature and the earth were widely accepted. The earth, for instance, was an immoveable sphere at the centre of the universe, made up of the four physical elements (earth, air, fire and water) plus aether, the divine substance, which made up the heavenly spheres and heavenly bodies (the rotating of the planets, furthermore, created a beautiful 'music of the spheres', which humans could not hear until they died and ascended to heaven). For many centuries science, along with philosophy and the arts, was inextricably linked to Christian theology and the church. The world was ordered, and everything had its place; any deviation from the norm was the work of the devil.

And so, when Nicolaus Copernicus (1473–1543) climbed the steps of the capitular church of Frauenburg in Polish Prussia during the early 1500s and began recording his astronomic observations, he was embarking on a project that would shatter the concept of the known universe. Copernicus first proposed his radical theory of heliocentrism (the sun being at the centre of the solar system) in 1510 but, fearing the condemnation of his peers and perhaps the pope, it wasn't until the end of his life that he published *On the Revolutions of the Celestial Spheres*.

Despite the monumental significance of his discoveries, Copernicus would remain largely unknown until Galileo championed his work nearly a century later.

Galileo Galilei (1564–1642), whom Albert Einstein called the 'father of modern science', remains one of the giants of the Scientific Revolution. Expanding on Copernicus' findings, Galileo was one of the first to use the newly invented telescope, and proved that the moon was covered with craters, and was not a perfect sphere as was commonly accepted. He also observed and documented sunspots (which would later cost him his eyesight), the phases of Venus and the moons of Jupiter. He developed laws of falling bodies based on experiments which he analysed mathematically. According to Galileo, mathematics was 'the language with which God has written the universe'.

Galileo was outspoken in defence of heliocentrism and scientific observation – excoriating those who defended their primitive ideas with biblical references. Eventually his radical thinking earned him a summons from the Catholic Church. In 1632 he was tried before the Inquisition and forced to recant. Yet the ideas would take root, transforming society and laying the foundations for today's thinking.

THE FERVOUR OF ENLIGHTENMENT

In Lisbon, early on the morning of 1 November 1755, when half the town was attending All Saints' Day mass, a terrible earthquake struck the city. The devastation was near total, with tens of thousands killed. For 18th-century thinkers, the repercussions of the quake went far beyond physical destruction. Lisbon, after all, was in a Catholic country, and the quake struck on a Catholic holy day, levelling nearly every church in town. Normally, natural disasters would be chalked up to the wrath of God, but the scale of this disaster seemed impossible to explain.

The great French writer Voltaire (1694–1778) was in Switzerland when the quake struck, and the catastrophe left a deep impression on him. Along with the disastrous Seven Years' War, it would lead him to abandon the optimism of his youth, and reject the widely accepted philosophy of Leibniz, who believed in a rational, well-ordered universe.

Voltaire was born and educated in Paris during the austere reign of Louis XIV, when France was the dominant ruler of Europe. He published thousands of works, earning a reputation as a poet, historian, dramatist, philosopher and confidant of kings. His outspoken attacks on the intolerance of the church and hypocrisies of the *ancien régime* would land him in the Bastille and send him into exile on several occasions. A great wit and social critic, Voltaire would become a symbol of the intellectual ferment of his time, the age of the Enlightenment, when the 'light of reason' illuminated the dark, superstitious times of previous eras.

Voltaire's record of the quake appeared in his satire *Candide* (1759), a farcical but caustic novel in which he puts his characters through a veritable hell, suffering through shipwreck, earthquake, war, murder, rape, forced prostitution and burning at the stake among other trials. *Candide* took aim at the savagery of colonialism, slavery, the Inquisition and other accepted norms of his day. Despite official condemnation, the book enjoyed enormous success. It is still widely read, and its dark cosmic vision is no less relevant 250 years later.

Candide is just a small part of the legacy of Voltaire, whose advocacy of civil liberties and religious tolerance were the pinnacle of Enlightenment thinking. As the great humanitarian of the 18th century, his philosophy would be carried forward by the ideas of 'liberty, equality and fraternity' that would sweep through Paris just 11 years after his death. Despite the enormous bloodshed the French Revolution unleashed, a new society emerged – based on religious tolerance, with serfdom abolished, and a new justice system prevailing that is still the basis for the civil law system in France.

☆ COMMUNIST MILITARY PARADE IN THE FORMER EAST GERMANY

☆ SOLIDARITY MEMBER AT THE SITE OF 1980 STRIKE, GDAŃSK, POLAND

☆ BIRMINGHAM'S 'GOLDEN BOYS' TRIBUTE TO THE INDUSTRIAL REVOLUTION

DYNAMO: THE RUSH TOWARDS MODERNITY

Sometime in the early 1800s, a group of masked men gathered on the moors outside Nottingham, England, and subsequently stormed a textile factory in Birmingham, attacking the machines with sledgehammers and pickaxes. It was one of many such attacks by a group of skilled artisans who felt marginalised by the rise of automated factories. They were known as Luddites, taking their name from their mythical leader King Ludd, and grew to such numbers by 1812 that they were staging pitched battles against the British army.

Around the same time in Birmingham, beneath a full moon, coaches bearing well-dressed gentlemen pulled up at the Soho residence of the respected industrialist Matthew Boulton. In attendance were some of England's most prominent scientists, inventors and natural philosophers. They were men at the cutting edge of history, all part of the great movement spurring the Industrial Revolution. They called themselves the Lunar Society, meeting every month on the full moon to discuss the continuous advances unfolding in science and industry.

Their ranks included Erasmus Darwin (grandfather to Charles Darwin), pottery magnate Josiah Wedgwood, arms manufacturer (but Quaker) Samuel Galton Jnr, and the chemist and philosopher Joseph Priestley, among dozens of others. Their most famous member was James Watt, the Scottish engineer and instrument maker, whose improvements to the steam engine were driving modernisation.

Despite the efforts of the Luddites, they could not halt the massive changes to society, as manual labour was replaced with machinery. England led the way – driven in part by wealth and resources from its colonies – though the changes quickly spread to other parts of Europe. Along with Watt's perfected steam engine came a rash of other inventions affecting the textile industry, mining and agriculture. Road, river and rail transportation dramatically improved, and enormous factories appeared in the countryside. The nature of labour changed, as did the make-up of the population, with workers flooding into cities to work in large mills. Some towns, such as Manchester, grew tenfold in less than a generation.

For some, the age of the factory heralded a dark, dehumanising era. The growing tensions in society helped fuel Romanticism, a movement of largely English poets, dramatists and philosophers who trumpeted the virtues of imagination, individualism and a respect for nature. They lived through a Europe plunged into war and revolution that now embraced the appearance of 'dark, satanic mills' as William Blake described them. Humanity for Blake, Coleridge and Wordsworth was headed down a path of self-destruction, with Mary Shelley's *Frankenstein* a poignant allegory of society run amok.

EUROPE UNDIVIDED

In many ways, the 20th century in Europe was a return to the Dark Ages, a time of irrationality and spiritual blindness that led to catastrophic wars. An estimated 40 million Europeans lost their lives in World War II, around 26 million of them were civilians.

For many, the war's end didn't bring freedom from tyranny. By 1946 an ugly split had emerged, and by the 1960s this split was concrete – the Berlin Wall being the archetype of the East–West divide, with communism on one side and democracy on the other.

Despite Marx's utopian socio-political vision, the states that adopted communism – usually under puppet regimes installed by the Kremlin – utilised particularly gruesome methods of repression. Untold millions from dozens of countries were killed in purges or sent to work and die in gulags in eastern Russia.

Eventually, the communist system showed signs of decay. Corruption and gross mismanagement by party officials contributed to its collapse, but ordinary citizens played the biggest role. Poland was one of the first countries to bring the Eastern bloc, and ultimately the Soviet Union, to its knees.

Solidarność, the Solidarity movement, began in 1980, when a group of workers at the Gdańsk shipyards staged a strike. The movement was led by Lech Wałęsa, an idealist who climbed over the steel fence of the Lenin Shipyard and became at one stroke the leader of the Solidarity movement. Although not a gifted speaker, Wałęsa was courageous, with a clear vision of liberating Poland from oppression. Unable to silence the uprising, the government met nearly all of the workers' demands: the right to strike and form unions; as well as unprecedented reductions in censorship.

The word of Solidarność spread, with nearly one million workers abandoning the Communist Party.

Under pressure from Moscow to crush the movement, the government responded. On a single night in December 1981, the police arrested some 50,000 Solidarity activists and imposed martial law. Wałęsa was imprisoned and Party Secretary Jaruzelski, hoping to quell the rebellion, introduced limited economic reform (trends repeated in Russia under *perestroika*). However it was too little, too late. Wałęsa had become a celebrated figure. In 1983, he was invited to a private audience in Rome, where he received the blessing of Pope John Paul II (also a Pole and an immense source of Polish pride). Later that year, he was awarded the Nobel Peace Prize. Fearing the government would prevent his return, Wałęsa sent his wife to accept the prize, and donated the money to the Solidarność movement. Finally in 1988 the government agreed to round-table talks which led to parliamentary elections. In 1990, Wałęsa was elected president, becoming the first democratically elected leader in Poland's history.

The profound events that transformed Poland would appear in different guises all across Eastern Europe as Soviet satellites freed themselves from the yoke of communism. Today the Iron Curtain seems a relic of the past, but no-one in the 1980s could have imagined that the unification of East and West and the creation of a European Union was less than a generation away.

THE AUTHORS

LAETITIA CLAPTON (COORDINATING AUTHOR)

Since living in Canada as a baby, Laetitia Clapton has had the travel bug. She studied French and German at Cambridge University and got under the skin of French life teaching English in Normandy. Trips around Europe, the USA and Australasia swiftly followed, with the fascinating continent on her doorstep remaining a favourite – coordinating and writing for *The Europe Book* has been her dream job. A freelance writer and publishing consultant, Laetitia has also written for Lonely Planet's *England, Great Britain, The Travel Book* and *The Cities Book,* and has appeared on *Richard & Judy,* CNN and the BBC to talk about travel.

BRETT ATKINSON

Brett Atkinson first made the long journey from New Zealand to Europe as an excited Kiwi doing his 'Overseas Experience' in 1985. He's since returned to honeymoon in Hungary and Croatia, written about the past in Slovenia and Bosnia, and explored the future of the Czech Republic for Lonely Planet.

DAVID ATKINSON

David Atkinson recently authored the new edition of Lonely Planet's *Wales.* David is a full-time travel writer based near Manchester, UK. He divides his time between Lonely Planet assignments and freelance articles for publications such as the *Observer, Weekend FT* and *Wanderlust Magazine.* Read more at www.atkinsondavid.co.uk.

CAROLYN BAIN

Having traipsed through almost 30 European countries, Melbourne-based Carolyn prefers those places with a strong Mediterranean flavour – the perfect combination of sun, sea, history and fine food make her favourite places shine. For Lonely Planet she has repeatedly visited Malta and Greece, plus Scandinavian destinations including Sweden and Denmark.

ALISON BING

Alison writes for Lonely Planet's *Italy, USA* and *Morocco* guides, and holds degrees in art history and international diplomacy – perfectly respectable diplomatic credentials she undermines regularly with opinionated culture commentary for radio, newspapers and art publications such as *Flash Art, Sculpture* and *artUS.* Thanks to: Laetitia Clapton, Susan Paterson, Marco Marinucci.

BECCA BLOND

Becca Blond was born in Switzerland, raised in Washington DC and now lives in Boulder, Colorado, with her fiancé and their oversized bulldog. Over the last four years Becca has authored nearly two dozen titles for Lonely Planet, including the Switzerland and Liechtenstein chapters of two editions of *Western Europe.*

MICHAEL BOOTH

Michael Booth is the author of Lonely Planet's *Copenhagen Encounter.* His book *Just As Well I'm Leaving,* about his experiences living in Denmark and his obsession with the life and travels of Hans Christian Andersen, is published by Vintage. He has just finished *Sacré Cordon Bleu,* a memoir of his year spent in Paris learning to be a chef (Jonathan Cape, 2008).

CHRIS DELISO

Chris Deliso is an American writer covering the Balkans, Greece and Turkey. He has contributed to Lonely Planet's *Greece* and *Bulgaria.* Chris' interest in the region started while studying for a masters degree in Byzantine Studies a decade ago at Oxford, and continued through living in İstanbul, Crete and, since 2002, the Republic of Macedonia.

PETER DRAGICEVICH

After a decade chained to a desk in various newspaper and magazine offices in the antipodes, Peter's spent recent years tracing his roots across Europe. Books for Lonely Planet include *Eastern Europe, Europe on a Shoestring, Mediterranean Europe, Vietnam, Sydney* and *Walking in Britain.*

LISA DUNFORD

Lisa's grandfather emigrated from the Carpathian Mountains, which were for a time in Czechoslovakia. After college, she worked for the US embassy in Bratislava and danced as Slovakia became a nation. Lisa's been an author on Lonely Planet's *Czech & Slovak Republics, Eastern Europe* and *Europe on a Shoestring,* among others.

MARK ELLIOTT

In over a dozen trips since 1995, Mark Elliott has crisscrossed Azerbaijan by train, horse, foot and sturdy 4WD. He has written three definitive books on travel within the country, makes regular presentations on the nation's lesser-known delights and provides predeparture cultural briefings for oil-industry expatriate executives before they're sent to Baku.

STEVE FALLON

Steve can't remember a time that he wasn't fascinated by travel. After receiving a BSc in modern languages from Georgetown University, Washington DC, he moved to Hong Kong where he worked as a journalist for more than 12 years. He lived in Budapest for three years in the 1990s and visited Slovenia frequently for work and pleasure. He now lives in London.

DUNCAN GARWOOD

Duncan moved to Rome just in time to celebrate the new millennium in the capital. Some seven years later and he's still there, living in the green hills just south of town. He's worked on various Italian guides for Lonely Planet, including the past two editions of the *Rome* city guide.

WILL GOURLAY

An Australian with a yen for southern Europe, Will has taught in Turkey, studied in Spain and nursed hangovers everywhere from Thessaloniki to Tbilisi. When not obsessing on all things Turkish, he works as a commissioning editor in Lonely Planet's London office. He is currently plotting a Balkan odyssey with his children.

PAULA HARDY

For the last five years Paula has heroically endured thousands of dishes of pasta, braved exploding volcanoes and worshipped faithfully at the altar of the sun god in the process of researching Lonely Planet guides to *Italy, Sicily, Sardinia, Andalucía* and *Morocco.* When not struggling to write them, Paula can be found commissioning Lonely Planet's Italy books in London.

STEVE KOKKER

Steve has long found life in Eastern Europe more thrilling and full of exciting possibilities than back in his otherwise-great hometown of Montreal. A frequent visitor to the region since 1992, he has spent most of his time in Estonia, Russia and elsewhere in Eastern Europe since 1996. Steve has worked on Lonely Planet's *Eastern Europe, Russia & Belarus* and *Romania & Moldova.*

VICTORIA KYRIAKOPOULOS

Victoria Kyriakopoulos is a Melbourne-based freelance journalist and travel writer. A regular visitor to Greece since 1988, she worked in Athens for four years, where she edited the magazine *Odyssey* and covered the 2004 Athens Olympics. She is the author of Lonely Planet's *Best of Athens* and *Crete* and contributing author of *Greece.*

LEANNE LOGAN

Leanne has clocked up nearly two decades and countless kilometres researching, writing and coordinating guidebooks for Lonely Planet – from Africa and Asia to the Pacific and Europe. Throughout it all, the diminutive duo of Belgium and Luxembourg have remained a personal favourite – for reasons greater than beer and chocolate.

KARI LUNDGREN

With a stewardess mother, pilot father and Viking roots, Kari began exploring at an early age, sailing up the coast of Norway to 80 degrees north when she was 12 and across the Atlantic at 15. She is a coauthor of Lonely Planet's *Norway*.

VESNA MARIC

Vesna has been a travel writer for four years now, covering Europe and beyond. She lives in London, a city she adores (even more so after she's been away for a while).

TOM MASTERS

Tom Masters is a London-based writer and producer, currently working as a producer for Lonely Planet Television in the UK. Since 2003 he has authored Lonely Planet titles including *Eastern Europe, London, Maldives, St Petersburg* and *Georgia, Armenia & Azerbaijan*. More of his work can be seen at www.mastersmafia.com.

BECKY OHLSEN

Becky Ohlsen blames her weakness for IKEA, Vikings and pickled herring on the Stockholm-based side of her family. She has indulged in these and other Swedish specialities while researching Lonely Planet's guides to *Stockholm, Sweden* and *Scandinavian Europe*. She has also contributed to *Seattle, USA, England* and *Walking in Britain*.

FRAN PARNELL

Fran Parnell's passion for Ireland and Iceland developed while studying Anglo-Saxon, Norse and Celtic at Cambridge University, and is kept aflame by frequent wanderings in both countries. She hopes other visitors will be similarly enchanted. Fran has contributed to many Lonely Planet guidebooks, including *Ireland, Iceland, Best of Reykjavík* and *Scandinavian Europe*.

LEIF PETTERSEN

In 2003 Leif Pettersen was 'Kramered' into abandoning an idiot-proof career with the Federal Reserve Bank of Minneapolis and embarking on an odyssey of homeless travel writing. He writes an almost-award-winning, 'slightly caustic' blog at KillingBatteries.com, where he dishes on travel writing, Romania, Italian internet, Berlin, Jesus and his remarkable-gift-for-hyphenation.

RICHARD PLUNKETT

Richard Plunkett lives in Melbourne and is currently studying law. He has written and contributed to 20-odd Lonely Planet books, most recently *Western Balkans* and *Georgia, Armenia & Azerbaijan*. Low points of his travels include eating goose-fat soup in Uzbekistan – he mistakenly thought the white lumps were tofu.

ROBERT REID

After studying Russian in the Oklahoma plains, Robert (www.robertreid.info) headed to Eastern Europe and hasn't stopped going. He's updated the Bulgaria chapter twice for Lonely Planet's *Eastern Europe* guide and written about Bulgaria in places such as the *New York Times* and *Houston Chronicle*. He is based in Brooklyn, New York.

TIM RICHARDS

Tim spent a year teaching English in Kraków in 1994–5, and has recently researched the rapidly evolving Poland on assignment for Lonely Planet. When he's not on the road, Tim lives in Melbourne, Australia, and writes on various topics including travel and the arts. You can see his work at www.iwriter.com.au.

MILES RODDIS

Miles, no heavyweight himself, specialises in exceedingly small nations and wrote the Andorra and San Marino chapters. He writes at greater length for Lonely Planet guides to Spain and France, Andorra's neighbours, and for the guide to Italy, which surrounds tiny San Marino.

REGIS ST LOUIS

Regis' fascination with European languages, cultures and history has led to extensive travels across the continent. He has covered numerous destinations for Lonely Planet, including Portugal, Estonia and Russia, and his travel essays have appeared in the *Chicago Tribune*, the *Los Angeles Times* and other publications. He lives in New York City.

ANDREA SCHULTE-PEEVERS

Andrea was born and raised in Germany and has built a career on writing about her native country for almost two decades. She's authored or contributed to nearly three dozen Lonely Planet titles, including all editions of *Germany, Berlin* and *Munich & Bavaria* as well as the new *Berlin Encounter*.

SIMON SELLARS

Simon Sellars is based in Melbourne. His writing has specialised in travel, in sound art/music, in film/animation, in JG Ballard and in social welfare, but he continues to be inspired by everything from the topography of cereal boxes to the anthropology of non-place urban fields. For more information, see www.simonsellars.com.

DAMIEN SIMONIS

A friend doing some matchmaking once reported glowingly that Damien 'has lived around the Mediterranean'. A Sydneysider with itchy feet, he has indeed spent years living and travelling from Alexandria to Athens, Venice to Nice, Tangier to İstanbul, and Malta to Mallorca. His base is now Barcelona.

ANDY SYMINGTON

A background in dubious activities – whisky vendor, theatre administrator, archaeologist, tomato salesman – equipped Andy to write guidebooks, of which he now has many under his belt. Finland and Scotland are two of his most-loved places and he has covered both for Lonely Planet. Whisky, saunas and cricket are among his debatable passions.

WENDY TAYLOR

Wendy Taylor graduated from UC Berkeley in 1995 with a degree in Slavic Languages and Literatures. She has written for several Lonely Planet titles, including *Russia & Belarus, Eastern Europe* and *Europe on a Shoestring*. She specialises in Belarus, where she recently spent six months studying, translating, writing, editing and working for democracy.

KERRY WALKER

Kerry grew up in Essex and now lives in the Black Forest. After completing a languages degree, she spent four years trotting the globe; Austria was her first experience with proper knee-deep snow. Kerry has recently penned guides to Vienna, Geneva and Strasbourg, and is currently writing Lonely Planet's *Austria*.

CLIFTON WILKINSON

Born and brought up in Northeast England, Clifton regularly enthrals his Lonely Planet colleagues with his Tales of Darlington, and when not commissioning others to write Lonely Planet's Britain guides, he's always happy writing about the country himself.

NICOLA WILLIAMS

Nicola Williams, a British journalist forever on the move, moved from Latvia via Lithuania to France a decade ago (home today is a hillside house with a Lake Geneva view). When she's not working, she can be found skiing in the Alps; strolling Paris, Florence and Milan; or flitting between family in North Wales, London and Germany.

INDEX

THE EUROPE BOOK
SEPTEMBER 2008

PUBLISHER Roz Hopkins
COMMISSIONING EDITORS Ellie Cobb, Janine Eberle
DESIGNER Mark Adams
PROJECT MANAGER Ellie Cobb
LAYOUT DESIGNER Jim Hsu
COORDINATING EDITOR Susan Paterson
ASSISTING EDITORS Jocelyn Harewood, Anna Metcalfe, Anne Mulvaney
CARTOGRAPHERS Wayne Murphy, Paul Piaia
MANAGING EDITOR Imogen Bannister
IMAGE RESEARCH Craig Newell
PRE-PRESS PRODUCTION Ryan Evans
PRINT PRODUCTION MANAGER Graham Imeson
DELIVERY MANAGER Jenny Bilos

PUBLISHED BY
LONELY PLANET PUBLICATIONS PTY LTD
ABN 36 005 607 983
90 Maribyrnong St, Footscray,
Victoria, 3011, Australia
www.lonelyplanet.com

Printed by SNP Leefung Printers Limited
Printed in China

ISBN 978 1 74104 733 2

PHOTOGRAPHS
Many of the images in this book are available for licensing from Lonely Planet Images.
www.lonelyplanetimages.com

LONELY PLANET OFFICES

AUSTRALIA
Locked Bag 1, Footscray, Victoria, 3011
Phone 03 8379 8000 Fax 03 8379 8111
Email talk2us@lonelyplanet.com.au

USA
150 Linden St, Oakland, CA 94607
Phone 510 250 6400 Toll free 800 275 8555
Fax 510 893 8572 Email info@lonelyplanet.com

UK
2nd fl, 186 City Rd, London, EC1V 2NT
Phone 020 7106 2100 Fax 020 7106 2101
Email go@lonelyplanet.co.uk

PHOTO CREDITS

FRONT COVER Man on Charles Bridge, Prague; David Hanover // Corbis. **INSIDE FRONT COVER** (from left) The Älplerletze ceremony, Germany; Stefan Puchner // Corbis. A shepherd in the Făgăraş Mountains; Staffan Widstrand // Corbis. **BACK COVER** (from left) Opera at Vienna's Staatsoper; Roland Schlager // EPA / AAP. St Basil's Cathedral, Moscow; Jamie Baker // Everynight Images. Bullfighters, Spain; Matias Costa // Panos Pictures. Puffin, Iceland; Joseph Van Os // Getty. **INSIDE BACK COVER** (from left) Windmills in Kinderdijk, The Netherlands; Jochem Wijnands // Picture Contact / Alamy. Hundertwasserhaus, Vienna; Jean-Pierre Lescourret // Corbis. **SPINE IMAGE** The Matterhorn, Zermatt, Switzerland; nostroom // iStockphoto **p2** Snow-laden branches and street light, England; Mark Bolton // Corbis. **p4** (clockwise from left) Building covered in red ivy, Oxford, England; Glenn Beanland // Lonely Planet Images. Man at Mont Blanc's Medieval Week market, France; Guy Moberly // Lonely Planet Images. Harvesting barley in Gronsveld, The Netherlands; Frans Lemmens // Photolibrary. Couple relaxing, Bucharest, Romania; Tim Dirven // Panos Pictures. Island of Ærø, Denmark; Yann Arthus-Bertrand // Corbis. **p5** St Basil's Cathedral, Moscow, Russia; Jamie Baker // Everynight Images. **p6** (from left) Arched gate, Cyprus; Tomek Sikora // Getty. Girl studying *The Birth of Venus* by Alexandre Cabanel in the Musée d'Orsay, Paris, France; Fred de Noyelle // Corbis. Inuit children, Greenland; Ira Block // Getty. **p7** Brazen Head pub, Dublin, Ireland; Amantini Stefano // 4Corners Images. **p9** Staircase in Livraria Lello e Irmão bookstore, Porto, Portugal; Anders Blomqvist // Lonely Planet Images. **p12** (from left) Roland Schlager // EPA / AAP. Stefano Renier / Grand Tour // Corbis. Christopher Furlong // Getty. **p13** (clockwise from left) Gary Vestal // Getty. Victor Fraile // Reuters / Picture Media. ML Sinibaldi // Corbis. Tiit Veermae // Photolibrary. **pp20-1** Eilean Donan Castle, Scotland; Macduff Everton // Getty. **pp50-1** Dirt road through Tuscan countryside, Italy; Massimo Borchi // Corbis. **pp86-7** Maribor Bridge and Drava River, Slovenia; Walter Bibikow // Getty. **pp124-5** Man floating in waters at Sithonia, Halkidiki, Greece; Naki Kouyioumtzis // Getty. **pp168-9** Matryoshka dolls, Azerbaijan; Stephane Victor // Lonely Planet Images. **pp204-5** Inuit hunter and his huskies jump summer sea ice, Greenland; B & C Alexander // Arcticphoto.com. **p255** Inuit woman smoking a pipe, Qaanaaq, Greenland; B & C Alexander // Arcticphoto.com.